BROADWOOD
BY APPOINTMENT

BY APPOINTMENT
TO HER MAJESTY THE QUEEN
PIANOFORTE MANUFACTURERS
JOHN BROADWOOD AND SONS LIMITED, LONDON

BROADWOOD
BY APPOINTMENT
A HISTORY

David Wainwright

QUILLER PRESS
LONDON

First published 1982
by Quiller Press Ltd
11a Albemarle St
London W1X 3HE

Frontispiece: John Broadwood, aged 79. Engraving by W. Say,
from a portrait by John Harrison, 1811 *(John Broadwood & Sons Ltd)*

Production in association with
Book Production Consultants, Cambridge.

Typeset by Goodfellow and Egan Phototypesetting.
Cambridge

Printed in Great Britain at the
Cambridge University Press, Cambridge

Contents

List of Plates

Foreword

By Mr Peter Smith
President of the Royal Warrant Holders Association

T he privilege of service to the Royal Family is greatly valued for those honoured to receive the warrant.

A number of Royal Warrant holders are proud to look back on continuous service over many years. Not all can claim a record as long and enduring as that Broadwood, who have made fine instruments for the Royal Family since 1740.

It is a tribute to the craftsmanship of past generations of skilled workmen that so many of these remarkable musical instruments survive, several in the Royal collections and all admired and honoured, to the present day.

Such a fine tradition finds a proper place among Royal Warrant holders, and it is therefore a pleasure for me to introduce such a remarkable story of devoted skill and craftsmanship.

Preface

John Broadwood was a Scottish cabinet-maker who came to London to seek his fortune. In due course in the classic tradition he married his master's daughter and inherited the business. His master was Burkat Shudi, a Swiss who, setting up his workshop in Soho in 1728, became one of the great makers of harpsichords in the eighteenth century. A friend of Handel, Shudi made harpsichords for the Prince of Wales; another of his fine instruments was played in London by the boy Mozart.

Having inherited a great harpsichord workshop, John Broadwood was intent upon improving the piano. He made scientific experiments and introduced a new technology; the result of which was to take Broadwoods into the leadership of piano manufacture. Having made keyboard instruments for the Royal Households since 1740, Broadwoods continue to hold the Royal Warrant for Pianoforte Manufacture.

Soon after he came to London in 1710 from Switzerland, Burckhardt Tschudi anglicised his name to Burkat Shudi, the form that he used throughout his life, even on legal documents; the only exception seems to be his signature on harpsichords destined for Europe, such as those for Frederick the Great. His daughter Barbara Shudi, who married John Broadwood, used the English form consistently, and gave it to their eldest son (James Shudi Broadwood).

In the nineteenth century the family, investigating its Swiss origins, adopted the Swiss form when naming two sons (James Henry Tschudi Broadwood, b. 1854, and Henry John Tschudi Broadwood, b. 1856). Later, it came to be believed that the Swiss form was more 'correct' and the family therefore revised entries in some reference books to give the founder's name as 'Burckardt Tschudi' and his grandson as 'James Tschudi Broadwood'. This was an error.

There is much technical detail in the manufacture of musical instruments, and technical advance and change are clearly of importance in the history of Broadwoods. I have tried to describe these changes, and their significance, as simply as possible in non-technical language, strengthened in this resolve by the comment of John Broadwood's friend Tiberius Cavallo, when reading a paper on musical temperament to the Royal Society in 1788: 'I have endeavoured to explain this subject in the most familiar manner, avoiding as much as possible the mathematical language and symbols; having found, by experience, that intricate mathematical disquisitions, especially on this subject, are understood only by a few able mathematicians, but that they are neither comprehended, nor even read, by those who might wish to understand, or to use them.'

It has not been possible to include all source materials in this book. I hope therefore to produce an associated volume to make more material available; enquiries should be addressed to me c/o Quiller Press.

East Molesey, Surrey,   1982 DAVID WAINWRIGHT

Chapter I

The Shudi Workshop

1728–1761

John Broadwood was born in Oldhamstocks, on the border of Berwickshire and East Lothian, on 6 October 1732 (Old Style). He was baptised nine days later in the parish church of St Helen, Cockburnspath—the larger coastal village on the main road from London to Edinburgh. The village of Oldhamstocks lay some three miles from the coast, and had for centuries been a trading centre for the farming communities in the Lammermuir hills. The name is Saxon and means 'old settlement'; the village's importance had been underlined in 1672, when an Act of the Scottish Parliament empowered it to hold fairs on the village green, at which the local farmers might buy what they could not provide for themselves. So the village supported a smith and a carpenter. The carpenter, or 'wright', provided woodwork from farm implements to furniture. The village wright of Oldhamstocks during the early eighteenth century was John Broadwood's father James, as *his* father John had been before him. Old John had married well; his wife was a Knox, related to the famous Scottish protestant reformer.

The Broadwoods have been traced back[1] to a Northumberland family of 'Statesmen' or 'Estatesmen', who held lands to the south of Hadrian's Wall, that formidable barrier between England and Scotland. They claimed to be descended from the Romans, and that their ancestors were men of that Roman Legion raised in Thuringia who, when their service with the Imperial Army ended, chose to stay in Britain. Those who remained were granted lands beside the Wall on condition of 'horning'; that is, they must defend it and give warning of the approach of Picts or Scots.

But the lands were meagre and would only support limited numbers; so the younger sons were sent out to seek their fortunes elsewhere. Some remained in Northumberland, where there are still Broadwoods or Braidwoods.[2] There are references to a 'Broadwood-hall' in the grieveship of Allendale, near Hexham. But other Broadwoods migrated north into Berwickshire and became tenant-farmers on land belonging to the Dukes of Roxburgh near Dunbar. That was early in the sixteenth century; certainly this branch of the family had been established on the border of Berwick and Lothian for at least four generations at John Broadwood's birth.

John learnt his craft of joiner and cabinet-maker from his father. From the land he drew a love of the countryside, and of country pursuits, in particular wildfowling on the coast. It was not so isolated a life as all that; at Cockburnspath cross-roads he would see the stage coaches, laden with the wealthy and successful, pausing for their last change of horses as they came up from London, before the 30-mile run into Edinburgh. There was

Oldhamstocks, the birthplace of John Broadwood *(from a watercolour by Alexander Carse, 1796) (National Galleries of Scotland)*

political excitement, too. When John was thirteen, Bonnie Prince Charlie rode through Haddington with his troops on their campaign south to take England. Nor, at that place and that time, was the education of a village carpenter's son primitive, for in Scotland by the beginning of the eighteenth century each parish had its school, where the children were taught—and well taught—reading, writing and arithmetic, and in many schools some Latin as well. The elders of the kirk examined the children in their catechism, and saw to it that they all read their Bible. Edinburgh, 'the Athens of the North', was flowering into a centre of intellectual life. It would have been in his Scottish boyhood that John Broadwood gained the love of books and learning that remained with him for life.

A historian has written of that period in Scotland:

It is difficult not to believe, as so many contemporary commentators obviously did, that the stimulus of education did give the rural population the tools to make the best of the remarkable opportunities that opened in eighteenth-century Scotland, not often by making them bookish, or by encouraging them to go on to higher

14

education, or even to desert their agricultural calling, but by opening their intellectual horizons and thus breaking the mental cake of irrational custom, so that they could make the very best of the agricultural revolution. It was not without irony that a system of schools originally intended to make the population fit citizens of a Godly Commonwealth came instead to fit them for the role of pioneers in a successful materialist state.[3]

By the time John Broadwood was in his late twenties, a skilled carpenter and joiner, his two younger brothers James and William were also of an age to help their father. Three sons were too many in such a business and the eldest began to consider seeking his fortune elsewhere. Legend has it that he walked to London with half-a-crown in his pocket, and took employment (as if fortuitously) with the leading London harpsichord-maker, Burkat Shudi.

The legend is inherently improbable. The Broadwoods of Old-hamstocks were, and remained, well-to-do, and it is unlikely that the eldest son set out on such a journey with so little provision. Another family legend, much more credibly, says that he came to London in 1761 with a letter of introduction to Shudi from the local laird. The local laird was Sir John Hall of Dunglass. His father, Sir James Hall, had been one of the Improvers, a remarkable band of Lothian landlords early in the eighteenth century who recognised that the Industrial Revolution would be carried forward by innovative technologies. They appreciated that these changes would have to be learnt by the young men on their estates. Around 1720, Sir James Hall sent three of his tenants' sons, at his expense, to study the new farming methods being introduced by John Cockburn of Ormiston. Other lairds sent the brightest young men to London, to learn new crafts and skills.[4] So John Broadwood was far from the first in that region to take the high road to London. The Hall family remained his life-long friends, and he always acknowledged his indebtedness to them. There is in the Broadwoods' possession a fine gold table snuff-box given to John Broadwood in 1801 by Sir James Hall, grandson of the 'Improver', son of Sir John and himself probably the first scientific geologist, who was born in the year that John Broadwood set out for London; and in 1802 John Broadwood sent up to Dunglass a fine grand piano (No. 2231) with, on the nameboard, the Hall coat-of-arms and the initials H.H. (for Lady Helen Hall: she was the second daughter of the fourth Earl of Selkirk, and Sir James Hall married her in 1786). The piano was charged to John Broadwood's personal account. It was a special and valuable present, and suggests a particular association.

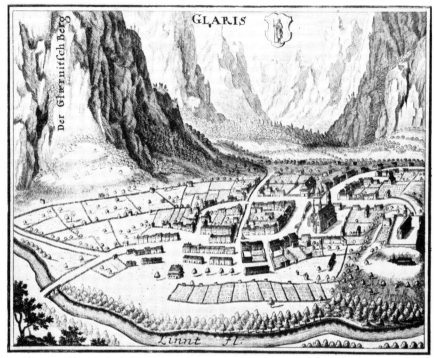

Glarus, birthplace of Burkat Shudi. Engraving by G. Bodenehr,18th century *(The Broadwood Trust)*

John Broadwood began to work for Burkat Shudi in mid-September 1761. London was in a state of excitement that month, and particularly the aristocracy who were Shudi's clientele, for the new young King, George III, was crowned in Westminster Abbey on 22 September. As so often at the beginning of a reign, there was a mood of buoyant optimism and celebration, which doubtless Shudi shared since the new King was the son of that Prince of Wales who had been his patron.

In fact Shudi had maintained his allegiance to the Prince of Wales at the expense of the favour of King George II, who had given his patronage to Shudi's principal rival, Jacob Kirkman. Between them, the two men shared the best part of the London harpsichord trade. It was a considerable achievement for Shudi, who had come to London from Switzerland at the age of sixteen.

Burckhardt, Burckat or Burkat Tschudi was born in Schwanden on 13 March 1702, the son of Josua Tschudi, a man of some substance—a wool-merchant, councillor and surgeon.[5] The Schudis or Tschudis were a well-established family. They could trace their origins directly back to one Johann, who had been Mayor of Glarus in 870. Their ancestor Heinrich (1074–1149) had been appointed Feodary (land-holding tenant) of the Glarus region in 1128 by the Abbess of Seckingen: Heinrich was the first to adopt the surname of 'Schudi'. For five hundred years the family had borne as its badge a pine tree, uprooted and decorated with nine bloody pine-cones. The badge dated from the exploit of an ancestor, Rudolf Schudi, who about 1280 faced an invading Austrian army, tore up a pine tree and laid about him, accounting for nine of his assailants.

But in Burkhardt's boyhood the family motto *Semper Virens*, 'always flourishing', was being challenged by events. The wealth of Schwanden came from its wood. For centuries the town provided school slates for almost the whole of Europe, and these slates were mounted in wooden frames. The town also exported wooden cabinets and tables. Joinery and cabinet-making were important trades, and from Schwanden came furniture in the various woods that were ousting oak—walnut, cherry, hornbeam and pine. Now the pine tree, the spruce fir, came to have a particular significance for it was used for *Geigenspelten* or fiddle-boards. It proved to have remarkable properties of resonance; and it was from the forests of central Europe that the violin-makers of Northern Italy (and particularly those of Cremona, such as Stradivarius and the Guarneri family) in the sixteenth and seventeenth centuries obtained the wood for the instruments that earned them a world-wide reputation. Spruce fir was also the wood used for the soundboards of keyboard instruments such as harpsichords and spinets—the heart and voice of those instruments.

By the beginning of the eighteenth century the staple source of the Tshudis' and the town's wealth was running short. The woodworkers turned themselves to wood merchants. But then the local parliament decided that deforestation had become so much of a threat that for ten years, in no community or parish might wood be sold outside the country. Many families were put out of business. The elder Tschudi, in common with other people in the town, bought a loom and began a new trade in cotton goods. But there was little future for young men like Burkhardt who had been taught the trade of joinery and cabinet-making by his uncle Josua. At the age of sixteen he decided to uproot himself and emigrate to seek his fortune.

He came to London. It was no casual decision. In London there was a place for a skilled young cabinet-maker who was prepared to work hard. Two men from Schwanden, Jakob Wild and Johann Wild, were established in London as merchants (perhaps wood merchants); the

Schwanden parish records also establish the presence in London at this time of one Hans B. Zopfi, a maker of strings for keyboard instruments; Stahelin, who was a picture-framer; and later members of the Blumer family became London harpsichord-makers—all, it will be noted, wood-based trades, or associated with them. So young Burkhardt was entering what was already a thriving little Swiss community in London.

The city to which Burkhardt Tschudi came in 1718, the fourth year of the reign of George I, was in process of expansion. Daniel Defoe defined its sprawl:

> When I speak of London, you expect I shall take in all that vast mass of buildings, reaching from Black-Wall in the east, to Tot-Hill Fields in the west; and extended in an unequal breadth, from the bridge, or river, in the south, to Islington north; and from Peterburgh House on the bank side in Westminster, to Cavendish Square, and all the new buildings by, and beyond, Hannover Square by which the City of London, for so it is still to be called, is extended to Hide Park Corner in the Brentford Road, and almost to Maribone in the Acton Road, and how much farther it may spread, who knows? New squares, and new streets rising up every day to such a prodigy of buildings, that nothing in the world does, or ever did equal it, except old Rome in Trajan's time . . .[6]

The population of London at the time is generally supposed to have been around 600,000. The foreign immigrants tended to congregate in the narrow streets of Soho—the Swiss (not a great many of them), the Huguenot French, in flight from religious persecution, and the Germans, who had come over with the new King from Hanover, where he was Elector (and King George I never, throughout his life, cared to try to speak anything but German).

There was a tradition of the manufacture of keyboard instruments in London. In the seventeenth century there was Charles Hayward, from whom Samuel Pepys bought a spinet. John Player was another established maker. But the best-known London makers were the Hitchcock family of Holborn. There may have been as many as a dozen craftsmen making instruments in London at this time. However, the best harpsichords were acknowledged to be those made by the Ruckers family in Antwerp, a business continued through a nephew by the Couchets. Ruckers harpsichords—the earliest now known is dated 1573—had a peculiar beauty of tone and reliability in use. One of the London makers had learnt his skill in the Ruckers workshop[7]: that was Hermann Tabel, a Fleming, who by 1717 or 1718 had his business in Oxendon Street, south of Piccadilly. He moved to Swallow Street, St James's, in 1724.

Not much is known about Tabel other than that he took as his apprentices, in the second and third decades of the eighteenth century, the two men who were to become the leading harpsichord-makers in London. In the 1720s Burkhardt Tschudi worked for him, and in the 1730s, Jacob Kirkman. Evidently he made well, and taught well. One of his harpsichords survives;[8] and because Tschudi, when he started making on his own account, copied most of his master's design, it is worth describing here.

It is dated 1721 and numbered 43, which suggests that Tabel had been in business for about four years, since at that time harpsichord-makers produced ten or a dozen instruments a year. It has two manuals, with two 8-ft sets of strings and one 4-ft, with a lute stop. The case is veneered in walnut with cross-banding; the interior is of sycamore with walnut stringing. There are finely chased brass hinges; the soundboard has a gilt rose with a viscount's coronet (the Ruckers put roses into their sound-boards—Kirkman was to continue this tradition, but Shudi never did).

Evidently this instrument was made for a man of title. Music in the early eighteenth century was the prerogative of the Court and the nobility. There were practically no public concerts as we know them today. Musicians were the servants of rich men, who might themselves be amateurs at the art and participate in small chamber orchestras (as Frederick the Great was to play the flute each evening with his musicians at Potsdam). Apart from the occasional gatherings of musicians in the upper rooms of inns to make music together, there was no way in which a composer or executant—or, for that matter, an instrument-maker— could obtain commissions other than by introduction to the Church or to this comparatively narrow circle of the salons of the Court and the nobility.

How, then, could a young Swiss harpsichord-maker in London in the 1720s break into this charmed circle? There were two men available to introduce him: Johann Jakob Heidegger, and George Frideric Handel. Heidegger was known to fashionable London as 'the Swiss Count'. He was German, and he was no Count. But his charm of manner, overcoming an extraordinary ugliness, gained him the entree to the salons. He was manager of the opera house, and an impresario; but he had climbed to that eminence from humble origins. He grew up in Zurich (40 miles north-west of Schwanden) and worked his way through Germany as a valet. Finding himself in London in 1707 penniless, he enlisted in the Queen's Life Guards. But he talked himself into the

Georg Frideric Handel. Portrait by Philipp Mercier *(by permission of the Rt Hon the Earl of Malmesbury)*

confidence of the rich, and persuading them to back his plans for an opera season began a career as a producer at which he proved to be a great success. When therefore the 26-year-old Handel arrived in London, speaking no English but with a European reputation as an operatic composer already forming, it was Heidegger who could take him round and open the most important doors, as the diarist Mary Granville (Mrs Delaney) records: 'In the year '10 I first saw Mr Handel who was introduced to my uncle by Mr Heidegger, the famous manager of the opera . . . We had no better instrument in the house than a little spinet of mine, on which the great musician performed wonders. I was much struck with his playing . . .'[9]

Though Handel was at this time officially Kapellmeister to the Court of the Elector of Hanover, he remained in London, living at Burlington House:

> Handel . . . apparently did little except continue his tour of the town's organs, and fraternise with the St Paul's Choir at the Queen's Arms Tavern in St Paul's Churchyard, where he idled hours away with a harpsichord at the weekly evening meeting. Society still strove to pamper him, but he moved little in the Burlington circle outside Burlington House. The dinners and social functions of the town had small attraction for him, but a harpsichord and a beer-mug in the house of a musical friend, however lowly in birth, made him a happy man.[10]

This pleasant existence was disrupted when in 1714 Queen Anne died and was succeeded by the Elector of Hanover. Handel's ostensible employer arrived in London to find his musical director already ensconced. However, King George appears to have overlooked Handel's pluralism, and appointed him music-master to the Princesses. When the King returned to Hanover in 1716 Handel considered it discreet to go back with him. In Anspach he encountered an old friend from his university days, Johann Christoph Schmidt, who was living with a large family in penury. Handel persuaded Schmidt to return with him to London, and he later became the composer's manager.

In the spring of 1717 the King returned to London, with Handel not far behind. That summer he wrote a series of harpsichord 'lessons' for the Princesses (harpsichord suites were generally known as 'lessons' throughout the eighteenth century since most of them were written as tuition for well-bred daughters of rich patrons). On one still July evening, when the King was sailing down the river to Chelsea, a new orchestral suite was played on board an accompanying boat: the 'Water Music'. It was a busy period for Handel; in 1719 he became director of the Royal Academy of Music, founded with the King's patronage to put on operas at the King's Theatre in Haymarket.

Though his fortunes fluctuated Handel made London his home, and became a naturalised British citizen in 1727. He was a popular guest at dinner-tables. 'The style of his discourse was very singular; he pronounced the English as the Germans do, but his phrase was exotic, and partook of the idiom of the different countries in which he had resided, a circumstance that rendered his conversation exceedingly entertaining.'[11] After dinner he would play the harpsichord, as attractively as ever. But he spent more time at home in his house in Brook Street, playing his favourite Ruckers harpsichord, its keys hollowed out like a spoon with use.

English was always a foreign language to Handel, and so he welcomed the opportunity to speak his native German. He was often to be found in Meards Street, Soho, where his business manager and friend Schmidt (who had anglicised his name to John Christopher Smith) lived at No. 18, and his friend the young harpsichord-maker Burckat Tschudi (who had anglicised his name to Burkat Shudi) lived at No. 1.[12] The Smith family had been in their house by Wardour Street since it was built in 1723. Shudi was in business on his own account by 1728,[13] having probably left Hermann Tabel's workshop that year. He had married Catherine Wild, the daughter of his compatriot Jakob Wild, who doubtless underwrote the new business as Shudi's marriage portion. Jakob Wild took a lease of a new house in Meards Street in 1732, but the family were living in the district, and perhaps the street, before that. Certainly Handel visited Shudi, and was 'a constant guest at his table, ever well covered with German dishes and German wines'.[14]

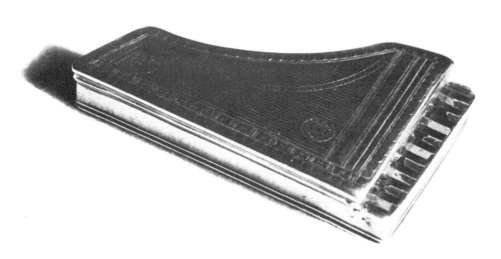

Shudi's snuffbox *(John Broadwood & Sons Ltd)*

In 1729 Handel went to Italy in search of opera singers and returned with the soprano Anna Strada del Pò. Anna Strada was a waddling woman with an ill-favoured face and at first she was nicknamed 'the Pig'. But her voice was superb. Handel relentlessly toured her round the fashionable salons, accompanying her on the harpsichord. The season at the King's Theatre was a success, and Handel gave Anna Strada a harpsichord made by Burkat Shudi. It is exactly on the pattern of the only Tabel harpsichord known to survive: the naturals are black and the sharps veneered and inlaid with ivory slips. The nameboard is inscribed 'Burckat Tschudi, Londini, fecit 1729'. Behind the nameboard is inscribed: '*Questo cimbalo e del^a Sig^ra Anna Strada 1731, London*' (This harpsichord was given to Madam Anna Strada 1731, London.)[15]

This would have been a remarkable advertisement for a harpsichord-maker still in his twenties and starting in business. In the years that followed, Shudi enlarged his trade, both as a maker and a tuner. The first written reference to the latter trade is in the Diary of John Hervey, first Earl of Bristol:

1733: April 11. Paid B Shudi for tuning the harpsichord, £0.17.6.

This is probably the bill for a year's tuning, or seven visits.

Soon the house in Meards Street must have been crowded with the paraphernalia of babyhood. Two girls were born (Sarah and Susanna), then a boy (Jacob, in honour of his grandfather) and then another girl (Margaret). But by 1736 all the little girls had died. The boy Jacob died in May 1736 at the age of three, a tragedy that may have been slightly eased by the birth to Catherine in the following month of a son, Joshua, followed eighteen months later by another son, Burkat. These children, the fifth and sixth to be born to the young couple, survived babyhood.

No doubt the presence of two small active children in a comparatively constricted house, particularly when the house was in the name of Jakob Wild and his wife, persuaded the Shudis to look for a house of their own. Although the business remained in Meards Street for the time being, and until Jakob Wild's death in 1741, Burkhardt Shudi and his family in 1739 took the lease of a house a few hundred yards to the west down Brewer Street, in Great Pulteney Street.[16] It was no less convenient for the Court at St James's, the Prince of Wales's house in Leicester Square, and for Shudi's fashionable customers in the great houses of the newly built Hanover and Cavendish Squares. Great Pulteney Street was on the site of Windmill Fields, to the east of Gelding Fields (which became 'Golden Square').[17]

The Pulteney family became tenants in 1575; and as the leases of the old houses fell in, early in the eighteenth century, Sir William Pulteney gave building leases to various craftsmen for redevelopment. Some were bricklayers or carpenters, but the leaseholder of what were to become Nos. 32 and 33 (London streets were not numbered until some years later) was Michael Helm, a victualler.

Account of Samuel Blumer, 'late foreman to Mr Shudi', 1753 *(The Broadwood Trust)*

Account of Burkat Shudi to HRH The Prince of Wales, 1750–1 (Royal Library, Windsor Castle)

Harpsichord by Burkat Shudi for Frederick Prince of Wales, 1740. Kew Palace *(Photo: A. C. Cooper Ltd)*

It was a tall, elegantly proportioned red-brick house of four storeys and a basement, with a frontage of 19 feet directly to the street. Shudi's rival Jacob Kirkman took a house in the same street in the same year (though at the other end, and on the east side). Samuel Blumer—a member of another Schwanden family—also had rooms in the street (and advertised himself as 'late foreman to Mr Shudi', a tribute to Shudi's growing reputation). John Clegg, the tragic young violinist who went mad yet drew crowds to the lunatic asylum to listen to his brilliant virtuosity, lived next door. A few years later, so did Michael Christian Festing, perhaps the greatest violinist of his day.[18] The street must have vibrated to the sound of strings.

In 1740 Shudi made a two-manual harpsichord for his patron, Frederick, Prince of Wales. It was No. 94, the case in burr walnut crossbanded with plain walnut (see above). As a result of this patronage, when in 1742 following the death of Jakob Wild he moved his business out of the Meards Street house, Shudi was able to advertise: 'This is to give notice that Burkat Shudi, Harpsichord Maker to HRH the

Prince of Wales, is removed from Meard's Street, in Dean Street, Soho, to Great Pulteney Street, Golden Square.'[19] His sign—for lacking street numbers, it was the custom for traders to hang out a distinguishing sign—was 'Ye Plume of Feathers'; that is, the Prince of Wales's crest.

This was a gesture of some significance. For the relations between Frederick, Prince of Wales and his father King George II had for some years been publicly acrimonious. In 1742 they had only just become grudgingly reconciled; and so Shudi's announcement had a particular meaning.

Despite the partisanship of society, Shudi prospered in those years. He was wealthy enough to afford the grand gesture. His staunch Protestantism led him to an admiration of Frederick the Great of Prussia, who was then the Protestant champion in Europe against the Catholics. Whether Shudi ever met Frederick is unknown; but other members of the Tschudi family were European diplomats and there may be an association through his relatives. When in 1744 Frederick captured Prague, Shudi built a grand and opulent harpsichord, lavishly gilded, and sent it to Frederick as a present. Frederick acknowledged it by sending Shudi a ring bearing the King's portrait.*

To mark the completion of this harpsichord, Shudi commissioned a picture (see Plate 2). It is a family conversation-piece and shows him in the parlour of the house in Great Pulteney Street, tuning a harpsichord. The harpsichord is on a particularly ornate stand, and tradition has it that this is indeed the one that he shortly afterwards presented to Frederick the Great.† Also in the picture are Shudi's wife Catherine, and their family at that date—the elder son, Joshua, and the younger, Burkat. The family cat is also included. On the wall is a mountain landscape near Schwanden, and portraits of the Prince and Princess of Wales.

The picture was painted to fill a particular space in the panelling above the fireplace in the little front parlour of the Great Pulteney Street house, where it remained for 150 years. The artist is unknown. Sir John Millais attributed it to Zoffany (who indeed liked to include cats in his pictures), but other experts discount this. Hogarth has been mentioned, and Mercier has also been suggested, because of his association with the Prince of Wales and because at about this time he painted a famous portrait of Handel with a harpsichord (see page 20). Yet another

---

* This ring, 'with the King of Prussia's picture', was bequeathed by Shudi to his friend John Snetzler, but has been lost.

† The whereabouts of this instrument, if it still exists, are unknown.

attribution is George Knapton, since in some lights a capital letter 'K' is allegedly to be identified faintly on the canvas.

The picture shows a confident and prosperous craftsman, surrounded by his growing family and demonstrating the best produce of his skill. It exudes prosperity and authority. Shudi was now the sort of master that the best craftsmen would be eager to work for. He would take on young craftsmen, teach them the secrets of the trade, and then they would start as makers on their own; and another young man would be taken on. So, in September 1761, John Broadwood (slightly older than most apprentices: he was nearly twenty nine) joined the Shudi workshop in Great Pulteney Street.

In the busy harpsichord workshop he was at first given the simple rough joinery to do, until he had proved himself: such work as glueing together the base-boards for the harpsichords that his distinguished master would finish. In the evenings he would climb the stairs in Great Pulteney Street to the attic that he shared with two or three other workmen. One was Andrew Clark. From the name we may deduce that he was a fellow Scot. Clarks farmed in the Lammermuir hills, and some are buried near the Broadwoods in Oldhamstocks churchyard. Clark had been working for Shudi for two years, so it is possible that he was a boyhood friend of John Broadwood. Another of Shudi's workmen in 1761 was probably a young immigrant who had arrived from Saxony the year before – Johannes Zumpe. Charles Burney tells us that when Zumpe first came to London he went to work for Shudi; and he came to London in 1760. It would not have been surprising that John Broadwood's first friends should have been Scots and immigrants from Europe, for in the 1760s Scots were much disliked in London; there was a lingering prejudice that they must be Jacobite and Papist. John Broadwood was neither, but the Scots accent is instantly distinguishable, and prejudice never stops to reason.

Chapter II

John Broadwood Joins the Business

1761–1769

T he second half of the eighteenth century was an age of scientific enquiry. Within comparatively few years Dr Joseph Priestley discovered oxygen; Benjamin Franklin made a major contribution to the understanding of the power of electricity; William Herschel advanced the study of astronomy, and Gilbert White's *Natural History and Antiquities of Selborne* examined in scientific detail the natural phenomena of the earth. It was in the year that Broadwood came to London that George III ordered lightning conductors to be installed on the roof of his new home, Buckingham House, following Franklin's discoveries.

The spirit of experiment was therefore in the air. Man was learning to harness natural forces and apply them to his service, in ways that were shortly to lead to the Industrial Revolution. This was Broadwood's world, and it was inspired by intellectual and scientific excitement.

It is no accident that many musical instruments were developed and changed in the eighteenth century. This is true of brass—particularly the trumpet—and woodwind, especially the oboe, clarinet and flute. Improvements were also made to that popular domestic instrument, the harp. But it was most marked in the change that overtook keyboard instruments, a change that happened most rapidly during John Broadwood's lifetime, and to which he was himself to become one of the most important contributors.

The limitations of the harpsichord were set out as early as 1713 by François Couperin, who wrote in the preface to his first book of harpsichord pieces: 'The Harpsichord is perfect as to its compass, and brilliant in itself, but as it is impossible to swell out or diminish the volume of its sound I shall always feel grateful to any who, by the exercise of infinite art supported by fine taste, contrives to render this instrument capable of expression.' Throughout Europe, harpsichord-makers were experimenting with ways of achieving this. They began with the patterns of the past, and one of those patterns was the clavichord, the small chamber instrument in which the key when depressed sent up a small metal tangent to touch the string instead of plucking it, as with the harpsichord. But the clavichord produced only a very small tone.

The credit for inventing an instrument that most nearly approximates to the modern piano is now given to Bartolomeo Cristofori (1655–1731), keeper of musical instruments to Prince Ferdinand dei Medici. Cristofori took the harpsichord as a pattern, and replaced the harpsichord jacks with small hammers tipped with soft leather. Cristofori also devised an escapement system, by which the key, returning to rest, brought a damper into contact with the string. Thus while the key remained depressed, the string would continue to vibrate. The action was primitive, and was only effective for comparatively slow passages of music; but it did enable the player to achieve a variety of tonal effects, depending on whether he depressed the key firmly or lightly.

Cristofori is known to have made at least three of these instruments by 1709, and probably made about thirty before he died. Cristofori's invention was described in print, with a drawing of the action, by a Rome journalist, Scipione Maffei, and others began to copy it. In 1711 an English monk in Rome, Father Wood, built an instrument apparently to this design, and sold it to Samuel Crisp, a friend of Dr Johnson and the Burney family. Crisp brought it to London, and sold it to Fulke Greville, after which it became widely known in musical circles.[1]

But the most important adoption of the invention seems to have been in the workshop of Gottfried Silbermann at Freiberg, near Dresden. Silbermann was an organ-builder and clavichord-maker. He began to make the new instrument, and demonstrated one to Johann Sebastian Bach on his visit to Dresden in 1736. The elder Bach was not much impressed; but his son Carl Philipp Emanuel Bach, who was clavier player to King Frederick of Prussia, was more interested and ordered several. Silbermann improved the action; and it may be because of his tradition of clavichord-making that he adopted the clavichord form, with the keyboard on the long side, rather than the harpsichord shape.

In 1755 a young man from Cambridge, the Rev. William Mason, bought on a tour of Europe a 'square pianoforte' and wrote enthusiastically to his friend the poet Thomas Gray: 'Oh, Mr Gray! I bought at Hamburg such a pianoforte, and so cheap!' On his return to England he talked so enthusiastically about this instrument that it was assumed in some quarters that he had invented it. Mason's pianoforte seems to have been a combined pianoforte and harpsichord.

A variety of these combined instruments survive, some with a barrel mechanism like a hurdy-gurdy, others combining the chamber organ with the harpsichord controlled by a single keyboard, the 'organa' or 'organised harpsichord'. Another extraordinary instrument of this period, though described (in the *Gentleman's Magazine* of 1759) as an 'electrical harpsichord', seems from its specification to have been more like a set of tubular bells in the form of musical glasses. Shudi certainly made 'organised harpsichords', though it is probable that the organ mechanism was supplied by his friend John Snetzler.

When the Seven Years' War effectively closed down Silbermann's workshop in Freiberg, his apprentices looked for work in that musical city of Europe that was still at peace. The first of them to reach London was apparently Americus Backers, a Dutchman, who set up in business in Jermyn Street. More followed, until eventually twelve were in London, for which reason they came to be known as 'the Apostles'. Among them were Zumpe, Pohlmann, Beyer, Buntebart and Schoene. Johannes Zumpe, as we have seen, took employment with Shudi; and it may have been from Zumpe, in the harpsichord workshop at Great Pulteney Street, that John Broadwood received his first introduction to the instrument with which his life was to be so closely associated—the piano-forte.[2]

If the first rule for luck in life is to be in the right place at the right time, John Broadwood followed it, for he arrived in London on the very eve of the first great commercial development of the piano. If the second rule is to seize new chances as they arise, then he did that too; for while his working loyalty was unswervingly to his employer Shudi in the making of harpsichords, he had the imagination to see that the piano would supersede it, and accordingly kept himself abreast of its changing technology.

In the 1760s Burkat Shudi was one of the two acknowledged great makers of harpsichords in London. The other, Jacob Kirkman, had overtaken him in business. Shudi's grandson acknowledges[3] that Kirkman had 'for many years, the greater part of the business in London' and suggests that this was because of Shudi's 'un-accommodating and independent deportment', which implies a strength of will and an unwillingness to compromise for commercial advantage. Kirkman became 'Harpsichord-maker to the King', while Shudi retained his allegiance to the Dowager Princess of Wales, the King's mother.

Perhaps the proudest point in the last decade of Shudi's career was when, in 1765, Frederick the Great of Prussia ordered four fine harpsichords for his New Palace at Potsdam. Two of them survived into the present century, Nos. 511 and 512, and William Dale gives this description of them:

> The pattern of the 'furniture' of both is the same. The keyboards are of the beautiful Hitchcock style, the sharps being inlaid with a slip of ivory. They have the full number of stops—machine, lute, octave, buff, first unison and second unison, and the Venetian swell was applied. Full directions for the working of these stops are given on No. 511, showing how novel the improvements were . . . . Here . . . are two fine and carefully constructed harpsichords made by Shudi in the zenith of his career, made certainly for Frederick the Great, when he had nearly completed

the *Neues Palais* at Potsdam, and according to Burney placed the one in the apartments of his sister the Princess Amelia and the other in that of his brother Prince Henry. Burney describes only the first one, No. 511, on oxidised silver legs. Both are inscribed 'Burckhardt Tschudi, fecit, Londini, 1766' . . .[4]

The use of his original German name-form is significant, since in England he invariably signed himself 'Burkat Shudi', even on legal documents.

A published affidavit of the period asserts that 'the greatest part of the work of the said Harpsichords was done by . . . Andrew Clark and John Broadwood, under the direction of their said master, Burkat Shudi; and particularly . . . John Broadwood remembers his having glewed up the founding boards of all the said Harpsichords, and his having assisted his said master Burkat Shudi, in putting the sounding-board (after [he] had wrought and finished the same under the immediate direction of . . . Burkat Shudi), into the first of the said Harpsichords sold to his Prussian Majesty.'

By the time he had been working for Shudi for three years, Broadwood had graduated to be one of his most trusted craftsmen, working on the most prestigious instruments. One of those harpsichords was to be heard in London, before its despatch to Potsdam, under the hands of a remarkable young prodigy: Wolfgang Amadeus Mozart, aged nine.

The Mozart family had left their Salzburg home nearly two years earlier, travelling from court to court giving concerts. Arriving in London in April 1764, the boy was soon playing before King George III and Queen Caroline. The father Leopold Mozart's contacts were excellent; top of the list was Johann Christian Bach, music master to the Queen.[5] Others on the list were 'Mr Tschudi Claviermacher in Pultney Street near Brewer Street', 'Mr Kirkman Claviermacher, Broad Street, Golden Square', 'Mr Neubauer Claviermacher, in Litchfield Street, St Anns Soho' and 'John Zumpe at the Sign of the golden guitar in Princes Street, Hannover Square' (the last, two of the Apostles).

The most fashionable small concert room in London at this time was Hickford's Room in Brewer Street. It had been taken over in the 1730s by the Hickford family, who promoted concerts by such contemporaries as Handel, Arne and Boyce.

Hickford's Room was only a few yards round the corner from Great Pulteney Street. On 13 May 1765 Burkat Shudi and his workmen set up there one of his 'Frederick the Great' harpsichords, for young Mozart. A month later the *Europaeische Zeitung* in Salzburg printed an account of the

Mozart at the harpsichord in Paris *(from the portrait by Carmontelle) Musée Condé, Chantilly (Photo Giraudon)*

occasion, which, from its florid tone (apart from the misprint of Shudi's name) was probably written by Leopold Mozart himself, ever promoting his brilliant son:

London, 5 July 1765. The very famous clavier maker Burkard Thudy [*sic*] of this city, a Swiss by birth, had the honour of making for the King of Prussia a wing-shaped instrument with two manuals which was very much admired by all who saw it. It has been regarded as particularly noteworthy that Mr Thudy connected all the stops to a pedal, so that they can be drawn by treading, one after another, and the decrease and increase of tone may be varied at will, which *crescendo* and *decrescendo* has been long wished for by clavier players. Mr Thudy has moreover conceived the good notion of having his extraordinary instrument played for the first time by the most extraordinary clavier player in the world, namely by the very celebrated master of music Wolfg. Mozart, aged nine, the admirable son of the Salzburg Kapellmeister, Herr Mozart. It was quite enchanting to hear the fourteen-year-old sister of this little virtuoso playing the most difficult sonatas on the clavier with the most astonishing dexterity and her brother accompanying her extempore on another clavier. Both perform wonders.[6]

This is a remarkable account for several reasons. It suggests that the harpsichord played by the young Mozart was the first to which Shudi had added the 'machine stop', controlled by a pedal. The 'machine', which was just coming into use at this time, was added to the majority of Shudi's harpsichords from this year, and was adopted by his friendly rival, Kirkman. There is however a curious anomaly in the report. If young Mozart played the new harpsichord he can hardly have used the pedal which was the remarkable feature of that instrument. His feet would not have reached it. The famous portrait of him done in Paris by Carmontelle two years earlier, evidently playing a Taskin harpsichord (see page 35), indicates that his feet were then some eighteen inches from the ground. It is scarcely credible that he could have grown enough in two years to reach the pedal. Presumably the stops were pre-set for him.

There is another puzzling feature of these Frederick the Great harpsichords. Dale says that they were fitted with the Venetian swell. In that case there should have been two pedals (and the photographs in Dale's book show only one).

For some years harpsichord-makers had been experimenting with ways of achieving variations in volume by fitting shutters to the lid. The

Shudi's 'Venetian swell', closed (top left), part open (top right), and (below) fully open, showing mechanism. National Trust, Benton Fletcher Collection, Fenton House *(Photo: Graham Miller)*

'nag's head' swell was in fairly common use, and some makers adopted a formidable device that lifted and closed a section of the lid by means of a pedal. Shudi invented the 'Venetian swell' which is a complete inner lid, made from slats of wood laid lengthwise in the pattern of a Venetian blind, and worked by a pedal. It was much the most effective of the 'swell' mechanisms devised for the harpsichord, and was soon widely adopted, probably under licence from Shudi, who also built them into older instruments made both by himself and by other makers. He patented the device on 18 December 1769, as

> a piece of mechanism or machinery by which the Harpischord is very much Improved, invented by him the same Burkat Shudi . . . The said piece of mechanism or machinery invented by him the said Burkat Shudi Doth consist of a cover extending the Breadth of the Harpsichord and from the front Board of the Harpsichord to the Ruler, of an indefinite Number of Valves which with their Frame extend the Breadth of the Harpsichord, and the length thereof from the Ruler to the small End, which Valves are opened and shut by a Number of small levers equal to the Number of Valves inserted or fixed in an Axis, Spindle or Bar turned by a Pedal.[7]

With this invention, Shudi had brought the harpsichord to a new pitch of refinement. He regarded it as a notable development that would maintain the harpsichord unchallenged as the consort of the organ among keyboard instruments.

There is no mention of the piano in Shudi's papers. That is not surprising. He was a harpsichord man. It may not be too fanciful to visualise old Shudi, master craftsman, observing his young workmen interesting themselves in these newfangled little German pianos, and tolerating their activities as the misguided folly of youth, which they were free to pursue so long as they did not do it in his working time.

The reputation of Shudi's harpsichords was indeed to survive for many more years. There were fine examples all over Europe, and Mozart played another of them in Naples in 1772, as Leopold Mozart noted in a letter: 'Yesterday evening we called on the English ambassador, Hamilton*, a London acquaintance of ours, whose wife plays the clavier

---

* (Sir) William Hamilton (1730–1803), diplomat and antiquarian, had been ambassador to the Court of Naples since 1764. His first wife, Miss Barlow, whom he married in 1758, was a gifted musician. She died in 1782, and Hamilton married for a second time—Emma, the Lady Hamilton who was to captivate Nelson.

with unusual feeling and is a very pleasant person. She trembled at having to play before Wolfgang. She has a valuable instrument, made in England by Tschudi, which has two manuals and a pedal, so that the two manuals can be disconnected by the action of the foot. We found at Hamilton's house Mr Beckford* and Mr Weis, also London acquaintances.'[8]

The Hamiltons' harpsichord had earlier been admired by Dr Charles Burney, who on his tour of Italy in 1770 'found three English harpsichords in the three principal cities of Italy, which are regarded by the Italians as so many phenomena. One was made by Shudi, and is in the possession of the Hon. Mrs Hamilton at Naples. The other two, which are of Kirkman's make, belong to Mrs Richie at Venice, and to the Hon. Mrs Earle, who resided at Rome when I was there'.[9]

Shudi's 'unaccommodating and independent deportment' was demonstrated in a public squabble with his nephew Joshua, the son of his elder brother Nicholas. In 1742 Nicholas had to fly from Schwanden when, in a fight in a public house, a man who had tried to intervene between Tschudi and an adversary was killed. Nicholas came to London, and then emigrated to America where he died in 1760. His son Joshua, having been a seaman, arrived on his uncle Burkat's London doorstep and was taught joinery. At some time before 1767, possibly after another family quarrel, he left, set up on his own as a harpsichord-maker, and started to put about that he, Joshua, was the real maker of the 'Frederick the Great' harpsichords.

Burkat Shudi announced in furious newspaper advertisements that Joshua was 'only a joiner', and that his, Burkat's, 'mistery' or skill had never been passed to anyone. Joshua countered in the *Gazetteer* of 12 January 1767 that 'harpsichord makers must be joiners, and is the comon course of our business . . . If he never comunicated his mistery, as he calls it, to any one, what figure will his apprentices make.'[10]

On the day that broadside was published three of Shudi's workmen, Andrew Clark, Thomas Nixon and John Broadwood, swore an affidavit that 'Joshua Shudi never did begin and finish any one Harpsichord during the time that this deponent hath worked for the said Burkat Shudi'. This affidavit, published in the *Public Advertiser*, describes precisely what each of the workmen did do, particular in making the 'Frederick the Great' harpsichords.

Joshua Shudi remained in business as a harpsichord-maker until his early death in 1774, after which his widow Mary advertised that she was

---

* Peter Beckford MP, discoverer and patron of Muzio Clementi.

continuing to trade, describing her late husband as 'nephew and disciple of the late celebrated Burkat Shudi'.*

Joshua's rhetorical jibe, 'what figure will his apprentices make', must have hit home. For in January 1767 Burkat Shudi was approaching his sixty fifth birthday. Of the two sons in the famous family portrait, the elder (also, poignantly, named Joshua) had died at the age of eighteen in 1754. The younger son, Burkat, was now in his mid-twenties, but while he worked for his father there is no evidence that he had inherited any of his father's skill. Shudi had married for the second time in 1759, and his new wife (Elizabeth Meyer, daughter of another London Swiss family) had presented him with another daughter; so that there were three daughters to be provided for: Margaret (who was twenty in January 1767), Barbara, who was eighteen, and the baby Elizabeth. What would happen to them were anything to befall their father? Burkat Shudi needed to ensure the succession, both as a matter of pride in the workshop that he had himself created, and as security for his beloved daughters.

It was inevitable that living and working in the same house the workmen became part of the family. As he gave more and more challenging tasks to John Broadwood, and saw them accomplished with a craftsmanship and skill that rivalled his own, Shudi must also have observed the affection growing up between his best craftsman and his second daughter Barbara. As affection ripened into a deeper love, Shudi did nothing to discourage it. Eventually, on 2 January 1769, John Broadwood married Barbara Shudi. He was thirty six, and she was a month short of her twenty first birthday. Truly, Shudi gained a son, and a son capable of carrying on one of the great harpsichord workshops. Thereafter the harpsichords sent out from Great Pulteney Street, unless they were Shudi's alone, bore the inscription 'Burkat Shudi et Johannes Broadwood'.

Throughout the 1760s, while devoting his energies to the harpsichord business, Broadwood was becoming more and more interested in the development of the piano. If his fascination was first aroused by his fellow-workman at Shudi's, Johannes Zumpe, he must have watched eagerly the commercial success Zumpe soon achieved from his workshop in Hanover Square with his little 'square pianos'. This is substantiated by the account[11] written by John Broadwood's son, who says that

---

* Only two harpsichords bearing Joshua Shudi's name have survived into this century, one of them dated two years after his death. There appears to have been a third Shudi making harpsichords in London at this time, named Bernard; Boalch, in *Makers of the Harpsichord and Clavichord*, says 'that Bernard was related to Burkat Shudi is beyond doubt', but no Shudi of that name appears on the very detailed Shudi family tree.

Zumpe 'on his return from Germany, where he had been to visit his relations, brought back with him the first of these instruments seen in England, and about the years 1768 or 1769, began to make them'. (James Shudi Broadwood is wrong in his dates: Zumpe was making them several years earlier than that.)

They were in length about four feet, the hammers very lightly covered with a thin coat of leather; the strings were small, nearly the size of those used on the Harpsichord; the tones clear, what is now called thin and wiry;—his object being, seemingly, to approach the tones of the Harpsichord, to which the ear, at that period, was accustomed . . . Beyer, Buntebart and Schoene—all Germans— soon after this introduction by Zumpe, began making Pianos, and by enlarging them, produced more tone in their instruments.

Zumpe began to manufacture them in quantity, selling them at £50; he was followed by his compatriot Johannes Pohlmann. The first recorded advertisement for a piano in Britain is in 1763; in *Mortimer's Directory* Frederic Neubaur announces the sale of 'harpsichords, piano-fortes, lyrichords and claffichords'.

Four years later, at a benefit performance of *The Beggar's Opera* at the Theatre Royal, Covent Garden, Miss Brickler sang 'a favourite Song from *Judith*, accompanied by Mr Dibdin, on a new instrument, called a PIANO-FORTE'. In the following year, at a concert at the Thatched House, St James's, Johann Christian Bach played a solo on a Zumpe pianoforte.

The little square pianoforte was thus not only a great success in the home, but also making its first appearance in the concert hall and theatre. There is a suggestion, though no more,* that Broadwood may himself have been making them by 1770, within a year of coming into partnership with Shudi.

Simultaneously with this flowering of the 'square', several makers were experimenting with the development of what was to become the 'grand', based on the harpsichord shape and frame.

The story was passed down from John Broadwood to his son James Shudi Broadwood, and is thus given by *his* son: 'John Broadwood, then

*H. F. Broadwood's *Observations* on the *'Notes'* of his father, James Shudi Broadwood (1862) contains the assertion in a footnote that 'We have traces, in some shreds remaining of old books, of a Piano (i.e. a small F.F. square) of 1770'—but there is no indication whether this refers to one of Broadwood's own make, or whether it was a square by some other manufacturer in which he was dealing.

41

Grand by Americus Backers, late 1760s. National Trust, Benton Fletcher Collection, Fenton House *(Photo: Graham Miller)*

with his apprentice Stodart, in the employ of Burkhardt Shudi, used to go of an evening to Jermyn-street, to assist Backers in bringing his mechanism to perfection. This was the case, and hence the dying man recommended the further care of his invention to his friend John Broadwood.'[12]

Americus Backers is recorded as living in Jermyn Street (under the name 'Andrew Backus') from 1763 to 1778.[13] He may have worked for the Hitchcock spinet workshop on his first arrival in London. The link between Backers, Broadwood and Stodart in the development of what came to be known as the 'English Grand Action' is interesting, and it is true that a surviving Backers grand, numbered 21* is dated 1772 and has an action very like that later adopted by Broadwood. Robert Stodart was in 1777 to take out the first patent using the word 'grand' in association with the piano. From the Backers dating, it is therefore reasonable to suppose that those evening sessions in the Jermyn Street workshop when the three men worked to perfect their new piano action took place at some time in the late 1760s, and certainly before Shudi's retirement.

Little is known of Stodart's early life, though H.F. Broadwood says that 'R. Stodart was a private in the Royal Horse Guards, a corps for admission to which the private had to pay £100; having little duty, and consequently much leisure, he apprenticed himself for three years to John Broadwood'. This sounds like an early instance of moonlighting in the Blues, but cannot be precisely accurate. Up to 1788 (when the Regiment was reformed, partly because of this abuse) 'Private Gentlemen' paid 100 guineas for admission to the ranks of the Troops of Horse Guards, which were permanently based in London; but it is improbable that even in those rough and ready days, a Trooper could have taken a formal apprenticeship while still officially in the Army.[14]

Whatever the truth of Stodart's status, he was assuredly at Broadwood's right hand as he worked on the new piano action; and by the time Broadwood took over effective management of 'Shudi & Broadwood' their development of the piano action was well advanced.

* The property of the Duke of Wellington, and now in the Russell Collection at Edinburgh University. Another Backers grand, undated, is at Fenton House, Hampstead.

Chapter III

Shudi and Broadwood

1769–1795

*T*he quiet lodgings of Dr Manette were in a quiet street-corner not far from Soho-square . . . There were few buildings, then, [1775] north of the Oxford-road [Oxford Street], and forest-trees flourished, and wild flowers grew, and the hawthorn blossomed, in the now vanished fields. As a consequence, country airs circulated in Soho with vigorous freedom, instead of languishing into the parish like stray paupers without a settlement; and there was many a good south wall, not far off, on which the peaches ripened in their season.

The Doctor occupied two floors of a large still house, where several callings purported to be pursued by day . . . In a building at the back, attainable by a court-yard where a plane-tree rustled its green leaves, church-organs claimed to be made, and silver to be chased, and likewise gold to be beaten . . .

Charles Dickens: *A Tale of Two Cities*

W ith John Broadwood's marriage, old Burkat Shudi, his wife and their youngest daughter Elizabeth moved out of Great Pulteney Street to their new house in Charlotte Street off Tottenham Court Road, leaving 'the workshop' to John and Barbara. Her elder sister Margaret, still unmarried, and young Burkat remained behind together with the workmen who 'lived in'. Like many young wives faced with the responsibilities of housekeeping for the first time, Barbara began an accounts book[1], solemnly inscribing the first page 'this is the Book belongs to Barbara Broadwood'. Sensibly she started it with an inventory: 'A List of Mr Broadwood's Cloathes', though it is not exhaustive and looks as though it consists only of the items that might go to the laundress—'12 Shirts Ruffelld, 9 plain ditto, 12 Neck Cloath' and ending with '3 Night Caps' and '8 pocket Handkerchiefs'.

Then there is a list of harpsichords that were probably being built on the date of the hand-over. There were twelve of them, of a total value of over £500, the first being 'Dutchess of Marlborough £78.15'. The

'This is the book belongs to Barbara Broadwood' *(Barbara Broadwood's household book, 1769) (Bodleian Library, Oxford)*

47

following pages are given over to shopping lists, of which this, from 12 March 1770, is typical:

	£	s	d
A Bullox Heart	0	1	2
Gravy Beef	0	0	2
Potatoes	0	0	1½
herbes	0	0	2
Paid the Baker	0	0	11½
Wood	0	0	2
Bakeing	0	0	1
paid peggy	0	1	0
half a pound of Butter	0	0	4½
three pounds of Soap	0	1	6
half a pound of Soap	0	0	3
Starch	0	1	6
Tea	0	0	7½
Suet	0	0	2
Eggs	0	0	2

The following week she was a little more extravagant, and bought 'A Leg of Mutton' for 1s 10d.

From time to time, no doubt when John was out when people called with orders, she jotted down business requests in 'her book', as this entry in 1772 shows:

Lady Moores Thitchfield Street Harpd. & Guitar Came Home.
Mrs Walker to tune Some Morning this Week at Nine o'Clock Lower Grosvenor St
Mr Gould Lower Grosvenor to tune a Spinnet on Mon Morn
Lady Beauclerk Somerset House to tune Her Harpd. on Monday Morning.
Lady Edgcumb at Two o'Clock Monday Morning
Lady Walgrove Whitehall
Miss Colebrooke Monday Morning Arlington St
Miss Lawes Spring Gardens to tune her Harpd. Friday Morning between the Hours of Twelve and Three.

How John Broadwood coped with four tunings on that Monday morning we cannot know; but the list indicates the fashionable character of his clientele and the demand for his services.

Signatures and seals of John Broadwood and Burkat Shudi, 1771 *(The Broadwood Trust)*

Barbara made some entries in the book which, tantalisingly undated, give other glimpses of domestic life. One page is headed 'Five pieces of Handkerch' and lists various names: 'Mrs Rector, Mrs Wild, Mrs Ruff, Mrs Calwell, Mrs Bates, Mrs Hands, Mrs Beck, Miss Shudi, Mrs Motrey, Mrs Patadergell, Mrs Broadwood, Mrs Jenny and Mrs Newby.'

There are numbers before each name, and a sum of money after it varying from 7s. to one guinea. Was this a sewing-circle of wives held at Great Pulteney Street? Mould suggests* (convincingly) that Mrs Wild was probably the wife of Jacob Wild, brother of Barbara's uncle; Mrs Bates may have been the wife of Joah Bates who conducted the Handel commemorative concert, while Mrs Beck could be the wife of the piano-maker Frederick Beck.

After little more than a year, old Burkat was clearly confident that his son-in-law was running the business competently, and by a series of legal indentures he formally made it over to him. On 7 March 1771 he leased John Broadwood the premises in Great Pulteney Street and Bridle Lane at a rent of £50 a year. He did however reserve 'sufficient and convenient room in the said messuage for the harpsichords now belonging to the said Burkat Shudi until such time as the same shall be sold, and particularly the use of the dining room for the new harpsichords belonging to the said Burkat Shudi . . .'

* 'The Broadwood Books' by Charles Mould (articles in *The Harpsichord Magazine*, 1973–4)

By another indenture of the same date, Burkat Shudi licensed John Broadwood to continue the business, together with the use of the Venetian swell, Broadwood to pay a royalty for each harpsichord sold varying from 16 guineas for a double-manual with five stops, to five guineas for a single-manual with two stops.

By yet a third indenture on the same date, John Broadwood contracted that in consideration of the sum of £500 paid to him by Burkat Shudi as Barbara's marriage portion, should Barbara or any of their children survive him, his executors would pay £1000 for their support. As yet there were no children; but in fact Barbara was just three months' pregnant and a daughter (named Catherine Margaret) was born the following September. Next year they hired a maid, as Barbara recorded in her book: '1772 Ann Davies came to my Service. Agreed Six Pounds Wages and her Tea – for Washing the Child's things Ten Shillings per Year.'

A son and heir (named James Shudi) was born at Great Pulteney Street on 20 December in that year. Old Burkat was able to see and hold his grandson, who was to carry his business forward to still greater times. Diligently John paid his father-in-law due royalties, presenting him with detailed accounts. These indicate that in the year 1772 he sold twenty two harpsichords, of which nine were double-manual and thirteen single-manual, some with and some without the Venetian swell. Including the house rent he paid Shudi £219 17s, after discounting various domestic items which show that he carried out other filial duties: 'Making Boards round the garden in Charlote Street . . . 16.0'.

In July 1773 Burkat Shudi, precise as ever, made his will; on 19 August, he died at his home in Charlotte Street at the age of seventy one. The scale of his bequests implies, apart from the business, a personal estate of some £8000, together with the freehold house in Charlotte Street. Most touching, perhaps, is the careful apportionment of his proudest possessions. The 'family picture' was to go to Barbara Broadwood; his daughters were to have, as well as the portraits of themselves, 'one of my double-keyed Harpsichords of my own making'. His great friend and executor, the organ-builder John Snetzler, was to have 'my Ring with the King of Prussia's picture'. John Broadwood was to inherit the rights in the Venetian swell, provided that he paid young Burkat an annuity of £40 (John signed the necessary legal document in the following month). Probably it was old age that made Shudi forget, when first drafting the will, that the family home in Schwanden was still in his name; a few days later he added a codicil bequeathing it to his sister Barbara, who lived there.

Burkat Shudi remembered his particular friends. John Keble, who was to have 'two guineas for a Ring', was organist of St George's, Hanover Square. John Snetzler was one of the leading organ-builders of the day, and a fellow Swiss (he was born in Schaffhausen).

An endearing picture of him in 1765 survives in this anecdote, which though written of the astronomer Herschel, well describes the dedication of the German-Swiss instrument makers.

About this time a new organ for the parish church of Halifax was built by Snetzler . . . Mr Herschel and six others were candidated for the organist's place . . . The second performer was Mr Wainwright, afterwards Dr Wainwright, of Manchester, whose finger was so rapid that old Snetzler, the organ-builder, ran about the church exclaiming, 'Te devil, te devil, he run over te key like one cat, he will not give my piphes room for to shpeak.' [Herschel] ascended the organ loft and produced from the organ so uncommon a fulness, such a volume of slow, solemn harmony, that I could by no means account for the effect. 'Aye, aye' cried old Snetzler, 'tish very goot, very goot indeed. I vil luf tish man, for he gives my piphes room for to shpeak.' Having afterwards asked Mr Herschel by what means . . .he produced so uncommon an effect, he replied, 'I told you fingers would not do' and produced two pieces of lead from his waistcoat pocket. 'One of these,' said he, 'I placed on the lowest key of the organ, and the other on the octave above: thus by accommodating the harmony I produced the effect of four hands instead of two.'[2]

When in March 1771 John Broadwood became effective head of the business, he began a Journal[3] in which to record orders. The entries, at least in the early years, are very brief and often consist merely of names— the names of the people who had booked tunings. Addresses, in that compact society, were unnecessary. The principal musical events were also familiar, so that the hiring of a harpsichord for a concert was simply entered ast 'Oritorio', or 'A reharsle', without any need to put down where. Only after a few years is the 'Thatched House', the main music room of the period, identified by name.

In the early 1770s John Broadwood was conducting four types of business. He was making harpsichords, and already as an acknowledged master selling them abroad as well as at home. He was hiring harpsichords for domestic use and for concerts. He had an extensive tuning business (the instruments soon went out of tune and had to be adjusted at least once a month), covering London and the home counties,

1773
Octobr 29 Sent a Delista Harp for
hire to Sir T. Rinnal
for the use of Miss Palmer

30 Sent for the Sngl Harpsichord
that was hired to Lord
Sandwick home

Novr 4 Mr Dashwood Harp
& Pianoforte

Novr 5 Sent mr Colike Harpd to Clapham
Dutches of Bedford Harpd tuned
Mr Lavance Red Loyn spinet
Mrs Grass Mr Bach

6 Lady Mayne   5

9 Miss Phips Lady mulgrave

10 Mr Duvalé new Court
Mr Rogers
Mrs Lecoke
Sent mr Reny new Harp
home to Keny Street

13 Tuned a Spinet at } Paid 5
Lord Bruces

Lady Edgcombe
16 Repaired any thing mr Dinols
16 Mr Callioh Paid for his Harp
17 Miss Walter at Bunny Hill
Mr Pother
Mr Grennough

1773
Novr 19 To tuning Miss Scot Harp & other
Pianoforte — saw Bill —   13 6
To Lord Spencer Pianoforte
To miss Perren Harpsichord
22 To mr Dashwood Pianoforte
in John Street
20 To mr Leatham Harp
22 Miss Pelham sent home Harp she hired
23 Tuning Lady Charlot Tufton

Mr Story Harp
24 To mr Nicod Harp
To mr Lecoke
25 Repaired a H

26 To mrs Burnal at Putenham — 10 6
mrs Boult at Do your bill 1 0 6
27 Mr Altham Harp at Thunder

29 Mr Cleark Harp Repaird
and Sent home —
Lady Chalvien Murry hired a Harp
30 Miss Phippe Bought a new
Harp and was sent home —
Mr Johnne at Clapham

Decr 1 To Dutche of Bedford —
To unpacking miss vennons
Harpsichord — — —
2 To mr Dashwood Piano forte
in John Street
To Barron Aughar Harp
To mrs Brudnaill Harp

Two pages from the Broadwood Journal, 1773 *(Bodleian Library, Oxford)* and dealing with instruments other than those of his own make. Finally, he was selling a variety of musical instruments.

The day of Shudi's death, 19 August 1773, is recorded in the Journal simply with a dash (his burial in the grounds of the Tottenham Court Road Chapel a few days later is not recorded). On the following day, the Journal notes: 'Sent the Empress Harpd on Board of Ship.' This was the double-manual (No.691) made to the order of the Empress Maria Theresa (and now in the Brussels Conservatoire). In the following pages are more instances of the aristocratic customers whom Broadwood served: the Duke of Leeds, the Duchesses of Bedford and Richmond and the 'Dutches of Malbury'—presumably that Duchess of Marlborough who ordered a harpsichord two years earlier.

John Broadwood's spelling of names, in the custom of the time, could be arbitrary; as when on 29 October he noted the sending of 'an Octave Harpd for hire to Sir Jos Rennals for the use of Miss Palmer'. Sir Joshua Reynolds frequently hired harpsichords from Broadwood, and may well have included at least one in his paintings; for there is a link between Broadwoods and a Reynolds portrait through the tuning entry for 20 August 1773: 'Miss Pain at Enfield Chase Paid 7s 6d' (See page 54).

With the aristocracy, the arts are well represented in the Journal. 'Mr Bach' appears once—presumably Johann Christian Bach, the youngest son of Johann Sebastian and known as 'the London Bach', who at this time was living in Soho Square and was a leader of London's musical life.

In March 1774 there was another order from a distinguished artist:

Mr Dashwood and Gardine bought a harpsichord, No.708, for
   Mr Gainsborough, painter in the Circle, Bath.
March 11. Mr Gainsborough's harpsichord was packed and sent
   to Bath.

'Gardine' was Felice de Giardini, the Italian violinist who was leader of the Pantheon Concerts. In later years, when Gainsborough moved to London, his name figures regularly in the Journal; evidently he had a tuning contract with Broadwood.

The ready availability of Gainsborough's harpsichord implies that by 1774 John Broadwood had reversed his master Shudi's policy of only making to order, and was now making for stock. But the evidence is that he continued Shudi's practice of making the whole instrument himself, rather than buying in ready-made parts. He supplied parts to other makers, and as he allowed other makers to use Shudi's patent Venetian swell (Kirkman was the most distinguished of his rivals who adopted it),

Mrs Paine and her two daughters, by Sir Joshua Reynolds *(Lady Lever Art Gallery, Port Sunlight)*

so on request he would add devices patented by others. Thus he added the celestine stop, invented by his neighbour, Adam Walker. This was a downstriking hammer which hit the strings at a point where a silk band revolved against them, activated by a treadle. This gave a sustaining effect. There is a note that Broadwood paid Walker £9, perhaps a royalty for the use of the device.

Broadwood bought mahogany in considerable quantity (on 8 June 1784 he paid a Mr Compton £62 6s 11d for 'Mohogeny at Sale', and another entry records the receipt of '2 cart loads of Mahoganey from Mr Alldee'). Some of his wire came from 'Willm Taverner Brass Copper and Iron Wire Drawer No 4 Peter Street, Half Moon Alley, Bishopsgate Without'. A printed label found on one harpsichord suggests a source of ivory for keys: 'William Drane/Comb maker/ (No. 25) Aldgate Street/ makes and sells all sorts of Ivory, tortoiseshell, horn and Boxcombs, wholesale and retail sells also Ivory, Bone and Hard-wood-Turn'.[4]

A note in October 1782 that 'Mr Williams Bought 6 sounding boards' suggests that Broadwood was supplying parts for the manufacture or repair of instruments.

Orders came in from all over the world. In 1775, probably as a consequence of the success of Empress Maria Theresa's instrument, an order arrived for a harpsichord for Dr Josef Haydn in Vienna (No.762, now in the Kunsthistorisches Museum, Vienna). Harpsichords went to Russia, Denmark, Portugal, Italy and France, and a number to the West Indies—Barbados, St Kitts and Jamaica. Agents' names appearing in the Journal include Mr Brooks, Oporto; William Ware, Belfast; Corri & Sutherland, Scotland; Neil Stewart, Edinburgh; Mr Obert, Boulogne; and Leotard Cazenove, France (via Dunkirk). There were also agents in America.

Sales could be erratic, but the hiring and tuning business provided continuing employment. Sometimes the demand was such that the family's own domestic instruments had to be sent out, as shown by an entry that 'Burkat's harpsichord' was 'sent on hire to Miss Chumley'. Two instruments that were regularly on hire had been made by the Ruckers in Antwerp many years before; their reliability was such that they were regularly in use until finally sold off, one in 1790 and the other in 1792, when the harpsichord was going out of fashion.

The usual charge for hiring was 10s 6d per month, but tuning charges varied with the frequency and distance. On 31 July 1772 'Miss Naville at Ipsom' paid 5s, but the 'Princess Amelia at Gunnessbury' £1 1s; 'Miss Secan at Rigate' paid 10s 6d, but 'Lady Chesterfield by yᵉ Qarter' paid £1 1s. The larger sums were probably a contract for several visits, for in July

1772 'Mrs Williams of Little Teatchfield agreed to pay a Guinea for five times'. The basic charge seems to have been 5s, but 7s 6d for those living further out such as Miss Pain at Edmonton, and 10s 6d for those in the depths of the country at 'Bekenham' or 'Tames Ditton'.

Broadwood also sold guitars when they were fashionable (the harpsichord-makers began to fear for their trade, Kirkman bought up a supply and put them in the hands of street singers, so that the aristocracy, seeing them played by vulgar folk, abandoned the fashion and returned to their keyboards.)[5] Broadwood also sold 'clavierorgana', the combined harpsichords and organs made by Shudi and Snetzler.

The reference to the hiring of 'Burkat's harpsichord' is the last certain reference in the records to Burkat Shudi the younger. There is no indication that he took any practical part in the business, certainly after his father's death; nor is there any reference to the date on which Broadwood stopped paying him the annuity of £40 to which he was entitled under his father's will. Some have suggested that he dropped out of the business in the 1780s; others have put the date of his death at 1792. The only clue may be in the fact that all Broadwood harpsichords bore the names 'Shudi & Broadwood' until 1793; and only one is known— supposedly the last harpsichord made by the firm—bearing the single name 'Johannes Broadwood' (now in the Russell Collection, Edinburgh); that is No. 1155, dated 1793.

The early summer of 1776 found London in a fever of political excitement. The American colonies were in rebellion, and the American Congress passed the Declaration of Independence on July 4. On that date John Broadwood despatched a single-manual harpsichord to a Mr Organ at Bath. Two days later he went down to Beckenham and tuned Mr Bennet's harpsichord. The Journal has no further entries for five days. After a blank space on the page, there is a note that he tuned for Lady Chesterfield on the 11th (presumably an unavoidable contract) and that Miss Ride paid her bill. Another gap follows. On the 16th he went out of town again, tuning at Wimbledon and Putney, and on the next day went to tune for Lady Cranborne 'in the country'. Not until the 19th did he get back to business, and 'shipp'd a large harpsichord for Mr Greville'.

The writing in the Journal on these pages is uncharacteristically tight, small and tense. For John Broadwood had personal worries that must have far outweighed the nation's concerns in his mind. The family records explain this apparently desultory abandonment of the business for ten days, represented in the Journal simply by blanks. On 8 July 1776 his beloved wife Barbara died at the age of twenty seven, probably in bearing her fourth child, a boy who was given his father's Christian

A Broadwood harpsichord of 1793 (probably the last made). The Russell
Collection of Early Keyboard Instruments, Edinburgh *(Photo: Tom Scott;
copyright, University of Edinburgh)*

name. She left her husband with three small children to bring up—
Catherine Margaret, aged nearly five; James Shudi, aged three-and-a-
half; and baby John. (Another daughter had died in infancy: the baby
was to die at the age of four.) Probably their spinster Aunt Margaret, who
still lived in Great Pulteney Street, took the place of their mother as best
she could. Margaret was dedicated to good works: she lent £1,000 of her
patrimony, a huge sum, to the Wells Street Chapel.

The Journal indicates that for a week following his wife's death John Broadwood did virtually nothing in the business. In the second week, he took himself alone out of town, using the tunings as a reason to ride out in the countryside that he always loved. This bereavement, at a time when his prosperity was increasing year by year, was a severe blow. The five years that followed seem to have been a fallow period in which his inventiveness flagged and his imaginative drive was curbed. Certainly his work on the development of the piano slowed down in those years: and it may be significant that it was in the following year, 1777, that the first patent was taken out for a grand piano (the first recorded use of the word 'grand' in this connection) not by Broadwood but by his young friend and former employee, Robert Stodart.

But when John Broadwood was working at full power again, through his tuning experience he was well placed to observe the success of the piano in fashionable society. For a time he was content to leave the market for grands in the possession of his friend Stodart, who had been one of his tuners, whose instruments he always admired, while he himself concentrated upon developing and improving the square, still in the 1770s a small, fragile box. From 1780 he remodelled and strengthened the case, moving the wrest pins from the soundboard to the left side of the back of the case. He further added a second soundboard beneath the first, linking them with a sound-post to improve the tone. These improvements were immediately successful, and he patented them in 1783, together with a brass under-damper that was a further refinement of the action.

The first identifiable reference to a square with these refinements is on 29 September 1783 when 'a P.F. with brass dampers' was sent to Miss Gibbs of Cork, at a price of £21. The first piano number quoted is 'Square piano No. 206', sold on 5 January 1784.[6]

In May 1781 he shipped a harpsichord and a pianoforte to Paris 'for Mr Clementi'. Muzio Clementi was a friend, and one of his sternest critics. Named by his contemporaries 'Father of the Pianoforte'—the legend is on his tomb in the cloisters of Westminster Abbey—he combined in one extraordinary personality the skills of virtuoso performer, composer, salesman, propagandist and charmer. Born in Italy, he was organist of a Rome church at the age of eleven; adopted by a rich Englishman, Peter Beckford, he was brought to England to continue his studies. By the age of twenty five he was conductor of the Italian opera in London. In 1781, when he ordered a Broadwood piano to take to Paris, he was embarking on the first of his continental tours. Later he was to buy out the London music house of Longman & Broderip, and later still to recruit his own piano-maker in Frederick William Collard. The flavour of

John Broadwood in middle age *(The Broadwood Trust)*

his criticism of those early pianos may be savoured in one broadside he fired back from Berlin to Fred Collard: 'The touch is both a lazy and lousy one—tho' 'tis thrummed on night and day, it is as disobedient as ever. Some radical fault. Rember a light, well-repeating touch is a grand article in Germany . . .'[7]

Through Clementi, Broadwood had the advantage of an informed judgement of piano developments in the major musical capitals of Europe at a vital period.

A few days before Christmas 1781 John Broadwood married for the second time. His new wife was Mary Kitson, the daughter of James Kitson of Doncaster. She was twenty nine, and soon was starting his 'second family' of six children, born between 1782 and 1793.

Square piano by John Broadwood, 1785 (with the double soundboard). Colt Clavier Collection *(Photo: Photographic Records Ltd)*

An analysis of the Broadwood Journal for the years 1772–1784* demonstrates conclusively that it was from 1783 that the pianoforte began to overhaul the harpsichord in popularity, and that it was in those years that the supremacy Broadwoods were to enjoy throughout Europe for many years was founded. The Journal records all transactions done by the firm—sales, hiring and tuning—and the entries are not always detailed enough to provide solid evidence of the numbers of instruments made and sold. But the number of transactions done rose from around 700 a year throughout the 1770s to almost 900 in 1784; and the number of references to pianos rises from under 50 per annum for most of the 1770s to over 250 in 1784.

But the increased sale of pianos was not at the expense of Shudi & Broadwood harpsichords. In 1784 John Broadwood sold thirty eight harpsichords, of which ten were double-manual and twenty eight single-manual. Some were secondhand but the majority were new; so he was probably making about twice as many harpsichords as Shudi had done in his best year. Yet in that one year, 1784, Broadwood sold 133 pianos, which means that he had multiplied his firm's production of keyboard instruments by well over ten times in twelve years.

* See Table I.

60

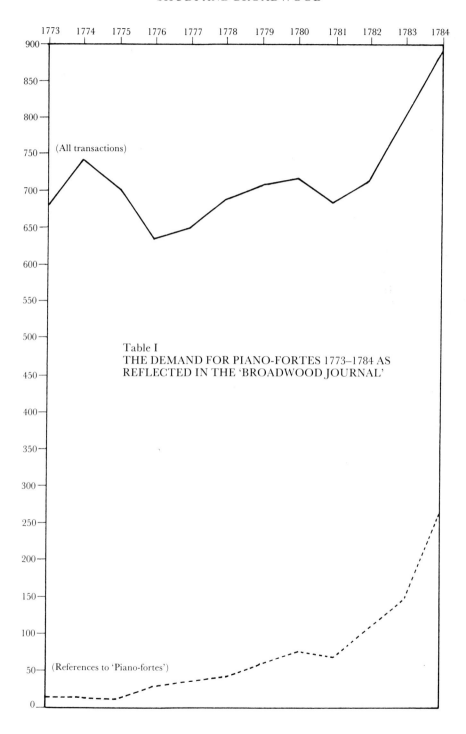

(All transactions)

Table I
THE DEMAND FOR PIANO-FORTES 1773–1784 AS
REFLECTED IN THE 'BROADWOOD JOURNAL'

(References to 'Piano-fortes')

The Journal indicates the pressure of demand. On 6 January, Giardini (who had ordered Gainsborough's harpsichord for him a decade earlier) ordered two pianofortes for the 'Marquis de Champunitz'. On the 28th a Miss Powies—who evidently had to be in fashion—'had a Piano till her own's made'. It took two months to make, and was sent to her on 17 March. On 17 January Messrs Corri & Sutherland of Edinburgh ordered two pianofortes which were 'shipp'd on board the Lovely Mary, Capt Bitson'. The pianos cost 15 guineas each, with 15s for a packing case and 5s for shipping. This was the first of an astonishing series of orders from that firm; by the end of 1784 they had ordered twenty one pianos in that year alone. It must have been a particular satisfaction to John Broadwood to know that his craftsmanship was so much in demand in his own country.

In April, Clementi ordered two more pianos; and his assiduity in promoting British pianos abroad paid off when on October 23 'Pascall Taskian' ordered four pianos, one plain and three inlaid. Taskin was the leading French harpsichord maker, and had been appointed Keeper of the King's Instruments to Louis XV. The order represented a notable tribute.

Despite the increasing popularity of the piano, Broadwood's international reputation for harpsichord-making remained unshaken in the 1780s. A Philadelphia lawyer and amateur musician, Francis Hopkinson, devised what he believed to be a better method of quilling the harpsichord, the essence of which was to give the quill greater strength and protection from breaking by adding a small metal staple. Hopkinson described his invention in a paper to the Philosophical Society of Philadelphia in December 1783; and in a further paper, read to the Society in November 1784, he described his practical progress in the intervening year.

> Wishing to bring my discovery to the test of full experiment and to the judgement of abler critics, I forwarded a description and a model of my improvement to a friend in London, requesting that it might be submitted to the examination of proper judges, and directing, in case it should be approved of, that an instrument made by one of the first artists and quilled according to my proposed method, should be sent to me. I have accordingly received an excellent double harpsichord, made by Messrs Shudi and Broadwood of London, and quilled according to my method: with this difference, I had rounded off the top of the tongue, and bending the quill over it, kept it in a horizontal position by means of a small

wire staple . . . But Mr Broadwood has left the tongue of its full
length and usual form: But made the hole, in which the quill is
commonly fixed tight, so large, that the quill has free room to play
therein; and then fixing the quill below, has bent it round and
brought it through the hole; which renders a staple unnecessary; the
top of the tongue answering the same purpose. The principle on
which the improvement depends is the same in both; but his is the
best method of executing it. He informs, however, that one
inconvenience occurs, *viz.* the quills being so forcibly bent in the
curved part, are liable, in some instances, to spring back, and so
become not only too short to reach the string it should strike, but the
projection of the curve will be apt to touch the string behind it, when
the stop is pushed back . . . I acknowledge that this inconvenience
occurs in some few instances in the instrument Mr Broadwood has
sent me; but would observe that as it does not *always* happen, it is a
fault in the execution and not in the principle.[8]

It is typical that not only was John Broadwood prepared to make a
'one-off' instrument to a novel specification, but he was concerned
enough, and interested enough, to make his own improvement to the
'improvement'. The despatch of this particular instrument is recorded in
the Journal:

1784 June 28			
Dr Mr Robt Bremner for a Double keyd Harpsichord	£	s	d
with five stops & two pedals & Patent swell &c	73	10	
Mohogoney Case			
To three extra row of Jacks	3	3	
To a sett of Tuning forks	1	1	
To a Leather Cover	1	11	6
To 50 Raven Quill		7	6
To 500 Crow Quill		3	
To a Pair of Plyers		1	3
To 13 yeards of Red flanel		18	
To a Packing Case & matts	1	2	
	81	17	3

Sent to Mr Hopkinson Philidelphi

(It is interesting to note that on the day Bremner, the agent, ordered
Hopkinson's harpsichord, he ordered for himself—a piano.)

63

In the following year Hopkinson made still more radical experiments, ultimately throwing out the quills altogether in favour of leather plectra. He wrote to his friend Thomas Jefferson (draftsman of the Declaration of Independence, and later to be third President of the United States), then Minister Plenipotentiary in Paris, that he had 'sent this Discovery to a friend in England—he was to offer for it 50 G^s but writes in answer that my Invention has been anticipated—I see I am to be defrauded both of the Money & Credit.'[9]

That friend could have been John Broadwood; for three months later Jefferson on a visit to London called in at Great Pulteney Street, writing in May to Hopkinson: 'I am just returned from a trip to England. I was in the shop of Mr Broadwood the maker of your harpsichord, and conversed with him about your newest jack. He shewed me instruments in his shop with precisely the same substitute for the quill, but I omitted to examine whether it had the same kind of spring on the back. He told me they had been made some time before your model came over . . .'[10]

Perhaps it was because of this slight misunderstanding that Hopkinson in the following year ordered a harpsichord from Kirkman, as did Jefferson; but more probably it was that already possessing a Shudi & Broadwood, he was interested to have a model from the other acknowledged maker.

The correspondence proves that Broadwood was using leather for plectra on harpsichords as a regular practice, as an alternative to quill. It also shows his continuing interest in the instrument, even though so much of his attention was now devoted to the improvement of the piano. There were still enough customers like Hopkinson determined to maintain their allegiance to the harpsichord, and derisive about the piano while recognising the failings of the older instrument. Even Hopkinson could write that 'although the three stops of a harpsichord should be quilled to the best advantage, the result of the whole will be an observable jingle or tinkling between the quills and wires, which depreciates the dignity and sweetness of the instrument. The best harpsichords are so censurable for this imperfection, that the *Forte Piano*, which is free from it, stands a chance of rivalling that noble instrument, for this cause only; being far inferior in every other respect.'

At least one other signatory of the Declaration of Independence was an admirer of Shudi & Broadwood harpsichords. He was Charles Carroll of Carrollton, Maryland. He had studied law in London as a young man, and perhaps obtained his introduction to Broadwood instruments through Joshua Reynolds (who painted his portrait). He ordered a Shudi & Broadwood two-manual instrument in 1785 through his London agent, probably as a wedding present for his daughter. This instrument was finally delivered in 1789.[11]

At this time Broadwoods still undertook the repair and indeed the substantial rebuilding of harpsichords, as this workmen's account shows.[12]

1788 April 5 Mr Compton. To repairing an old harpsichord of Ruckers.

	Days	Hours
Baldie repairing the case	20	5
Stephens putting on mouldings and setting out do.	5	6
Mr Duff finishing do.	7	-
In all 32 days 11 hours		

To Vineer, crossband & string for inside and out
To a new Top and front board for do.
To two new setts of keys for do.

As the demand for pianos built up through 1785 John Broadwood recruited more craftsmen (keeping an eye open for skilled Scots—James Forsyth, who was to become his strong right hand, was taken on that year).[13] He also felt the need for reliable clerical assistance. His eldest son, James Shudi, had been sent to France to learn the language, travelling to Paris and his school at the Barrière de Clichy in the care of Clementi. But he disliked the French, and pleaded to be allowed to come home. He was a bright, intelligent lad. John Broadwood allowed him to come home—to join the business.

'Barbara Broadwood's book' was brought out of the cupboard; and on the eve of his thirteenth birthday, James Shudi Broadwood was installed in Great Pulteney Street as ordering clerk. That seems to be the explanation for one cryptic entry, in between two other entries dated November 1785. It reads, in neat small copperplate:

Filii
Jacobus Broadwood filius primus natus
Guilliamus—secundi frati
Carolus—3.[14]

These would be the three sons of John Broadwood living at that date; for by now his second wife had borne him two more sons, William (who

65

died at the age of five) and Charles (who lived to be nineteen). Thomas, the most famous son of that second marriage, was not born until the December of the following year. So this entry could be young James's mark of his arrival; and there are other clues to both the family life and the business. Thus on 4 March 1786 it is recorded that 'Messieurs Ransom & Morland & Hammersley Received of John Broadwood . . .' a sum of money—the page is torn at the amount. Hammersley's were Broadwood's bankers; perhaps young James was showing off his skill at French appellations. His father may have been less amused by the caricatures of moustachioed faces (the enemy French?) that have been drawn in the margins. There is also the following list, of great significance for the business:

Waggons set out.
Albans St . . .
—windmill
Bury waggon . . .
Swaffham Waggon at four Swans Bishopsgate street,
    Tuesday 12 o'clock
Robert Burton Esq.
at Burtisham near St Ives, the Waggon sets out at
    Catherine wheel bishopsgate street W.
    at the Vine, ditto, th. Sat.
    12 at Noon.
Cambridge Waggons set out from the Bull Inn Bishopsgate Street
    every Tuesday Wednesday Thursday Friday before Noon.
    James . . .
Leicester Loughborough Derby &c &c sett out from the White
    horse Cripplegate sets off Tuesday at 12 o'clock
Saturday morning by Clarke & one . . .
the Bell Inn Wood (St) on Tuesday at 12 o'clock. By Clark.
Lewes Waggons &c by Shelley . . . Inn Borough every Wednesday
    evening & setts out on Thursday early.
Litchfield Staffordshire . . . Waggon sets out from the Castle &
    faulcon Aldersgate Street on Friday between 10 & 11 morning.
    Waggon sets out on Tuesday between 10 & 11
Hereford Waggon—Vaughan Waggon sets out from the Saracens
    head Friday street every Saturday at 10 o'clock
Birmingham . . . sets out every Thursday . . . o'clock from the
    Castle (& Falcon) Aldersgate Street

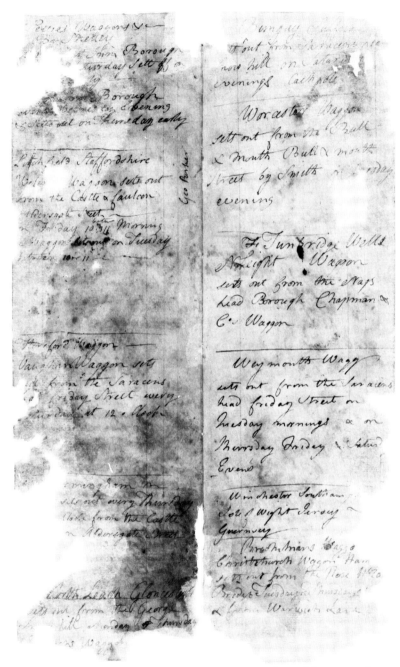

Broadwood Journal, 1785, showing the departure points of the carters' waggons
(Bodleian Library, Oxford)

North Leach Gloucester sets out from the George (Snow) hill
  Monday & Thursday . . . sons Waggon
Bungay Suffolk sets out from Saracens head Snow hill on Saturday
  evenings Catchpole
Worcester Waggon sets out from the Bull & Mouth Bull & Mouth
  Street by Smith on Tuesday evening
Tunbridge Wells Wheight (?) Waggon sets out from the Nags head
  Borough Chapman & Co Waggon
Weymouth Wagg. sets out from the Saracens head friday Street on
  Tuesday mornings & on Thursday Friday & Saturday evens.
Winchester Southampton Isle of Wight Jersey & Guernsey
  Bradnetman's Waggon Christchurch Waggon . . . sets out from
  the Rose . . . . Bridge Tuesdays Thursdays . . .
[two entries unclear]
Daventry & Northampton Waggon George Smithfield W & S aft.
  Adams Waggons.
The Northampton Waggon sets out from the Ram Smithfield on
  Tuesday & arrives at Northampton on the Friday following &
  sets out again on Friday & arrives at Northampton Tuesday.
The Stamford Hunts Waggon goes from the Castle & Falcon
  Aldersgate St on Tuesday & Saturday morning at 10 o'clock.
  From the White Hart . . . John St on Tuesday the Goods to be
  taken there the night before.
The Atherston Waggon sets out from the (Castle &) Falcon
  Aldersgate Street Wednesday morning . . .
Stafford Waggon at . . . every Tuesday morning.

This list, occupying five pages of 'Barbara's Book' in a childish hand,
could well be one of the early chores given to young James in Great
Pulteney Street. It demonstrates, by providing a detailed timetable of the
departure points of the carriers' waggons and the names of the carriers,
that transport was becoming increasingly important to a firm that no
longer concentrated its sales upon the fashionable world of the
metropolis, but was selling throughout the country.

The towns named are also significant, for with a very few exceptions on
the south coast (Weymouth and Southampton, for example) they are all
inland. Broadwoods sent pianos to the major coastal towns such as
Bristol, Liverpool and Hull, Glasgow and Edinburgh, by sea, on one of
the fleets of coasters that trimmed their way up and down the North Sea
and Irish Sea (the coasters were far cheaper than the carriers).

One further glimpse remains of James Shudi's boyhood. John

Broadwood was staunchly religious, and each Sunday morning shepherded his wife and children to the Scottish Chapel in Wells Street where they sat in a position of honour beneath the pulpit on the left side of the Minister. In old age one of James Shudi's boyhood friends, F. Dods, reminisced about the bleak Sunday discipline of those days:

> I cannot say that my respect for Wells Street and its institution increases—to me, especially as concerned with learning by heart the shorter Catechism first, and then the longer, at home, on Sundays, it was a scene of confinement and punishment—well calculated, if for any thing, to make religion hateful . . .
>
> But for all this, I do most highly respect the feeling which prompted a few Scotchmen, in an inferior station of life, take them all together, to combine their scanty means, and build a chapel for the sake of hearing the Gospel preached conformably to the faith of their fathers—it was a noble effort—and succeeded surprisingly.
>
> Have you the least recollection of old Hall, the original minister, whose widow your father long contributed to support? Or of James Hall, the shining Edinburgh preacher? (I have been at concerts with him, introduced by you)—or of Lawson, the original genius of Selkirk or of Ebenezer Brown (the son of old Brown of Haddington)— the most uncouth of creatures; yet I have known him fill the chapel almost to bursting.

The name of Hall thus recurs, but any link with the Lairds of Dunglass who first helped John Broadwood to London is obscure. The letter does establish Broadwood's part in the foundation of the Scottish Chapel, and confirms his lifelong allegiance to his Scottish faith and upbringing.

The Minister of the Wells Street Chapel from 1782 (until his death in 1827) was the Reverend Alexander Waugh. Although a Secession Minister, he took a leading part in the proceedings of the London Presbytery of the Scots Kirk, and was one of the founders of the London Missionary Society. He was John Broadwood's sole executor outside the family, and is described in his will as 'my trusty and well-beloved friend': he also received a personal bequest of £200. Most of the Broadwood children were baptised at Wells Street, beginning with James Shudi in 1773 and ending with Henry, twenty years later (old John is still described in the Register as 'harpsichord-maker' in 1793).

Several of John Broadwood's good Scots workmen also attended the chapel. The congregation included James and John Reid, James Forsyth, Thomas and John Black, John Murray, William Allen and Thomas

A Kensington terrace in 1811 similar to John Broadwood's High Row. *(Kensington and Chelsea Borough Libraries)*

Hopkins (the last, described as 'Pianoforte Maker' in 1800, is perhaps the Thomas Hopkins mentioned in John's will; so it is probable that he was working for his uncle).

The workmen continued to be members of the congregation well into the next century. There are Allens, Murrays, Blacks and Stewarts in the Register into the 1830s. By that time, the Broadwood sons, as country gentlemen, had been enfolded into the bosom of the Established Church of England.[15]

By 1787 pressure on space in Great Pulteney Street was acute. An additional workshop had been built on the roof, but the increasing demand for pianos and the still considerable order-book for harpsichords meant that the house was no suitable place for a family with three small children. In March 1787 John Broadwood took a lease[16] of twenty one years on a house 'in the country', as his family described it. The house was No. 14 Kensington Gore, in a terrace known as High Row. He also leased the adjoining house, No. 15, which was smaller but had a larger garden, running down to the market gardens which gave an open view at the back down to the village of Brompton. His rent was £25 a year for the larger house, and £10 for the smaller. The houses were the first 'middle-class housing' between Kensington Palace and Knightsbridge Barracks; the remainder of the road was lined, opposite Hyde Park, with large houses in their own substantial grounds. The Brompton Park Estate had built this single terrace about 1770, and it may be that Broadwood noticed it when on the way to tune Admiral Lord Rodney's harpsichord at Gore House, almost next door (the Admiral lived there for five years from 1784; later, Broadwood's neighbour in the big house—from 1808— was William Wilberforce).

The houses were demolished in 1851 by the Commissioners of the Great Exhibition, for the creation of Prince Albert's permanent centre for the arts and sciences in South Kensington; John Broadwood's house was approximately where the Royal College of Art now stands.

Some years later James Shudi Broadwood rented No. 21, the westernmost and much the largest house in the terrace. No. 14, into which the Broadwoods moved in 1787, was a conventional eighteenth century house, though with a view across the park to Kensington Palace. The street door led into a narrow hall, with a dining parlour off it, and behind that a 'small parlour' which housed the great iron chest with its immense hasps, bolts and locks which served John Broadwood as a safe and strong-box for some of his wealth. The parlour was served by a basement kitchen with a large range, copper kettle, copper chocolate pot and brass warming-pan. The scale of the Broadwoods' entertaining may be gauged from the stock of 'five dozen large plates, three dozen small plates' and also from the furnishings of the parlour itself—a large mahogany pillar-and-claw table, with twelve mahogany dining chairs.

In the cellar when John Broadwood died a quarter of a century later were 'fourteen dozen port wine' and 'four dozen Madeira', which suggests a generous host. The drawing room was on the first floor, with its view of the park. Apart from the inevitable 'piano forte with mahogany case', there was a square sofa with a loose cotton cover and two bolsters, six mahogany elbow chairs with cushions, and two mahogany circular card tables covered with green baize. The three tall windows were dressed with printed cotton curtains; on the walls were paintings and prints and a large mirror in a burnished gold frame. The floor was covered with a Turkey carpet, with an Imperial rug before the hearth.

The back room on the first floor, 'the small drawing room', was used by John Broadwood as his library, for the main furniture was a mahogany winged bookcase with glass doors, and drawers below. Among his books were twenty two volumes of the *Encyclopaedia Britannica* (the first edition was published in Edinburgh in 1768), four volumes of Burns' *Justice*, and four volumes of Blackstone's *Commentaries*, the leading popular Biblical work of the day. The three bedrooms and the servant's room were all furnished with four-posters, each bed with three blankets and a counterpane or quilt. The furniture in the main bedroom was mahogany, including a 'mahogany night stool and pan'. In that bedroom also—a protection against burglars, perhaps?—were kept 'a fowling piece and two pistols'. A comfortable house, then, but far from showy; the furniture good, well-crafted, but not florid; the house of a man who did not need to flaunt his considerable success in outward extravagance.

Following the dramatic success of his square piano, John Broadwood now turned his mind to the improvement of the grand. He turned to two scientists—Tiberius Cavallo, Fellow of the Royal Society, and Dr Edward Whitaker Gray of the British Museum. Both were customers of the firm. In October 1785 Broadwood sold 'Mr Carvalo' 'a sett of jacks' for one guinea. Dr Gray had bought a 'new pianoforte' as early as November 1783 for 20 guineas; subsequently he sold his harpsichord to Broadwood in February 1785, but then that July he found that he needed one for an evening's music, so Broadwood's workmen carted one to his chambers in King's Bench Walk, charging him 4s (there and back).

Tiberius Cavallo (1749–1809) was born in Naples, the son of a physician, but came to England as a young man and made a considerable reputation as a natural philosopher (or as we would say, an expert in the physical sciences). He was versatile in his interests. The inventor of several pieces of apparatus for chemical and electrical experiments, he specialised in work on the influence of light and air on plants, and on electricity (on which he wrote a treatise), in particular the medical applications of electricity. He was also an expert in acoustics, which evidently drew Broadwood's attention: Cavallo read a scholarly paper[17] to the Royal Society on 3 April 1788 concerning temperament in the tuning of keyboard instruments. The paper is especially interesting since, if Cavallo had been advising Broadwood on the development of the piano, he makes no mention of that instrument, referring only to the harpsichord and organ among keyboard instruments.

Dr Edward Whitaker Gray (1748–1806) was a botanist—which no doubt explains the link with Cavallo, over the latter's work on plants—and was appointed Under Librarian (he would today be called Keeper) of Natural History in 1787, a post he retained until his death. It was Dr Gray who, with Cavallo's advice and Broadwood's encouragement, experimented with the striking point of each string to establish the vibrating length that would give the best tone. Hitherto, grand pianos had a single bridge on the soundboard, in the style of the harpsichord. This meant that the bass strings were struck at a point nearer the wrest pin in proportion to their vibrating length than the treble strings: this produced a weak bass. Dr Gray demonstrated that if the string could be struck at about one-ninth of the vibrating length of the string, this would produce a better tone. To achieve this, John Broadwood divided the bridge, introducing a separate bass bridge. The innovation was immediately successful, and within a short time was adopted by all piano-makers.

There was another reason why Broadwood was able to enlarge his markets within a year or two. In 1789 the streets of Soho filled with

Edward Whitaker Gray of the British Museum, adviser to John Broadwood on the redesign of the grand. Portrait by Sir Augustus Callcott *(Copyright: The Royal Society)*

refugees from the French Revolution. The trades in Paris that had served the aristocracy closed down, and many craftsmen fled to London— among them the Erards, Sebastien and his nephew Pierre. They had been making square pianos in Paris from 1777 (before that date, most pianos in Paris were English imports, particularly those of Zumpe).[18] It is said that the Erards worked for Broadwood for a time before starting their own London workshop manufacturing harps and pianos. Thus at the most important phase in the development of the piano, the Parisian makers who might in other circumstances have offered a serious challenge were prevented by the Revolution from making any challenge at all.

Many Paris-based musicians came to London at that time, and in the years that followed. Among them (he arrived in 1789) was Jan Ladislav Dussek, then at the height of his popularity. Handsome, he was known as 'le beau Dussek', and is said to have introduced the fashion of pianists

A grand by John Broadwood, 1794 *(Photo: Sotheby Parke Bernet & Co)*

playing sideways to the audience because he wished his listeners to enjoy the beauty of his profile. Dussek had been born in Bohemia but had achieved fame in Paris, where he was a favourite of Marie Antoinette. It was Dussek who suggested to John Broadwood that a further half-octave in the treble, above the conventional five octaves, would add dramatic sparkle,[19] and they were probably added to the grand sold to 'Mr Duseck' on 20 November 1789. At first these 'additional keys', as they were known, were offered as an optional extra.

But by 1793 they had become usual, as Broadwood explained to Thomas Bradford of Charleston in a letter dated 13 November: 'We now make most of the Grand Pianofortes in compass to CC in alt. We have made some so for these three years past, the first to please Dussek, which being much liked Cramer Jr.* had one of us so that now they are become quite common and we have just begun to make some of the small Pianofortes up to that compass.'[20]

Dussek's pride in his new grand is illustrated by his lending it to Josef Haydn on the composer's first visit to London in 1791. Haydn lodged first with his impresario Salomon in Great Pulteney Street, (as Burney relates) 'having a room for composing at Shudi & Broadwood's pianoforte shop in the same street'.[21] Broadwoods took a grand, at Dussek's charge, to the Hanover Square Rooms on 11 March 1791, bringing it back the next day; the occasion was the first appearance of Haydn in Salomon's Concerts—a similar procedure was followed for each of Haydn's benefit concerts, on 16 May and 30 May. When Haydn moved out to the country—Lisson Grove—in June (where he composed *Orfeo ed Euridice*) Dussek lent his own grand to Haydn, and hired a replacement from Broadwood (that he did not simply order up another piano for Haydn implies a particular respect for his own instrument). J. B. Cramer, then aged twenty, was a frequent visitor to Haydn and on those visits he admired the Broadwood so much that he ordered one for himself.

Broadwoods supplied Cramer with a piano for his first recorded public recital, on 25 February 1793, at the Hanover Square Rooms, when he was twenty three. Poor Dussek was spoiled by his success, his story being encapsulated in Percy Scholes's summary[22] that he 'took too little exercise, became stout, found motion tiresome, took to lying in bed, felt bored, drank and died'. His contribution to the development of the piano was already largely forgotten when he died in 1812.

---

* Johann Baptist Cramer (1771–1858), pianist, composer and founder of Cramer & Co. He was the son of Wilhelm Cramer, at that time director of the King's band.

Having extended the compass of the keyboard to 5½ octaves, John Broadwood soon enlarged it still further, adding another half-octave in the bass to bring it to six octaves. Some pianos in 1793 and 1794 were made up to GG in the treble, but the first full six-octave grand was made in the early summer of 1794[23], probably No. 607.

Soon Broadwood grands were in as much demand as Broadwood squares. John Broadwood was obliged to find every inch of space he could in Great Pulteney Street and the mews round about. In May 1778 he had leased the adjoining house (No. 32) from Sir William Pulteney at a rent of £105 per annum. Three years later he leased No. 29 with a restricting clause requiring him 'not to carry on the trade of vintner, victualler, butcher, baker, cheesemonger, dyer, scourer, tallow chandler, soap-boiler, blacksmith, whitesmith, brazier, tripe boiler, brewer, distiller or any other dangerous, annoying or offensive trade'. It seems that No. 29 was an investment, for it was soon let as a dwelling house.

But it was in the mews at the back, Bridle Lane, that the greatest expansion took place. In 1785 John Broadwood bought the lease of a Bridle Lane mews from Job Jones, timber merchant. In 1791 at auction he paid £194 5s. for Lot 2: 'A leasehold double coach-house, with stall stabling, and coachman's room and loft over, situate near the Plaisterers' Arms on the East side of Bridle Lane, in the occupation of Alexander Ross Esq. and estimated worth Fourteen Guineas per annum. Possession will be given at Michaelmas next. Thirty years (wanting ten days) of the lease unexpired at Lady Day 1791, at a peppercorn rent.'

Subsequently he acquired the Crown Posting House, later known as 'Square Yard', on the corner of Bridle Lane and Silver Street. So by the turn of the century, Broadwoods occupied rather more than twice the space they had taken up thirty years earlier—three adjoining houses in Great Pulteney Street, and behind them nine adjoining mews properties, together with the former Crown public house. It was not the most convenient factory lay-out, but it did have two advantages: integral stabling for the horses with easy access for carts bringing in timber and leaving with pianos along the mews. Great Pulteney Street provided the elegant showroom frontage, Bridle Lane the working access.

On 4 June 1793 Broadwoods sent a harpsichord to St James's Palace as they did annually for the performance of the King's birthday ode. The harpsichord was used in rehearsal, but for the actual performance the director of the King's band called for a pianoforte. The harpsichord was never used again. The grand pianoforte 'with additional keys' had become established. Though the square was still the major selling line, the Broadwood ledgers for 1794–1796 demonstrate the growing

A square piano by John Broadwood & Son, 1795 *(Photo: Sotheby Park Bernet & Co)*

popularity of the grand, and the rate at which the fashionable world rushed to trade in not only harpsichords and small square pianos but also grands of earlier make for the new instrument 'with additional keys'.

They were not cheap. A grand sold at 70 guineas, a square with additional keys at 27½ guineas, a square with inlaid case 25 guineas, and the cheapest square at 20 guineas. The fact that the name of the instrument had not been finally set is shown by the various ways in which the same clerk inscribes it in the first two pages of the 1794 ledger, as Grand Pianoforte, Grand Piano, Grand Pianoforté, PianoForte, and Grand PianoForté[24]. Evidently the abbreviation 'piano' was already in use, at least in the trade. The one ledger entry in John Broadwood's own hand defines the instrument as a 'Grand Pianoforte'.

At this time Broadwoods were still selling harpsichords as well as pianos, though in very small numbers; they also dealt in spare parts and strings (even, on one occasion, cello strings), and of course employed repairers and tuners.

The export trade was also becoming important. In August 1794 they shipped six square pianos to Port-au-Prince, in three separate vessels, the *Herther* (Capt Edward Atkinson), the *Duchess of Portland* (Capt W. Elliott) and the *Triton* (Capt Forrester). Shipping charges were £1 on each consignment, and insurance was paid at 14 per cent on a cargo valued at £45 10s. Notably, Broadwoods had two agents in Port-au-Prince (now Haiti): Delonguemere & Co, and Etheard & Baudot (this illustrates how they had captured what would surely have been a French market). Sales to the West Indies were generally buoyant. Within a few months a grand and a square went to Mr Green in Antigua, and an inlaid square to Mr Lindo for Mr Cervetti in St Kitts (there were sizeable English colonies in those islands, augmented by Nelson's Navy). Europe was not neglected. A grand was sent to Alberto Albertini in Verona, Italy, and a pedal harp was despatched to Constantinople. In July 1796 two grands were sent to J. W. Haesler in 'Mosco'.

The American market was also growing. A grand was bought by Messrs Wignell & Reinagle[25] of Philadelphia. Mr J. J. Astor made a purchase in bulk on 16 July 1796. He bought six pianos, for which he paid £129 4s 1d, which would have meant six ordinary squares at 20 guineas each, with six packing cases at 10s 6d each. The additional 4s 1d was no doubt the cost of the extra sets of strings usually supplied with export sales. John Jacob Astor was setting the foundation of the fortune that was to make him a multi-millionaire. The son of a Mannheim merchant, he had come to London about 1778, having been preceded by his elder brother George who had set up as a maker of musical instruments, particularly flutes, in Wych Street, Drury Lane.[26] It is sometimes said that on first arriving in London the young Astors worked for Broadwood, but there is no definitive evidence of this. John Jacob Astor sailed for America in 1783 with a consignment of flutes. Later he began to trade in furs and began a transatlantic business, bringing furs to Europe and returning with musical instruments, including Broadwood pianos.

Square pianos survive bearing George Astor's name. It is uncertain whether he made them himself, or bought them on an 'own name' basis from Broadwood, for they are remarkably like Broadwood squares of that date.

Broadwood's trade now divided into two main parts—regular accounts, of customers whose pianos and harpsichords Broadwoods sold and regularly tuned, and what they called 'chance trade'—people who came into the showroom in Great Pulteney Street. Between February and

May 1794 there were forty six of these 'chance' sales, encompassing nine grands, nine inlaid squares, twenty six ordinary squares and two double harpsichords.

There was still a demand for harpsichords; Broadwood on two occasions gave 25 guineas for second-hand instruments (though it is not recorded whether they were Shudi & Broadwood, or by some other maker); the usual price was 12 or 15 guineas. His valuation of the small squares, which would have been ten or twenty years old, depended for their trade-in price on their condition and maker. Thus he gave good prices (usually 10 or 12 guineas) for squares by Christopher Ganer; once he gave 14 guineas for a Kirkman square, once 15 guineas for a Longman square, and even 20 guineas for a square by Haxby of York. The earliest squares, by Zumpe or Pohlmann, he usually allowed 4 or 5 guineas for. Earlier grands given in part-exchange for new Broadwoods were usually priced at 45 guineas; possibly those were early Broadwood grands, for he rated Stodart grands at 35 guineas.

He did not reckon to keep these second-hand instruments for long in Great Pulteney Street, but tried to sell them within a month or two, usually charging a 50 per cent mark-up. For example, on 6 February 1795 he took a double-harpsichord of 1775 from the Duchess of Rutland in part exchange for a new square piano, giving her 25 guineas for it. He sold the harpsichord on 7 April to a Mr Mielan of Leadenhall Street for £35. On 6 March he accepted two small squares—one a Schoene, the other a Ganer—from Mrs Banbury of Dover Street in part exchange for a grand, allowing her 15 guineas for the first and 12 guineas for the second: he sold the Ganer three weeks later to Mrs Spoor of Marylebone High Street for 18 guineas. In July 1795 he took a small Zumpe from Lady Cremorne in part exchange for a square, and allowed her 7 guineas, but sold the Zumpe within a fortnight to 'Mr Ostler at the Marquis of Stafford's' for 9 guineas.

Pianos of lesser quality acquired in part exchange deals he sold off in job lots. Thus in July 1795 Messrs Preston & Son bought seven secondhand small pianos from him for £44 2s. This seems to be an average price for what he had paid for them, which implies that he was selling them virtually at cost to get them out of the showroom.

By the mid-1790s Broadwoods had ceased to manufacture harpsichords altogether* (though the designation 'harpsichord-maker' appears on legal documents until well into the nineteenth century). For

---

* The last is believed to be No. 1155, dated 1793, now in the Russell Collection at Edinburgh University (see page 57).

some years, though, Broadwoods continued to trade in them, and maintain and restore them: thus in July 1794 a harpsichord belonging to Mrs Cole of Wandsworth Common was restored and re-strung, with the addition of a harp stop and what is described as 'a back machine' (presumably the machine stop); she was charged 5 guineas plus 15s for 'caravan from and to Wandsworth'.

Broadwoods had agents throughout the country. In 1794–1796 James Roche of Cork bought six grands and 13 squares; J. & W. Lintern of Bath took ten grands; Mr H. Hine, music seller, of Liverpool bought seven assorted pianos; and Mr Charles Nicholson of 3 Upper Dawson Street another seven. Discount for bulk orders had not yet been introduced, but the firm would accept barter, for Mr Hine paid partly with '54 gallons of Madeira wine @9s 6d' and Mr Nicholson also made part payment with 'a pipe of Madeira'.

The variety of the business is shown in the order from Mr J. G. Willetts of Pudsey, near Leeds, in October 1794. Mr Willetts was evidently a maker or repairer of both harpsichords and pianos, for Broadwoods supplied him with a swell for a Kirkman harpsichord, 'with all the machinery etc', 56 wrapped pianoforte strings, 50 raven quills and 6 dozen tongues (for harpsichords, clearly). Corri & Dussek in the Haymarket acted as agents for Scotland, for several of their orders are marked 'sent Edinburgh' or 'sent from Haymarket to D. Todd Esq. Glasgow'.

The Royal Family were regular customers. In the summer of 1795 the Prince of Wales bought two pianos, one an ordinary square and one with additional keys. Princess Sophia hired a grand in the spring of 1795 at the Queen's House, and Princess Elizabeth at Buckingham House employed Broadwoods to maintain her harp. She seems to have been extremely heavy-handed on the harp, since although Broadwoods put new strings on it and tuned it in March, it needed a complete new set of strings a month later, and in August it had to be repaired yet again (perhaps, charitably, we may assume they were different harps).

Her sister Princess Sophia's hiring is a reminder that this had now become a major part of the firm's trade. That musical patrons would sometimes hire instruments as a generous gesture to distinguished visitors is illustrated by Lady Warwick's hiring of a pianoforte 'with additional keys' at Hampstead from February to May 1795 'for Dr Haydn'. And what long-forgotten personal drama hides behind the hiring in April–May 1796 by M. de Carrière 'at the Fleet Prison'? The Fleet was the debtors' prison; but whoever else he did not pay, M. de Carrière seems to have paid Broadwoods.

Which came first, the development of the piano or the increasing demands of composers upon the instrument? It is a problem that has puzzled musicologists, but the most convincing theory is that of Philip James,[27] who quotes in support the distinguished scholar Professor E. J. Dent:

The death-knell of the harpsichord was sounded not by the introduction of the piano, but by the change in musical taste, which resulted in the perfection of that instrument. This is not a quibble, but an assertion of the principle that the invention of instruments does not create a new kind of music, but is in response to the demands of composers who are often in advance of the general taste. Professor Dent has concisely summed up this important question in these words: 'It is a mistaken view of history to suppose that makers of instruments preceded composers in the discovery of new possibilities. It is only the second-rate composers who are stimulated by mechanical inventions; the great composers imagine new possibilities and it is they who suggest to the instrument makers the directions in which they can improve their wares. At the beginning of the nineteenth century the pianoforte makers had little or no idea of producing the quality of tone which we now associate with this instrument. Old pianofortes often sound like harpsichords, not just because they are old, but because their makers meant them to sound like that . . . The advantage of the pianoforte lay not in its different tone-colour, but in its power of dynamic gradation.'

This theory is borne out in Broadwood's case by the influence on him of Clementi, the composer, and Dussek, the executant.

James Shudi Broadwood had grown to maturity with the piano. As a boy, he had listened to his father's discussions with Signor Cavallo and Dr Gray. His particular interest in acoustics and tuning dates from those days. In the business he had become his father's deputy. Production had vastly increased. By 1794 the firm had made over 500 grand pianos and over 1000 squares, most of them in the preceding decade. The administrative procedures needed to run a comparatively modest craft workshop had long since been overtaken by the requirements of a large business. It was James Shudi who revised the firm's methods of recording its flourishing activities. Over a period of four years from 1792 he introduced systems of business accounting,[28] set down in five series of ledgers, each dedicated to a distinct activity—orders, letters, tunings, the day's work in the factory, and the import of materials and export of finished goods. From 1796 each piano was numbered and the date of its manufacture recorded.

Broadwoods were now in the forefront of piano manufacture. James Shudi had been working in Great Pulteney Street for ten years, and personally knew every aspect of piano-making. In 1795 John Broadwood took his son into partnership, giving him a full half-share in the business; and its title changed to John Broadwood & Son.

Chapter IV

John Broadwood and his Sons

1795–1812

B *uonaparte's project was taking shape . . . The First Consul's purpose was plain. It was to make the sea useless to the country which ruled it. Similar threats had been made against England before. But they had done her little harm because, as long as the Baltic, with its all-important trade in grain, timber and naval stores, remained open to her ships, the closure of the remainder of the European coastline hurt Europe more than it injured Britain. Controlling the ocean routes, she could deny the colonial produce of the New World and the East to her foes while extending her own imports and supporting her elaborate structure of usury through trade with the Hanseatic and Scandinavian towns. On this basis the long war, which many had thought would be her ruin, had actually enriched her. So soon as she had established complete command of the seas over the combined fleets of France, Spain and Holland, her wealth and financial power, instead of contracting, had expanded. "Our trade," Pitt told the House of Commons in the summer of 1799, two years after Cape St Vincent and Camperdown, "has never been in a more flourishing situation." By the turn of the century British exports had reached a declared annual value of nearly forty millions, or half as much again as at the outbreak of war, while imports had doubled. Despite privateers the tonnage cleared from Great Britain to North Germany in the same period had trebled. The destructive effect of the war and Revolution on the Continent was making Britain the manufactory as well as the warehouse of the world.*

Sir Arthur Bryant: *The Years of Endurance 1793–1802*

I n 1795 Britain's trading links were stretched round the world, and the rewards of that trade flooded in from the East India Company, from the now British-ruled Canada, from the West Indies with their wealth of sugar and timber, and there was the promise of new riches to be mined in the British settlements in Australia. The American colonies had been lost, but the sea-lanes of the world were sailed by British ships and Britain was outward-looking. But Europe was in a ferment. Following the Revolution, the irreligious anarchists of France seemed bent on destruction, not only of their own domestic institutions but of those of Europe as a whole—and particularly the British supremacy. In 1793 Britain had declared war. But by April 1795 William Pitt's alliances had crumbled, the British Army had withdrawn from Europe, and as Parson Woodforde wrote in his Diary: 'Dread and terrible times appear to be near at hand.'

The main factor in the destruction of the Grand Alliance was the Treaty of Basle, whereby the states of northern Europe made their peace with France. The architect of that treaty was Manuel de Godoy, premier of Spain, who subsequently made an agreement with France to turn Portugal against England. Yet the following February Godoy—who in secret was intriguing to do Britain all the harm he could—found time to order a pianoforte from Broadwoods. Queen Maria Luisa of Spain, whose favourite he was, had caused him to be given the exotic title of

A 'sofa table' piano by John Broadwood & Son, 1803. Ham House *(Photo: Victoria and Albert Museum)*

A grand piano by John Broadwood & Son, 1798, with Wedgwood medallions
(Collection of the Albany Institute of History and Art, New York)

'Prince of the Peace' for his efforts at 'peacemaking' by the Basle Treaty;
this piano was to be a special thank-offering.

It was a grand with additional keys, in a satinwood case 'superbly
ornamented' with plaques by Wedgwood and Tassie, and on the
nameboard a portrait of Godoy by the Royal Academician miniaturist,
Taylor. The piano was ordered by Godoy from Grenier's Hotel, Jermyn
Street, on 8 February 1796, and shipped to Bilbao on 22 June.[1] The cost
of the piano and its transport was £257 4s 6d. Broadwoods must have
been glad that the piano was completed, shipped and paid for when, that

autumn, Godoy threw open the Spanish ports to the French Navy.

The designer of Godoy's rich and costly piano was Thomas Sheraton; his design was afterwards published in London. Sheraton had come to prominence at this time as one of the leading furniture designers through the publication, from 1791, of *The Cabinet Maker's and Upholsterer's Drawing Book*, sets of working drawings for furniture to rival those published by Chippendale forty years earlier (the Broadwood books of this period contain a reference to a 'Mr Chippindale', but this is probably Thomas Chippendale Jr, also a cabinet-maker and the son of the great furniture designer). Sheraton was a Soho neighbour of Broadwoods, first in Wardour Street and then in Broad Street, and it is said that he designed various pieces of furniture, especially a fine break-front bookcase and escritoire, for the main room in Great Pulteney Street.

A square piano by John Broadwood & Son, 1799 *(Photo: Christie, Manson & Woods Ltd; A. C. Cooper Ltd)*

An 'elegant' grand piano by John Broadwood & Sons, 1810. Colt Clavier Collection *(Photo: Photographic Records Ltd)*

Features of the standard Broadwood pianos of this period suggest the influence of Sheraton, in particular the use of satinwood banding inlay. It is curious, though, that his design for the Godoy piano does not include pedals; Dale says(in *Tschudi: the Harpsichord Maker*) that he made no provision for them, though they were of course added—unusually, on three separate suspended columns, rather than attached to the front legs.

The use of satinwood for the Godoy piano case illustrates a new experimentation in the use of woods.[2] Satinwood had long been used by Broadwood as a contrast to the darker mahogany, especially for the nameboard and cheeks above and beside the keyboard where its pale yellow colouring pleasantly complemented the ivory of the keys, particularly when the satinwood was outlined with ebony stringing. The best quality satinwood was imported from Puerto Rico, and the *Cabinet Directory* of 1803 describes it as having a 'cool, light and pleasant effect in furniture'.

Mahogany, however, had become the staple wood. When makers first began to turn to it from English walnut, it was because the planks were

A square piano by John Broadwood & Sons, 1815. Colt Clavier Collection
(Photo: Photographic Records Ltd)

larger, and the timber was more stable and less liable to warp or shrink. It
was therefore an admirable material for piano manufacture, since the
frame was less liable to distortion and thus to going out of tune quickly.
Mahogany was imported to Britain from the early eighteenth century, at
first from the islands of the West Indies, particularly Jamaica and Cuba.
From about 1775 Honduras mahogany, of still greater solidity and
strength, began to be imported.

The early square pianos relied almost entirely on the fine grain of the
wood for decoration. The tops were generally cut from the solid, the cases
veneered over a simple frame, with fruitwood stringing. In the last
decade of the century, perhaps under Sheraton's influence, the satinwood
of the nameboard and cheeks was often cross-banded with mahogany,
and the outer case of mahogany cross-banded with satinwood. The
company name was written in ink—at first *Johannes Broadwood*, and then
from 1795 in the English form *John Broadwood & Son, Great Pulteney Street,
Golden Square, Patent, London* with the year and number—on an inlaid
boxwood plaque.

The vast increase in production attained by John Broadwood was not,
of course, achieved in a social vacuum. It was a response to the increased
demand of a new market, in the homes of a newly refined middle-class.
Lord David Cecil has pointed out[3] that the later eighteenth century 'saw
the life of the country gentry noticeably more civilised than that of their

grandparents'. It was a change epitomised by the elegance of Gainsborough as against the rough bawdy of Hogarth, an age in which women gained greater social influence and were encouraged to cultivate the social graces. Among those graces was the ability to play the piano.

Jane Austen is the incomparable chronicler of that world, and in her novels may be found the customers for that immense number of square pianos. She herself played, as her niece Caroline recalled:

> Aunt Jane began her day with music—for which I conclude she had a natural taste; as she thus kept it up—tho' she had no one to teach; was never induced (as I have heard) to play in company; and none of her family cared much for it. I suppose, that she might not trouble them, she chose her practising time before breakfast—when she could have the room to herself. She practised regularly every morning—she played very pretty tunes I thought—and I liked to stand by her and listen to them; but the music (for I knew the books well in after years) would now be thought disgracefully easy— much that she played was from manuscript, copied out by herself— and so neatly and correctly, that it was as easy to read as print.[4]

Jane herself was somewhat sardonic about skill on the piano. She tends to apportion that skill to characters who are emotional, impetuous and perhaps not over-intelligent. Thus in the *Plan of a Novel* she writes:

> Heroine a faultless Character herself—perfectly good, with much tenderness, sentiment, & not the least Wit—very highly accomplished, understanding modern Languages & (generally speaking) everything that the most accomplished young Women learn, but particularly excelling in Music—her favourite pursuit—& playing equally well on the Piano Forte & Harp—& singing in the first stile.

That fashionable young woman Mary Crawford has firm ideas on musical ability (in *Mansfield Park*):

> 'Are they musical?'
> 'I do not at all know. I never heard.'
> 'That is the first question, you know,' said Miss Crawford, trying to appear gay and unconcerned, 'which every woman who plays herself is sure to ask about another . . . There is a beauty in every family.—It is a regular thing. Two [sisters] play on the piano-forte,

and one on the harp—and all sing—or would sing if they were taught—or sing all the better for not being taught—or something like it.

The piano was a social instrument, and Jane Austen nicely defines the way in which it was used by young women of the period to score off each other in company—or attempt to, as in this scene from *Pride and Prejudice*:

[Elizabeth Bennet's] performance was pleasing, though by no means capital. After a song or two, and before she could reply to the entreaties of several that she would sing again, she was eagerly succeeded at the instrument by her sister Mary, who having, in consequence of being the only plain one in the family, worked hard for knowledge and accomplishments, was always impatient for display.

Mary had neither genius nor taste; and though vanity had given her application, it had given her likewise a pedantic air and conceited manner, which would have injured a higher degree of excellence than she had reached. Elizabeth, easy and unaffected, had been listened to with much more pleasure, though not playing half so well; and Mary, at the end of a long concerto, was glad to purchase praise and gratitude by Scotch and Irish airs, at the request of her younger sisters, who with some of the Lucases and two or three officers joined eagerly in dancing at one end of the room.

In *Emma*, Jane Austen used a Broadwood square as the fulcrum of the plot, when the dashing young Frank Churchill orders a Broadwood to be sent anonymously to his secret fiancée Jane Fairfax, thereby occasioning a flood of gossip in Highbury:

Mrs Cole was telling that she had been calling on Miss Bates, and as soon as she entered the room had been struck by the sight of a pianoforté—a very elegant looking instrument—not a grand, but a large-sized square pianoforté; and the substance of the story, the end of all the dialogue which ensued of surprize, and inquiry, and congratulations on her side, and explanations on Miss Bates's, was, that this pianoforté had arrived from Broadwood's the day before, to the great astonishment of both aunt and niece . . .

Mrs Weston, kind-hearted and musical, was particularly

interested by the circumstance, and Emma could not help being amused at her perseverance in dwelling on the subject; and having so much to ask and to say as to tone, touch, and pedal, totally unsuspicious of that wish of saying as little about it as possible, which she plainly read in the fair heroine's countenance.

After a dinner party, they have songs round the piano.

At last Jane began, and though the first bars were feebly given, the powers of the instrument were gradually done full justice to. Mrs Weston had been delighted before, and was delighted again; Emma joined her in all her praise; and the pianoforté, with every proper discrimination, was pronounced to be altogether of the highest praise.

This scene, repeated as it was in a thousand homes as the daughters of the family demonstrated their sensibility and refinement drawn from the studies of Clementi and exercised in the many books of popular ballads of the day, epitomises the society that Broadwoods were serving so well. It is difficult to recognise in those sunlit drawing rooms, apart from the occasional hints given by the presence of 'officers', an England that was in the midst of a long, bitter and, as it must have seemed, interminable war with the French.

In December 1796 a French invasion force set course for Ireland; but encountering gales, it never landed. In February 1797 another French force crossed the Channel. After landing at Ilfracombe and burning a farmhouse the group crossed the Severn Estuary to Fishguard. The 'invasion' was, however, poorly provisioned and its leader surrendered to local volunteers. Fears of a full-scale invasion led the Bank of England to suspend cash payments; and the volunteer movement for national defence attracted many new recruits, among them James Shudi Broadwood, who in April 1797 was commissioned as a Lieutenant in the Royal Westminster Volunteers. At this critical point in the country's fortunes the Navy, driven to desperation by brutal conditions and poor pay, mutinied at Spithead and the Nore and for many weeks it seemed probable that Britain's last line of defence would crumble. Very little attention seems to have been paid in Britain to the exploits of a French general, Buonaparte, who having spent the previous year rampaging through Italy had now resoundingly defeated the Austrians.

But wars and rumours of wars do not always succeed in discomfiting human affairs. So on 11 July 1797, at St James's Church, Piccadilly,

James Shudi Broadwood married Sophia Bridget Colville.

That summer, London was enthralled by the presence in town of a popular hero of the day: Commodore Sir Horatio Nelson, who was recuperating after losing an arm at the Battle of Cape St Vincent. The Nelson household were customers of Broadwoods; three years earlier the then Mrs Nelson had hired a piano for her lodging at 17 New King Street, Bath; subsequently she bought it—a square with additional keys, on a French frame. The transaction was negotiated for her by Nelson's uncle, William Suckling of Kentish Town, an official in the Customs and Navy Office.

The immediate fear of invasion was to continue for some years. To pay for the war, Pitt imposed swingeing taxes; there was also a voluntary defence fund, to which everyone contributed; in February 1798 John Broadwood & Son paid £200. The workers at Broadwoods formed themselves into a Volunteer Company of the Royal Westminster Volunteers, and on 8 March 1799 James Shudi Broadwood was gazetted its Captain (he was also honorary Regimental Treasurer). They drilled and trained vigorously with all London: on his birthday, 4 June, old King George reviewed 10,000 Volunteers and Militia in Hyde Park and was delighted with their bearing. The Volunteers were to keep up their preparations for a further three years until in 1802 Nelson, having demonstrated Britain's sea-power in the victory at Copenhagen and, capping his triumph in containing Napoleon at the Battle of the Nile, relieved the immediate threat to London and the south and east coasts. The volunteers disbanded.

Against this threatening backcloth, business nevertheless prospered. As Pitt told the Commons in the summer of 1799, 'Our trade has never been in a more flourishing situation.' By this time John Broadwood was an extremely wealthy man. Like other rich and successful businessmen, he had begun to operate as a private banker, making loans and mortgages, and investing in other enterprises (particularly those of fellow Scots).[5] Between 1785 and 1797 he lent out more than £7,700. Sometimes these were personal loans, as for example the loan of £200 in 1789 to 'Ketita Kitson of Stainforth, Yorks'—no doubt a relative of his wife's.

Sometimes John Broadwood's business dealings concerned property, as the loan to John Fraser of Charles Street in 1790: 'Mortgage on property in Weymouth Street £600 and loan of £400.' Yet others were investments in shipping, a trade in which Broadwoods were closely interested through the import of timber, but—because of the ever-present danger from privateers and enemy warships—a high-risk enterprise fraught with hazard. Nevertheless John Broadwood invested very substantially:

Brig Duchess of York
1792, August 27
Cash paid Donald Deacon for one
    fourth share of the said Brig   518 17   6

Ship Sally
1792, May 11
Cash paid John Allday of Carlisle
    Street for ¼ share   173   0   0

John Broadwood was also generous to young musicians. In 1802 he gave a grand to George Smart, then organist at the St James's Chapel, Hampstead Road, and a pianist at the Haymarket Theatre. Smart was then twenty six. Later, as Sir George, he was to be organist of the Chapels Royal and conductor of the Philharmonic Society, and as such a correspondent of Beethoven. Smart recorded John Broadwood's generosity:

Mr Broadwood senior . . . showed me great kindness in the following matter. I purchased the lease of 91 Great Portland Street this year [1802] of Mr P. Meyer for the sum of eight hundred and fifteen pounds, together with some furniture left in the house. The lease expired in 1867. I was obliged to borrow from Mr Broadwood the sum of two hundred or three hundred pounds, and I offered to assign to him the lease as a security for repayment. This he declined, saying "It would cost you some money to make a legal assignment of the lease to me. If you are honest you will pay me when you have the means," which, thank God, I soon had. I shall never forget his kindness.[6]

As the new century dawned, family life for John Broadwood in his late sixties must have been very pleasant. His second wife had presented him with seven children. Though two had died (the eldest son of that marriage, William, at the age of five, and a daughter, Berberice, in infancy), there were two teenage sons (Charles and Tom), a daughter, Mary, and young Henry (born in 1793) at Kensington Gore. It was a civilised household, for despite the war French culture was still admired and Broadwood employed a French emigré, M. Du Bourblanc, to teach

Reeves Hall, East Mersea, Essex (John Broadwood's country house). *(Author's photograph)*

the children French. He also allowed this refugee to have his son to live in the house.

Perhaps it was for some relief from this household of children that in 1798 John Broadwood bought a country estate—Reeves Hall, on Mersea Island in the Blackwater estuary. It was a farm of 534 acres, with a neat red-brick manor house (see above), much of it seventeenth century though with some parts older (the manor has been traced back to 1254). Reeves Hall stands in an isolated fold of land on the north side of Mersea Island, looking across the marshes to the Pyefleet Channel and Pewit Island. East Mersea is a fishing settlement, and home of the men who cultivate the oyster-beds producing that staple of the Victorian diet the 'Colchester Native'. It is also a fine place for wildfowling. To John Broadwood's town friends this 'Sabine farm' may have seemed an odd, not to say dangerous retreat; it was a notorious haunt of smugglers, and on just the sort of isolated coast that might attract an invasion fleet. But it lies in relation to the sea-coast in much the same relationship as the

Cockburnspath of John Broadwood's boyhood, and was the perfect place to indulge his love of country pursuits, far away from the pressures of business. He later let out the farm, but played his full part as 'Lord of the Manor', presiding over the Court Baron and Court Leet.[7] It was evidence of the confidence he now reposed in James Shudi to conduct the business, for at Reeves Hall old John was two or three days' journey away.

Soon James Shudi was starting a family. His eldest son, John, was born in 1798 and daughter, Elizabeth, in the following year. Sadly, the daughter died at the age of six weeks. James Shudi felt that his young wife would be in healthier surroundings in the country, and in 1799 old John provided him with a loan of £3,000 to buy a country estate. It was Lyne Farm, a pleasant little Georgian villa in rural seclusion on the borders of Surrey and Sussex (highwaymen were still a hazard on the London road).

At Lyne in November 1800 Sophia gave birth to her second son, who was named James Preston. Their happiness was to be short-lived. With a fearful repetition of the tragedy that had befallen old John precisely twenty five years earlier, Sophia Broadwood died at Lyne on 26 August 1801. She was twenty two years old, and left James Shudi with his two small sons. Fate had not finished with the family. Little more than a year later, old John's daughter Mary died in February 1803 at the age of fourteen, to be followed two months later by her nineteen-year-old brother Charles.

Thus at the age of sixteen Thomas Broadwood was left the eldest son of old John's second marriage; and that summer he was put to work in the Counting House at Great Pulteney Street to manage the accounts.[8] Even then he was sharp with figures, a characteristic that never left him. His education had been in the style of the time for the son of a wealthy man: from the age of seven, boarding schools (first at Hockwell, and then 'a boarding school at Wimbledon kept by a Dr Lancaster'). From the age of twelve he had been tutored privately at home.

Joy returned to the family in the summer of 1804 when on 11 June, at Marylebone Church, James Shudi re-married. It must have delighted old John that James's bride was of a good Scots family, the Stewarts, though of a branch that had been 'out in the '45'. Margaret Schaw Stewart had been born in Dominica, where her father, Daniel Stewart, was an army surgeon. He had died two years later, leaving two small children whose mother sent them back to Britain for their education. The mother had remained overseas, marrying her cousin Dr Alexander Field and eventually settling in the southern states of America. Margaret

Stewart's brother Daniel was a soldier of fortune, spending some time in the southern states supervising the loading of ships (and acting as a local agent for Broadwood pianos).

That Mrs Field, Margaret's mother, was a woman of character is demonstrated by the one letter of hers that survives. This also indicates that at the time of the wedding and for some years afterwards, James Shudi had not met her; and indeed, because she had remained on the 'enemy' side during the American War of Independence, she was regarded with some suspicion. Margaret inherited her staunchness, determination and humour. She made James Shudi an admirable wife, bearing him thirteen children (eight daughters and five sons) between 1805 and 1822. The first-born, a daughter who was named Sophia as a gracious remembrance of James' first wife, arrived in April 1805, just six months before Lord Nelson was to achieve the first great victory of the renewed war against the French, and lose his life, at Trafalgar.

From 1802 Broadwoods were selling throughout the country. Their agents were of two kinds. The most numerous were music teachers, and the Letter Book contains many names of provincial organists who would have been the music teachers of Jane Austen's young ladies. Thus Mr Sweeney, Organist, Cashell, Ireland, ordered five squares in May 1802. The response to Mr Moore, Organist, Stratford on Avon, illustrates the beginning of such an association: 'In respect of returning the Instruments should they not be approved of, we certainly will not object to exchanging any you may not like, if *within six months* but the carriage and cartage must be at your expense. For ready money we shall be happy to allow you 5 per cent.' That was the usual discount for the local music masters whom they called 'our country friends'.

In those years Broadwoods were suffering the penalties of commercial success—an inability to satisfy demand. The office was overwhelmed with correspondence and sometimes it was a month before letters were answered. In addition (particularly at those periods of domestic bereavement) John and James Broadwood had to delegate the task of drafting replies to clerks who sometimes wrote injudicious letters which offended old friends. James Shudi had to pick up the pieces and write placatory letters, as this to Mr Lawton, Organist, Leeds, in December 1802: 'We certainly cannot advocate our regularity, but know the want of it has caused us heavy losses and subjected us to many insults. To another part of your letter we must answer that we have ever considered you as one of our best Country Customers, & have never considered your orders "insignificant".'

This pressure had evidently prevailed for some years; for in 1798 James Shudi had written to a complaining wholesaler: 'Do not think the pianofortes have been kept back from any wrong invective . . . Would to God we could make them like muffins! Stewart, and many others, have been waiting as long, or longer, than you have.'

The demand is reflected in the physical handling of pianos listed in the Porters' Books. Thus on one Saturday chosen at random (11 June 1803) there were twenty two outward removals of pianos on that day alone.

That James Shudi was desperately overworked is occasionally made plain in the firm's letters, as this in March 1802: 'We are particularly sorry you should have been kept out of your Money so long, which has been caused by the indisposition of Mr Jno. Broadwood in consequence of which Mr B [James Shudi] had more to attend to than he really could & amongst others you was forgotten . . .'

And this, written a few days after the death of John Broadwood's fourteen-year-old daughter Mary, in 1803: 'We have been so occupied with business and unfortunately with domestic distress . . .'

On top of all this, they were plagued with bad debts, and in 1802 applied an ultimate sanction to a number of defaulters: We cannot (you must be convinced) but feel extremely discontented with your treatment of us. Your Promises of Payment you have repeatedly broken, & at length seem to have forgotten entirely. We therefore shall think ourselves justified in imploying our Attorney to recover the debt & that you may be able to be provided we think Proper to give you this Notice.'

The problem was common in the luxury trades. In 1810 the firm of Josiah Wedgwood estimated its outstanding accounts at £41,477, or more than the total assets of the factory. One customer, the Marquis of Donegal, had not paid his bill for fifteen years, though continuing to order and be supplied.*

There was also a problem with customers who hired grand pianos on the promise of subsequently buying them or returning them, and in the event did neither. Broadwoods wrote to a Mr Eastin of Coscombe Hall, Worcester, quoting the leading legal authority of the day: 'We this morning received your favour of 12th Inst. in which you deny being indebted to us for hire of the Pianoforte we furnished you with and we beg to inform you that in a similar case Lord Mansfield said that the Instrument being had on hire was certainly not purchased "*till the money was paid for it*".' Mr Eastin had had his piano 'on hire' for six years.

*See Barbara and Hensleigh Wedgwood: *The Wedgwood Circle 1730–1897* (Cassell, 1980).

Customers' friends, then as now, were a peril in a trade that served fashionable society; and it is not difficult to picture the reasons behind this letter to Mrs Lawrell of Hatchlands. The lady had commissioned her friend Madam du Fresnoy to choose an instrument for her. 'Permit us to express a hope [wrote Broadwoods] that in selecting Madame du Fresnoy to make choice of an instrument you have selected a person on whose judgement you can depend and abide. We also beg to state that the Instrument you are going to return was chosen by Mr Field at the desire of Mr Lawrell & Mr Salomon, who had chosen one previously to Mr Field's making choice, on whose acknowledged abilities they chose ultimately to depend.' God save us, James Shudi must have said, from our 'friends' . . .

Perhaps because of the uncertainties of payment from provincial music teachers, Broadwoods began deliberately to create a network of agents throughout the country. They were for the most part retailers of musical instruments and music sellers in the main provincial towns, and they were offered substantial discounts. The terms are given in this letter to Mr Aspinall, Merchant, Birmingham, on 8 April 1802:

	£	s	d
A GPF Grand piano forte 6 Octaves	84	-	-
A Do. Additional keys	73	10	-
A Do. Ornd. Case	89	5	-
A Small PF Con. Con.	25	4	-
A Do. Additional keys	29	8	-
A Do. Do. with Damper pedal	31	10	-
A Do. Do. Ornd.	35	14	-

Above we have written out the prices we sell our Pianofortes at in London. On this we usually allow Merchants ordering one or two 10 per cent. for ready money. If the order is large we afford more. From your connection with Mr Storace we must consider you as a Wholesale Dealer, so allow Dist. of 25 per cent. but expect with an Order a Good Bill.

Similar terms were offered to Mr Boyton, Music Seller, of Park Street, Bristol, who had taken a number of pianos:

We hope you will soon contrive to dispose of them, of which we think there can be no doubt judging by the sale of towns of less importance than Bristol provided you keep them in good tune & order. In the advertisement you talk of putting in the papers we think you may with propriety call them 'Broadwoods improved & durable pianofortes' for even our opponents acknowledge their superiority in standing in tune & order. As you sell an instrument, if you write to us (we) will replace it.

In other business relationships, the music sellers were taken on as agents proper—that is, Broadwoods carried the financial overheads, the agents sold at an agreed retail price and deducted their 25 per cent as discount. The idea of advertising evidently appealed to James Shudi, for he wrote in 1804 to J. Bradley, a Liverpool agent who held a stock of six pianos: 'We wish you will advertize at our expense and as you sell one, on writing to us with a Bill for the wholesale Amount we will forward you Another.' These agencies, however, were not lightly given and Broadwoods took care to see that what would today be described as 'after-sales service' was adequate. Thus in 1802 they wrote abruptly to Messrs Miller & Wood of Edinburgh: 'As we are given to understand that our Instruments are not fairly dealt with at your House, we think it a Duty we owe ourselves to decline supplying you any longer with them. We therefore have not entered the order you have sent us in our Books.'

It is obviously a fallacy to suppose that because communications at the beginning of the nineteenth century were slow, word did not travel fast. This is confirmed in a further letter (of February 1803) to the firm's old friends and customers, Corri & Sutherland of Edinburgh, announcing the imminent arrival of a consignment of pianos. This further demonstrates James Shudi's wary eye for competition—and, indeed, the emergence of competition.

> We should have sent you the above long before now but have had so many more Instruments bespoke than we could readily make, that we have been necessitated to keep many waiting besides yourself, & to refuse many orders. We hope they will please you so well as to enable you to recommend them to Town as well as Country—being informed you scruple to do so—recommending in such cases Clementi's [and] our small ones for the Country, & Mr Tomkinson's Grand ones, like Leake's famous pills, for Town or Country, for Sea or Land—this being the case I am afraid the GPF you took from Mr Thompson will have a poor chance of sale, & if you think so too I hope for Old Friendship Sake that you will pack it up & send it us back with as little noise as possible, trusting that you will have a little regard for our reputation who have ever defended yours. When you have got Time pray acquaint me whether it is from the softness of their touch, or the hollowness of their Tone that you

think our small PF not so fit for the delicate Citizens of Edingboro'
as for the clumsy fists and dreary abodes of Clodhoppers; this I beg
as a friend for the sake of information and improvt.[9]

One reason for the delays in production was that Broadwoods were
scouring Europe (war or no war) for materials. In February 1804 they
ordered 400 lb of steel wire in four gauges from Mons. Lieber in Berlin,
informing him that 'we use a greater quantity of music wire than any
other manufacturer in this Kingdom and we think it will answer your
purpose to send us the best'. In June 1805 they bought 1,568 soundboards
as a job lot from Leipzig, shipping them through Hamburg.

If they had no pianos to sell (and in December 1802 they had to write to
a customer that 'from the great demand, we have sold everything we had
prepared for sale in the summer') they were overstocked with
harpsichords. That autumn they could offer an enquirer a two-manual
Kirkman in mahogany, and other two-manuals in walnut, together with
a range of single manuals. They had to stop taking harpsichords in part-
exchange, writing for example to Miss Banks of Salisbury: 'We know not
what to advise you to give for the Harpd. you mention. The last we sold of
the sort you say to be sold we got fifteen Pounds for, but we could not
ourselves buy any Harpds. the sale being so heavy and uncertain.'

The demand for pianos was not exclusive to Britain. The Charleston
agent, Eckhard, was selling in the southern states of America £500 worth
a year, despite the fact that Broadwoods would not allow him credit ('In
England we give a year's credit, which we do not find ourselves inclined
to do abroad'). There was a brief hiatus in September 1804 when
Eckhard cancelled his orders. James Shudi wrote cheerfully: 'We
suppose the rumour of an approaching Invasion of this Country had
induced you to suppose we shd. not be able to stand our ground, or some
other unfounded misrepresentation. We believe the ground we at present
occupy is perfectly secure, so much so that you need not feel the least
alarm about our stability. Enclosed you have our Statement of your
Account with invoice of goods shipp'd herewith . . .'

Other exports fared less well. In August 1802 Broadwoods had to write
to Mr John Rawlings of Cobham, Surrey, with the sorry saga of a grand
ordered by him for delivery to another Mr John Rawlings, of Bengal. The
grand was shipped in February 1801 in the *Windham*, in the care of the
Mate, Mr Brocas. At Spithead the clipper was given new orders, to sail
directly to China, not calling at India. So the unfortunate Mr Brocas
found himself stranded in Canton with a Broadwood grand. Being
unable to find anyone willing to take it to Bengal (and one may have some

sympathy with the unfortunate Mate scouring the dockside in Canton for a ship bound for Bengal, with some person willing to take responsibility for a Broadwood grand), he sold it to a Mrs Pattle, 'the only Lady in the Settlement'. Arriving back in London a year later he reported this to Broadwoods, who duly retailed the story to Mr Rawlings, saying that Mr Brocas would offer him '£100 to £110'. Mr Rawlings was furious; Broadwoods declined responsibility, but persuaded the Mate to admit that he had received 130 guineas for the piano in Canton, and would pay that over. There, alas, the story ends; there is no record of whether Mr Rawlings accepted.

Broadwoods had more trouble in India, as indicated by a notice that was drafted for insertion in the English language papers in the sub-continent in 1803:

John Broadwood & Son, Grand & small piano forte makers to His Majesty and the Princesses having received authentic information that Instruments of very imperfect nature are sent out for sale to India and their name affixed as if manufactured by them think it necessary to acquaint the Gentry in India that none of the numerous Piano Fortes introduced into Asia by officers of Indiamen and others for sale within these 6 years last passed are of their manufacture. They beg to declare that none of the pianofortes that have mahogany fronts or name boards that have any painted ornaments or that have brass clamps on the corners are of their manufacture with the exception of two Grand pianofortes with brass clamps sent out 9 years ago, and one small one sent in 1800.

Such misrepresentation was, of course, a tribute to the value that the name 'Broadwood' had now achieved across the continents. But it was a business malpractice that was to plague the company throughout the nineteenth century.

James Shudi's admirable clarity of expression is apparent in the company's letters; from time to time they display also his irrepressibly puckish humour. This could get him into trouble (perhaps in those times when, overburdened, his judgement slipped a little). On one occasion he nearly lost a friend through it.

The Fleet prison, in those years, housed debtors. But it was not unusual for wealthy men to send in appetising meals to those of their friends who, temporarily embarrassed, were housed at His Majesty's pleasure. One evening in November 1804 a friend and music seller from Bath, John Astley, came to dine with the Broadwoods at Great Pulteney

Street; and he 'dined out' on the story that his dinner the previous evening had been taken as a guest in the Fleet prison, where a mutual friend had invited him. The next day James Shudi, happening to be writing a business letter to the Linterns in Bath (music sellers who were friends of both the Broadwoods and Astley), added in passing that 'Astley had been in the Fleet'. The unfortunate Astley arrived back in Bath to discover that the word had gone round that he had been flung into the debtors' prison; his credit locally was ruined. Or so, deeply offended, he claimed, and both Thomas and James Shudi had to write abjectly contrite letters. 'I see I have thoughtlessly committed a great folly,' wrote James Shudi, humbly asking Astley 'to make me your Banker' for any loss he had suffered as a result of the joke.

In 1808 Thomas Broadwood, now twenty three, and firmly installed as company accountant (as he would now be called), in command of the books at Great Pulteney Street, was taken into partnership. James Shudi retained his half-share in the business, old John handed over one-quarter-share to his younger son, retaining one quarter-share for himself. It is a measure of the prosperity of the firm that in the years 1800–1808 John Broadwood received some £5,000 a year from the business, and James Shudi between £3,500 and £6,000 a year. As the income of a skilled workman in those days would be around £100 a year, the value of John Broadwood's annual profit from the company in those years may be something like £300,000 a year at 1982 prices. By the same measure, the cost of the finest grand, at £84, was about four-fifths of a skilled man's annual income, or around £5,000.

With the admission of Thomas Broadwood to partnership the name was once more changed; from 1 January 1808 it became John Broadwood & Sons.

Many attempts had been made in the eighteenth century to arrange the piano so that it would be more compact. The square did not have the sonority of the grand. It had occurred to a number of makers that if the piano could be placed upright (in the style of the chamber organ) a better sound could be achieved in less floor-space. Stodart had devised an 'upright grand' in 1795. In 1800 two manufacturers produced upright designs virtually simultaneously—Matthias Müller in Vienna and John Isaac Hawkins in Philadelphia. Hawkins's design was patented in England by his father, Isaac Hawkins of Dolby Terrace, City Road. It has many interesting features, not least an iron frame far in advance of its time. Two years later Thomas Loud of Hoxton patented an upright and noted the possibility of 'oblique stringing' to gain string length without excessive height.

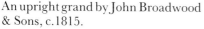

An upright grand by John Broadwood & Sons, c.1815.

Upright grand open, showing the bookshelves *(Smithsonian Institution, Washington)*

James Shudi, writing many years later, gave the credit for the successful development of the upright to William Southwell, though he claimed the idea as his own. 'The Vertical or Cabinet Piano was first produced by William Southwell, from a sketch given him by James Broadwood about 1804; so little was it then appreciated, that the first manufactory in the line refused to purchase the patent he took out.'[10] Southwell had been a maker in Dublin, but came to London in 1794 and at his workshop first in Lad Lane and then in Broad Court, St Martin in the Fields, made a number of experiments in uprights. The 'upright grand' was a cumbersome piece of furniture, since it could be eight feet

The grand piano given to Beethoven by Thomas Broadwood. Manufactured in 1817, it was subsequently owned by Franz Liszt, and is now in the National Museum of Hungary at Budapest. *National Museum, Budapest. Photo by Károly Szelényi (Corvina Archives)*

Burkat Shudi, his wife Catherine and sons Joshua (left) and Burkat. The 'family portrait' was done in 1745 to fit the panelling in the parlour at 33 Great Pulteney Street, where it remained until early this century. The artist is unknown, though

it has variously been ascribed to Hogarth, Zoffany, Mercier and Knapton *(The Broadwood Trust)*

A Shudi and Broadwood two-manual harpsichord of 1770. This instrument, now the property of the National Trust (the Benton Fletcher Collection) at Fenton House, Hampstead, is No 625, dated 1770. There are two pedals, the left controlling the machine stop, the right the Venetian swell. The case is of burr walnut cross-banded with mahogany, inlaid with strips of boxwood and ebony *(Photo: Graham Miller)*

tall; as the tail of the piano was at the top, the available space was often filled with bookshelves which made the piece still more unstable.

No doubt because the factory was working at full stretch making conventional grands, Broadwoods did not at first move into the upright market, and in October 1798 wrote, in response to an enquiry, recommending Stodarts for this form of piano. That they were 'so little appreciated' probably reflects old John's opinion. Typically, they made experiments, and it is recorded[11] that 'an Upright Grand, no.2' was sold on 16 December 1799. That they were being made to order is indicated by a letter of 7 February 1803 to Mr A. Corfe, in the Close, Salisbury: 'The price of an Upright Grand pianoforte in a plain case is 25 gns. We can make a very handsome instrument for One Hundred Guineas and higher to any price. At £105 we would make the case either of Sattinwood or black rose wood whichever would best match the Gentleman's furniture. The height of the case will be 8 ft 3 ins, the width 3 ft 7 ins. Waiting the favour of your Answer giving us the longest time you can . . .Ps. The depth of the case is 1 ft 11 ins.'

As the demand built up, Broadwoods contracted with James Black to make them on an 'own name' basis at his factory in Percy Street. Many members of the Black family worked for Broadwoods, and James Black may have been one of many former employees who had gone out on his own. Certainly his standards of workmanship were admired, for he was used as an independent arbiter when—as happened from time to time—customers more familiar with the harpsichord criticised the piano tone. The 'upright grand' was so named until about 1812, when it began to be superseded by the 'cabinet' in which the lay-out was inverted, reducing the height.[12]

Hawkins's use of an iron frame was symptomatic of the increasing interest of piano manufacturers in the possibilities of using metal to strengthen the case. In 1808 James Shudi experimented with iron bars for this purpose, but was unable to achieve a result that satisfied him.

The stream of customers was unceasing and the demand for pianos apparently insatiable. There were many distinguished customers. Among them was a soldier, newly married, and Member of Parliament for Rye. On 17 September 1806 Sir Arthur Wellesley 'of Hastings, Sussex and 11 Harley Street' hired 'a small piano forte' until 7 January, no doubt for the amusement of his young bride. Sir Arthur was in one of his rare periods at home, between military service in India and his triumphs in Portugal and Spain, and later as victor of Waterloo; 'now Lord Wellington', as someone has added in impeccable copperplate beneath his name in the ledger. On neighbouring pages are the names of Captain

Lyne House, Surrey, the home of James Shudi Broadwood *c.* 1817 *(Brayley's History of Surrey)*

Worsley RN 'of Rippon, Yorks', Lady Rodney (wife of the Admiral), Mrs Siddons, and 'Miss Wedgwood, Etruria, Staffs' who sent her grand for repair.

The tradition of service to the Royal Households had been upheld continuously since Burkat Shudi made a harpsichord for the Prince of Wales in 1740. John Broadwood is named in the annual Court registers as 'Harpsichord Maker to the King' from 1793 to 1807, and as 'Harpischord and Piano Forte Maker to the King' from 1809 to 1812. The lists from 1814 to 1821 have Thomas Broadwood as 'Musical Instrument Maker in Ordinary to His Majesty' from 6 April 1813; he retained the appointment at least until 1836. It is curious that the Royal Warrant was passed on from John Broadwood to his younger son, and not to the elder; but it may be explained by the fact that James Broadwood was appointed Organ Builder in Ordinary to His Majesty on 4 November 1799, an appointment he held at least until 1821; he is further listed as holding that appointment in 1836.[13]

James Shudi's post as Organ Builder was no sinecure. In the autumn of 1802, for example, he was in correspondence with Lord Salisbury over the rebuilding of the organ at the Chapel Royal, St James's, offering three styles of repair, at £100, £200 or £300. The cheapest was chosen; and perhaps suspecting that his services were being regarded as expensive by the Royal Household, James Shudi pointed out that this price provided him with no personal profit 'as I consider the salary I receive thro' your goodness sufficient compensation for any trouble I may be at'.

For two years trade with the United States had been at a standstill through an Embargo Act of the U.S. Government. This had introduced difficulties in the supply of timber, and the export of pianos to what had been in earlier years a growing market. However, James Shudi's brother-in-law Daniel Stewart was able to write more optimistically from Petersburg, Virginia on 24 April 1809 (he was too optimistic; by 1811 the embargo was reimposed and the Americans were approaching a naval war against Britain):

My dear Broadwood

I wrote to you a few days ago and have now the pleasure to inform you that in consequence of arrangements since made between the American and British Governments the President has by proclamation put an end to the Embargo Laws with all their appendages from which I am inclined to hope everything will go on pleasantly in future. I now trust I shall be able to get rid of the Tbr. [timber] at a saving price and shall as soon as that can be effected, remit you for the Goods shipped over last fall, however the market has not advanced much as yet, owing to both the U States and Britain being shut out from the Continent. I mentioned to you in my last that as soon as it could be done I should order two pianos for friends here, you will now therefore be good enough to pack up two of your very best Square pianos with additional Keys, and send them by the first Vessel for Norfolk or City Point, you will please be particular in choosing them as it may lead to more extensive orders in your way of business in future, of course putting them as low as you can afford. You will also be good enough to select some of the newest Songs and Pieces of Musick for the piano and let them be packed up with one of them marking the case EBH the other without the musick you will have marked FA. I will thank you for this to procure some of the newest Songs and pieces of musick and pack in the case EBH, directing the parcel in which they will be put up to Miss Harrison of Brandon. I suppose three Guineas worth in each parcel will be enough—All these things you will consign to Messrs Holloway and Mr Canserd of Petersburg Virginia sending them Invoice & Bill of Lading and I will see that payment is soon forthcoming.—I shall go on North in a few days and shall be in all the principal Towns in that quarter before I return and if I meet any person in your way whom I think trustworthy I will endeavour to carve you out some business, for notwithstanding the good folks on your side are so musically inclined I suppose you would not wish them to monopolise utterly the products of your industry . . .

    With love to Margaret and Compliments to all friends,

      I remain &c, yours very sincerely, D Stewart.

Daniel Stewart did go north that summer, writing again from New York on 4 September 1809, with comments on British piano sales there:

I have met with a Mr Thomas Western, instrument maker & seller, Maiden Lane in this City, who wishes to establish a Correspondence with you, Calculating to import a number of instruments yearly, not knowing of your terms for satisfaction on this head I refer him to yourself. He has been long settled in this City where he has acquired some property, in Houses and offices, a respectable old Englishman, if you think that any recommendation.

Mr W formerly lived in St John Street, Golden Square and is known to a Mr Robt Macduff at present in your employ, he also refers to Mr Preston of whom you can inquire. But the best recommendation I know to be the Cash which Mr W speaks of sending forward with his order—I have advised him to write to you on the subject and you can arrange with him against a renewal of Intercourse.

There are others in your Line whom I will find out before I leave the City. Some whom I have spoken to think your instruments rather high, but they all acknowledge their superiority. You have also the Character of being rather hard in your bargains, obliging them to pay the money down in England upon receipt of the Instruments—You would probably extend your business here Considerably by Crediting responsible people and it will be in my power to obtain any information you may require on that head—Clementi & Co have sold a good many instruments to people in this Country but they do not stand the Climate like yours. Astor sells a good many but they, like Pindar's Racer, 'made to sell'.

Quality control, and particularly the concern over tuning which was James Shudi's special interest, seems to have pervaded the workshops; for it is recorded that on Primrose Hill in 1809 'two journeymen of Broadwood's fought [a duel] with no result over the tuning of a piano'.[14]

John Broadwood was growing old. On 4 April 1811 he formally retired from the partnership, handing over his remaining quarter-share to his son Thomas so that he would have an equal share with his elder brother James Shudi. Old John had transformed the business from a harpsichord workshop employing three men to probably the leading piano-making company in the world, employing a hundred. He had been in the forefront of the development of the piano and had seen his fellow-makers copy and adapt the ideas that he had pioneered. He had bred two sons in whose capable hands the firm would surely develop further; there were two grandsons, John and James Preston. In June 1811 Margaret Broadwood gave birth to the fifth child and first son of James Shudi's second marriage, who was to be christened Henry Fowler Broadwood. The old man could well be content.

At the end of June 1812 Dr Charles Burney, one of his oldest friends, wrote to him from Chelsea College:

Dr Burney sends his best compliments to Mr Broadwood, and shall be much obliged to him if he will have the goodness to let one of his ingenious Foremen regulate the Hammers and touch of his 6 Octave Piano Forte, of wch. each Octave is so ill voiced as to seem of a different register. It is only during the height of summer that Dr. B. has inclination to quit his bed room or strength to put down a key. He hopes his very worthy old Friend Mr. B. Jr. is well, & if able and willing to go out shd. be very glad to see him whenever he will favour him wth. his company.[15]

Old John would have remembered that piano well. It had been made for Burney by Merlin, apparently in 1777, and Burney claimed that it was the first instrument made with six octaves; he ordered it specifically for the playing of duets. There is some question, however, whether it was a piano or a harpsichord or both; and from Burney's Will it is evident that at some time in the 1790s he asked Broadwood to replace the action, for it is described as 'that by Broadwood in the Merlin Case'. Burney also had a small Broadwood square.

On a day in mid-July 1812 John Broadwood was dining with his son Thomas in the house in Great Pulteney Street, when he suffered a stroke. He could not be moved home to Kensington Gore, and lingering on for one day more, died on 17 July. He was in his eightieth year. His son recorded in his personal diary some years afterwards a truly heartfelt tribute: 'He . . . expired . . . leaving behind him few so good—and none that can surpass him ever, for uprightness and uniformity of conduct, & every virtue that should adorn a man, he left behind him an unspotted reputation. He was a *truly good man*, beloved by all who knew him, he was sincerely religious—he had many friends (few acquaintances perhaps), *no enemy*.'

So it happened that John Broadwood ended his days perhaps as he would have wished: in the house that he had first entered as an eager young cabinet-maker just over fifty years before, the house that had been his workshop and the foundation of his fortune.

He was buried in the grounds of Whitefield's Tabernacle in Tottenham Court Road, beside his first wife Barbara Shudi and their two children who had died in infancy, near the Sexton's Door on the left hand side going in.* By his will he made generous provisions. His sons James Shudi and Thomas had already been given the business. His widow Mary was to enjoy an annuity of £500 a year, which enabled her to live in comfort for a further twenty eight years. His youngest son Henry, then aged nineteen, was to receive Reeves Hall and a legacy of £20,000 on his twenty first birthday. There were other family legacies, to his daughter and son-in-law and their children, to his brother William in Old-hamstocks and his sister Naomi in Greenock. There were bequests to the Scottish Hospital and to the Society for Propagating Christian Knowledge in the Islands of Scotland. To James Forsyth, foreman at Great Pulteney Street for twenty five years, he bequeathed the very substantial sum of £500 'as an acknowledgement of his diligent attention to business'.

John Broadwood's personal estate, exclusive of the business, was valued at £106,364, with a further £20,000 in outstanding loans and bonds. In modern terms he was a millionaire. He had come to London to seek his fortune and he had found it. He had established a reputation for craftsmanship, and the highest standards of manufacture and of business dealing.

* The Chapel, and with it the grave, was destroyed by the last bomb to fall on London in the 1939–1945 war. The American Church in Tottenham Court Road is now on the site.

Chapter V

The Brothers in Partnership

1812–1836

*T*he abstract study of the nature of things—science—had been much pursued by the cultivated amateur: but the making of things, albeit with the assistance of new methods of inquiry, remained manual labour and thus to be comprehended within the proper tasks not of the gentleman but of what came to be called the 'practical man'. So there evolved and sharpened in the course of the 19th century two parallel distinctions between pure and applied science; and between the 'educated amateur' and the 'practical man'.

It was . . . precisely from the ranks of 'practical men' that these entrepreneurs were drawn. They came, in the main, neither from the gentry nor from the bottom of society. They were 'not typically very poor men who struggled to greater affluence through their creative efforts'. They came instead from what might be termed the middle order of Players, those just on the other side of the line; yeomen, traders, skilled artisans, from the 'respectable farming family' which spawned the ironmaster Richard Crawshay; from the linen-draper father of the great flax-spinner John Marshall; or from amongst the successful London silversmiths who were the ancestors to the future textile Courtaulds.

D C Coleman, 'Gentlemen and Players' in *Economic History Review*, second series, Vol XXVI No. 1, February 1973

For some time James Shudi and Thomas Broadwood had wanted to expand the business and increase production. While he was still a partner their father, with due Scots caution, had counselled moderation. There was a war on; shipping was uncertain and unpredictable, by the natural forces of the waves and wind and the human forces of privateers and the edicts of governments. But the domestic market was apparently ever-growing, and the brothers set out to satisfy it. Their first move (in April 1812) was to increase production capacity by buying up the premises in Henry Street, St Pancras, of John Andreas Stumpff, harp-maker. Curiously, in the legal document of this transaction, and in other legal documents for a further ten years, James Shudi and Thomas Broadwood continue to be described as 'harpsichord makers', although it was nearly twenty years since such an instrument had been made in their house.

The Broadwood brothers were now men of wealth and social distinction. James Shudi was settled with his growing family, spending the week at Kensington Gore, and the weekends at Lyne, with longer holidays for the shooting. Thomas in contrast, as a wealthy young bachelor took to travelling. When he was sixteen or seventeen, the Continent was closed by the war and his travels were limited to Scotland (with his parents) and Ireland (on his own). But in 1809 he embarked on a singular adventure. As he recorded in his diary: 'I sailed over to Gibraltar in the packet from Falmouth in 7 days, and from thence visited Ceuta in Africa & afterwards Malaga, Seville, Cadiz, St Lucar Ayamonte, Beja, Alcather de Sel & overland to Lisbon & from thence embarked in the packet for Falmouth (in 12 days).' Thomas was closely following the British armies; for it was on 12 May that Arthur Wellesley defeated the French at Oporto, causing them to retreat from Portugal; two months later, after the battle of Talavera, he was created Duke of Wellington. Whilst on this journey Thomas was given an audience by the King of Spain.

His next great adventure was in 1814 when, as it was then thought, Napoleon had been finally defeated and exiled to Elba. Thomas drove to Paris with his friend James Goding (a prosperous London brewer) 'with our own horses in his Gig'.

The Allied Army was then in Paris—in possession of the Town— [I] was present at a grand Review of 60,000 of the Allied Troops and rode on horseback down the line, in the train with the Emperor Alexander of Russia, the Emperor of Austria, the King of Prussia & the different princes and nobles of those potentates, from the

Champs Elisees [sic] to the Pont de Nuille [sic]. The Cossacks kept
the ground . . . .[1] Mr Goding returned to London by himself and I
went down to Lyons & returned by Paris & the Belgique Bruxelles,
Antwerp, Haarlem, Leyden, Amsterdam, the Hague, Rotterdam,
& by Helvoetsluys packet to Harwich & London.

Evidently rubbing shoulders with emperors was all in the day for
Thomas Broadwood now. In 1815, however, he did not travel (the British
Army under Wellington was assisting Napoleon's final downfall at
Waterloo). Instead, he bought himself a country estate—Juniper Hall, at
Mickleham in Surrey.[2]

In 1816, the war being over, there was a flood of wealthy Britons
travelling to those parts of Europe that had been closed to them for a
quarter of a century. That autumn and winter, Thomas Broadwood set
out on an extended tour of France and Italy, visiting most of the major
cities down to Naples before returning home in the Spring. Later, in 1817,
accompanied this time by his friend Goding, he explored Switzerland,
Austria and Germany. While in Vienna, Thomas took the opportunity to
meet the greatest living composer. As he wrote some years later:

> It was in August 1817 I had the pleasure of seeing Beethoven at
> Vienna. I was introduced to him by his friend Mr Bridi, a Banker at
> Vienna. He was then so unwell, his table supported as many vials of
> medicine and gollipots as it did sheets of music paper & his cloaths
> so scattered about the room in the manner of an Invalid that I was
> not surprised when I called on him by appointment to take him out
> to Dine with us at the Prater to find him declare after he had one foot
> in the carriage that he found himself too unwell to dine out—& he
> retreated upstairs again.
>
> I saw him several times after that at his own house and he was
> kind enough to play to me, but he was so deaf and unwell.[3]

On his return to London, Thomas Broadwood wrote to Beethoven
offering him a piano as a gift. Beethoven was delighted, and wrote:

My very dear friend Broadwood,
    I have never felt a greater pleasure than your honour's intimation
of the arrival of this piano, with which you are honouring me as a
present. I shall look upon it as an altar upon which I shall place the
most beautiful offerings of my spirit to the divine Apollo. As soon as
I receive your excellent instrument, I shall immediately send you

Montrischer Ami Broadwood!

Jamais je n'eprouvais pas un plus grand
Plaisir de ce que me causa votre annonce
de l'arrivée de cette Piano, avec que vous
m'honorès de m'en faire présent, je
regarderai come un Autel, ou je
deposerai les plus belles offrandes
de mon Esprit au divine Apollon.
Aussitôt come je recevrai votre Excellent

instrument, je vous enverrai d'abord les
fruits de l'inspiration des premiers
moments, que j'y passerai, pour
vous servir d'un souvenir de moi à
vous mon très cher B., et
je ne souhaite ce que, qu'ils soient
dignes de votre instrument.
          Mon cher Monsieur et ami
          recevés ma plus grande
          considération
          Je votre ami
          et très humble serviteur
          Louis Van Beethoven

Vienne ce 3me
Dumay Février
1818

Letter to Thomas Broadwood from Beethoven, 1818 (*The Musical Times, 15 December 1892*) the fruits of the first moments of inspiration I spend at it, as a souvenir for you from me, my very dear B.; and I hope that they will be worthy of your instrument.

My dear sir,
accept my warmest consideration,
from your friend and very humble servant,
Louis Van Beethoven
Vienna, 7th February 1818.[4]

Beethoven's music was highly regarded in London, at least by musicians if not by the general public. From its foundation in 1813 the Philharmonic Society performed his music at its concerts. Among the founders of that society were several friends and acquaintances of the Broadwoods, among them Muzio Clementi, Philip Anthony Corri (son of Domenico Corri who had gone into business with Dussek in the Haymarket where they were agents for Broadwood pianos), and J. P. Salomon.

There were other personal links between Broadwoods in London and Beethoven in Vienna. His family friend and former pupil Ferdinand Ries was now living in London (and acting as Beethoven's agent); and Ferdinand's younger brother Pieter Joseph Ries, formerly a clerk with the East India Company and a friend of Charles Lamb, was Broadwoods' foreign correspondence clerk for many years.[5] Another link was through the harp-maker Stumpff, who after selling his business to Broadwoods retired to Vienna, where his family was friendly with Beethoven.

The piano Thomas Broadwood sent to Beethoven was a six-octave grand, made in Great Pulteney Street late in 1817. The case was Spanish mahogany, inlaid with marquetry and ormolu, the brass carrying-handles formed as laurel wreaths. The piano was triple-stringed throughout, with two pedals, the left a soft pedal and the right divided into two, the right side damping the treble, the left side the bass. The conventional label was on the nameboard ('John Broadwood & Sons, Makers to His Majesty and the Princesses, Great Pulteney Street, Golden Square, London'). There were additional inscriptions: on the front was Beethoven's name, and above it the legend *Hoc instrumentum est Thomae Broadwood londini donum propter ingenium illustrissimi Beethoven.*

The names of five noted pianists in London who wished to be associated with the gesture were placed on the right of the nameboard: they were Kalkbrenner, Ries, Ferari, J. B. Cramer and Knyvett.

The piano was despatched by sea to Trieste, where it was put on a cart for the 200-mile journey overland to Vienna. At Trieste there was some

116

Beethoven's Broadwood beneath the portrait of Liszt, to whom it later belonged, in the National Museum of Hungary, Budapest *(Photo: Bakonyi Béla, Budapest)*

delay, for the customs demanded duty on it, and Beethoven had to enlist the influence of his patrons to obtain exemption. That this was achieved is indicated by a contemporary account in the Vienna *Gazette of Arts*:

A liberal Briton as representing his musical and scientific countrymen has offered at the Shrine of our Master a noble present . . . That respected Briton is Mr Broadwood of London, who selected the most perfect Grand Piano Forte perhaps ever constructed, and in testimony of his high esteem, addressed it, with all charges of its conveyance defrayed, to Beethoven's summer residence at Moedling, near Vienna . . .

The instrument is of such excellence that no other in our country can be compared to it. Its keeping tune may be conceived from the fact that at the beginning of January it was sent by sea from London to Trieste, and from thence about the latter end of May by land to Vienna, and finally to Moedling, where on arrival it was found perfectly in tune . . .

The Imperial and Royal Custom has afforded a gratifying proof of the public esteem of the talents of our Beethoven, by permitting a free entry of the Piano. Thus are Great Musical Talents distinguished in our native country, thus are they honoured by foreigners . . .

The piano was later transferred to the workshop of Frau Streicher, daughter of Mozart's piano maker Andreas Stein. While it was there, the London pianist Cipriani Potter (who was later to give the first London performances of several of Beethoven's piano concertos) was asked to try it, since it was said that while the tone was beautiful, the action was heavy. Potter reported to Beethoven that the piano was out of tune, at which the composer said: 'That's what they all say; they would like to tune it and spoil it, but they shall not touch it.' The only person allowed to tune it was Stumpff, 'who came with a letter of introduction from Broadwood'.[6]

In the early 1820s, Beethoven remained loyal to his Broadwood, taking it to Mödling for his holidays. He seldom allowed anyone else to play it (although it is recorded that when the young painter August von Klöber visited Beethoven to paint a portrait he found the composer giving a lesson to his nephew Karl on the Broadwood).[7] Later he allowed Ignaz Moscheles to borrow it for a recital in Vienna in 1823. By that time it had suffered from the composer's violent treatment, the result of his frustration at his increasing deafness. Although the Viennese maker,

Graf, put it into order for the concert, it was not regarded locally as being comparable with Graf's own instruments, perhaps because the audience was more familiar with the Viennese tone. Moscheles wrote: 'I tried in my Fantasia to show the value of the broad, full, although somewhat muffled tone of the Broadwood piano but in vain. My Vienna public remained loyal to their countryman—the clear, ringing tones of the Graf were more pleasing to their ears.'[8]

Nevertheless it was Moscheles who noted that of all his pianos, Beethoven preferred the Broadwood, using it until 1823, by which date he had virtually wrecked it in his desperate attempts to hear the sound. He asked Graf to build him a piano with four strings to each note.

That Thomas Broadwood regarded the gesture of giving a piano to Beethoven as a private and personal one is demonstrated by his insistence that the firm should not seem to be capitalising on it. When he sent an account of the affair to the publisher Novello in 1829, he gave him permission to print the quotation that indicated how highly Beethoven was regarded by his contemporaries, 'or any other part that does not require our house to be mentioned, or anything in the shape of, or that has the appearance of, a puff of our instruments or ourselves'.

There is no record that Beethoven did send Thomas Broadwood the 'first fruits' of that piano. In the summer of 1818, however, he was composing his Piano Sonata in B flat, one of those to the manuscript of which he appended the words. 'Sonata für das Hammerklavier', and the one that has subsequently borne the title 'Hammerklavier'. The last three piano sonatas—Opp. 109, 110 and 111—have been particularly associated with this piano.

His feelings towards his Broadwood were set down by a young poet, Ludwig Rellstab, who visited him about this time. His account also contains the only direct quotation from Beethoven about the instrument:

> Beethoven . . . rose, went to the window, and stood beside his piano. The sight of him so near to his instrument awakened a thought which I had not before ventured to entertain. Ah! if he would but sit down, and express his feelings in tones! In happy, anxious hopefulness, I went close up to him and put my hand on the piano, which was an English Broadwood. To make Beethoven turn round, I softly struck a chord with the left hand; but he did not seem to hear it. In a minute or two he turned round to me, and seeing that I was looking at the instrument, said 'It is a beautiful piano. It was sent to me as a present from London. Look at the names!' There I read the names: Moscheles, Kalkbrenner, Cramer, Clementi, and

Broadwood.* The incident was impressive. The wealthy, artistic manufacturer who presented it to Beethoven could not have devoted his instrument, which seemed a specially good one, to better purpose. The great artists mentioned had reverently subscribed their names as sharers in the scheme; and so this strange autobiographical page had come from far over the sea to lay the homage of the great at the feet of the highest and greatest. 'It is a handsome present, and has a fine tone', said Beethoven, looking at me and putting out his hands towards the keyboard, but without turning round. He struck a chord softly. Never will another fill me with such melancholy. He had C major in the right hand, and struck B in the bass; and looking at me, steadily repeated the wrong chord several times that I might hear the sweet tone of the instrument; yet the greatest musician on earth did not perceive the discord. I do not know whether Beethoven noticed his mistake; but, turning from me, he struck a few chords which were quite correct and in their usual positions, and then left off playing; and this was all I ever heard from him!'[9]

The eventual wreck of the Broadwood is recorded by Beethoven's friend Stumpff in 1824: 'What a spectacle offered itself to my view! There was no sound left in the treble and broken strings were mixed up like a thorn bush in a gale.'[10]

After Beethoven's death in 1827 his Broadwood was bought at auction by a dealer, Spina, who presented it to Liszt. He kept it in his library in Weimar, adding to it the silver music-stand presented to him by the people of Vienna. It was subsequently placed in the National Museum of Hungary in Budapest (see Plate 1).[11]

Thomas Broadwood's last call during his journey in Autumn 1817 was at Düsseldorf, where his nephew James Preston Broadwood was living. Of James Shudi's two sons from his first marriage, the elder, John, had matriculated at Exeter College, Oxford, and was beginning his career as a scholar,† an ambition that his father encouraged. Evidently it was James Shudi's intention that his second son, James Preston, should join the partnership. In 1817 the boy, then aged sixteen, was sent to Germany to learn the language, staying first at Düsseldorf and later

---

* Rellstab was wrong: Moscheles and Clementi did not sign the Broadwood.
† The Rev. John Broadwood (1798–1864) later became noted as a collector of folk songs. He took no part in the business other than as (after his father's death) leaseholder of the Horseferry Road factory.

moving to Leipzig, which his father describes as 'a Gay City & city of business—in which are many Merchants of the first connections, information and manners . . . Mr Cramer says Mr Peters is highly respected at Leipzig & will prove a good acquaintance for you' (Peters had founded his music-publishing business three years earlier).

In a series of letters James Preston's father and stepmother kept him informed of developments at home which demonstrate James Shudi's concern to interest his son in the business, and also his own close attention to it. 'Trade is getting better', he wrote in June 1817; and again, in January 1818, 'Our business goes on better than ever—presenting to us the means of acquiring every blessing in this life—purchasable'.

In March 1818 James Shudi put the case plainly to his son: 'Say . . . if you have still the wish to attend to my business in Pulteney Street—I have no doubt but I might possibly find some other line in trade for you—but am extremely doubtfull if I could find you one half so profitable or so certain—With attention you will be certain to become independent in circumstances & after a few years be entirely your own Master—but attention & a conciliating demeanour will be imperatively necessary at first.' That September James Shudi went down to Lyne for the shooting. But he was careful to point out to his son that the business did not run by itself.

> We had two days rain Saturday & Sunday which no doubt admitted of good hunting on the Monday—but I and Thomas were obliged to attend in Pulteney Street and must stay there all this week malgré all pleasures which may offer, being convinced that the most flourishing of businesses will languish wither & decay, if not attended to & cultivated by the master's eye (at least). We are selling so much that we cannot supply the demand and are therefore straining every nerve to do more & are about taking some large Premises to give us the means of doing so—I believe that business in every department is flourishing now.

This is the first reference to the development that was to lead, a few years later, to the leasing of a large factory in Horseferry Road, Westminster. But evidently James Preston made some response that his father considered pert, for James Shudi wrote: 'Our business in Pulteney Street increases faster than we could at all expect & I believe in spight of the insinuation in your last letter will continue to increase & I flatter myself will be a fortune to you as it has proved to your grandfather & myself.' The refrain recurring through the letters of 1818 is that 'business

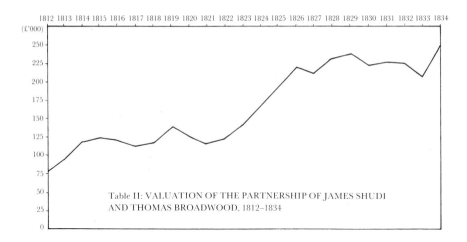

1812 1813 1814 1815 1816 1817 1818 1819 1820 1821 1822 1823 1824 1825 1826 1827 1828 1829 1830 1831 1832 1833 1834

Table II: VALUATION OF THE PARTNERSHIP OF JAMES SHUDI AND THOMAS BROADWOOD, 1812–1834

goes on better & better', a truth illustrated by the valuation of the firm which increased from £77,647 in 1812 to £138,537 in 1819 (Table II).

Among the musical associations of that 'better & better' trade was the despatch on Monday, 22 April 1816 of two grands (Nos. 2044 and 2053) to Messrs. Alexander Greig [*sic*] & Son, Bergen, shipped on the *Four Brothers*, Capt. William Mackgroeklin. Alexander Greig emigrated from Aberdeen to Bergen after the 'troubles', took up Norwegian citizenship in 1779, and built up a prosperous business shipping lobsters to England. He had special schooners built, and imported luxury goods (including Broadwood pianos) on the return journey. He became British consul at Bergen, though amending his name to 'Grieg'. After his death in 1803 the business was carried on by his son John, who became the father of the composer Edvard Grieg.[12]

Young James Preston travelled from Düsseldorf to Leipzig by post waggon and coach, much of the time sitting outside in a freezing December. When he came home the next year he was suffering from consumption and was put to bed at James Shudi's London home, 16 Lower Cadogan Place. In the spring of 1820 he was taken down to Lyne, where he died on 4 June at the age of nineteen. The heir whom James Shudi had planned to introduce into the business, whose training he had looked forward to supervising as his father had done his, was no longer there. James Shudi's second marriage had produced three more sons, but they were mere children: Henry Fowler was nearly eight, Thomas Capel was nearly two and Walter Stewart was just one year old. If James Shudi had visualised a retirement to the country pleasures of Lyne within a few years, that was now out of the question. It would be at least a decade before a son was ready to join the business.

The standard Broadwood square piano, in mahogany, with forte pedal, 1828. Colt Clavier Collection *(Photo: John Maltby)*

Meanwhile Thomas Broadwood was taking himself a wife. He married Annie Mundell at St Margaret's, Westminster on 23 February 1819. After a honeymoon in Switzerland, Italy and the Mediterranean they set up house first at 21 Upper Cadogan Place, later moving to No. 17 where his first-born son Thomas was born on 22 December 1821. It was a week of celebration, for on the previous day Broadwoods had delivered a new decorated grand (see Plate 8) to King George IV at the Pavilion, Brighton.

The character of the firm's clientele is shown by the entries in the Porters' Day Books. Within a few days, in spring 1820, a square was sent to Lord Rosebery at 13 Piccadilly, a grand on hire to Lord Shaftesbury in Grosvenor Square, and a grand to Mrs Gladstone in Grafton Street.

Exports were booming: eight squares were despatched to Warre & Co, Rio de Janeiro, eight more to Mr Rausch, New York, and four to Mr Codman, Quebec. A grand went to Daniel Elliott Esq, 'Civil Service, Madras', and another to 'Miss Colvin, care of James Colvin Esq, Calcutta'.

On the same day, 21 December 1821, that the King's piano went to Brighton, seventeen other instruments left Great Pulteney Street. They included an upright grand to Lady Knatchbull at 50 Wimpole Street. A square was sent to the Revd. Mr Bethell, 'Eaton College, Berks' for which a Mrs Franklin received three guineas for the introduction; the piano was delivered to the Old White Horse Cellar in Piccadilly, to go by Atherton's waggon: carriage cost sixpence. A grand and a square were sent to the West India Export Dock for shipment on the *Fortitude* (Capt. Butcher) to Miss Andrews of Hindsburg House, Barbados; a square went to Leadenhall Street on its way to Bombay with Capt. Fendall of the 4th Light Dragoons, a passenger on the *Demira*.

In 1825 Thomas Broadwood bought an estate near Crawley in Sussex where he built a substantial new house, Holmbush.[13] He became a Justice of the Peace for the County of Sussex, as James Shudi was in Surrey. Both the Broadwood brothers had thus achieved the transition from urban craftsmen to landed gentry. James Shudi marked this social elevation in 1824 by obtaining a Grant of Arms, which was registered on 9 April. The design included a quartering of the Tschudi arms 'in memory of his late honoured Mother who was a representative of a branch of the ancient family of Tschudi': for the crest he took the pine-tree and its blood-red cones.*

Their younger brother Henry† had scaled even higher social heights. Inheriting Reeves Hall and £20,000 at the age of twenty one, he had become a man-about-town with perhaps the most fashionable of all addresses—No 1, Albany. In December 1826 he was appointed a Gentleman of His Majesty's Most Honourable Privy Chamber to George IV, an appointment he kept during the reign of William IV.

---

* Ermine two Pallets Vair Argent and Gules on a Chief Azure an Amulet between two Pine-Trees eradicated Or, And for Crest on a Wreath of the Colours a Pine-Tree eradicated fructed proper surmounted by three Arrows two in Saltire the points downwards and one in fess the point towards the dexter also proper encircled around the Stock by an Amulet Or.

† Henry Broadwood (1793–1878), youngest son of John Broadwood, Member of Parliament for Bridgwater 1837–1852. He had no part in the firm, though his extravagant life-style was a source of perpetual anxiety to his brothers.

Cabinet upright by John Broadwood & Sons, 1834. Russell Collection of Early Keyboard Instruments, Edinburgh *(Photo: Tom Scott, copyright University of Edinburgh)*

With the ending of the war, great changes took place in the style of furniture and in the methods of manufacture. The florid intricacies of the carver's art and of inlay became too expensive, and in the post-war years of high living costs a new simplicity was required. This was further encouraged by the introduction of steam-powered machinery for woodworking. In 1793 Sir Samuel Bentham, naval engineer and brother of Jeremy Bentham, took out an all-purpose patent for machines for 'planing, moulding, rebating, grooving, mortising, sawing, in coarse and fine woods, in curved, winding and transverse directions—and shaping wood in all sorts of complicated forms'.[14] Despite this, at Broadwoods as at the majority of furniture makers, 'the only process which was mechanised to any extent was the heaviest process, the sawing and planing of the planks'.[15]

Two innovations in finish were introduced at this time. The first was French polishing, said to have been brought to Britain in 1814; this gradually overtook the time-consuming and even more laborious process of repeated wax polishing, and achieved the high glassy shine that became fashionable. The second was the increased use of brass inlay for decoration. Shudi had used cast brass for the furniture of his harpsichords (one of 1770 has decorative carrying-handles in the form of laurel wreaths that are very like those Broadwoods put on to grands, as for example Beethoven's). Brass inlay in the form of scrolls and banding was a feature of the nameboard of Broadwood squares from the early 1800s. Later the brass ornament became highly ornate, particularly in contrast with the most expensive rosewood veneer (see the example of the 1834 cabinet upright page 125). This was peculiarly English, and indeed a London, speciality. 'The ornaments, cut out of sheet brass in simple scroll and floral forms and classical patterns, were inserted into the veneer which was fretted to correspond, and the exactness of finish is admirable. Several drawings for inlay of this character are preserved in a portfolio in the Victoria and Albert Museum, dating from 1816. The presence of this brass inlay on furniture is evidence of origin in London; for such metal work was a specialised trade, carried on in London in the neighbourhood of St Martin's Lane and Long Acre.'[16]

In 1823 James Shudi and Thomas Broadwood leased a factory in Horseferry Road, Westminster, from the Grosvenor Estate. This enabled them to plan production on a logical system, with each constituent part of the instrument made in a rational sequence so that the timber and materials could be brought in at one side of the site, and the almost completed pianos despatched from the other, for transport to Great Pulteney Street for finishing and final tuning. The choice of Horseferry

Road was sensible, both because it was mid-way between the wood wharf on the river and Soho, and because the Westminster area was a centre for furniture manufacture and thus provided a ready pool of skilled craftsmen.

Broadwoods were now among the largest purchasers of wood in London. Thomas Broadwood was buyer, at auction 'by the candle'* in City coffee-houses such as Garraway's; and the timber trade admired his purchase in 1823 of what was said to be the finest log of Honduras mahogany ever grown. Logs were bought uncut, and therefore buying required judgement and entailed risk. This particular log—'the finest in regard to figure and quality'—contained 390 cubic feet at broker's measure (4684 feet of inch) and was bought for £1,781 0s 6d; it proved to be so sound that it could have been sold cut for more than £2,000. Broadwoods were so pleased with the purchase that a section of the finest plank was mounted, polished, and displayed on the wall.

The decade from 1820 saw the introduction of two radical improvements in piano structure. The first was the systematic introduction of metal to strengthen the frame. The second was the invention of the double escapement action.

Makers had been attempting to marry wood and metal in the piano case for some years, and Hipkins records[17] that 'James Shudi Broadwood tried iron bars to resist the treble strain in 1808, and again in 1818, but was not successful in fixing them'. It was a problem that concerned all piano makers, and it was solved by William Allen, a tuner employed by Stodarts. Working with Stodart's foreman, James Thom, he devised a system of parallel metal tubes, linked to metal plates—brass above the brass strings of the bass, iron above the iron strings. Devised as a system of stabilising the tuning, it was patented in 1820; but its main achievement was in permitting the introduction of thicker and heavier strings, and was thus the point of transition from the lighter case of earlier years. At about the same time one of Broadwood's workmen, Samuel Hervé, designed a fixed metal string-plate which was introduced into Broadwood squares from 1821.

In 1827 James Shudi Broadwood patented a combination of metal string-plate and fixed metal bars. There were four bars, set diagonally with no bar parallel to the long side. This was a complex arrangement since the bars had to be adjusted with absolute precision; and the scale was divided at the points where the bars passed. However, this

---

*The final bidder before a candle snuffs out is the purchaser, a practice still maintained in some French wine auctions.

A Broadwood grand in India, 1824: the Winter Room in Sir Charles D'Oyley's house at Patna *(Collection of Mr & Mrs Paul Mellon)*

development enabled Broadwoods to launch a new range of semi-grands in 1831, followed in 1834 by a new range of boudoir or cottage grands. These proved commercially successful on the domestic market at which Broadwoods were aiming.

The second major development was made in Paris, by Erards. Sebastien Erard had revived and expanded his workshop on his return from London, where he had left his nephew Pierre to manage their successful London factory. In about 1810 Sebastien made a grand for Napoleon; an inventive maker, he introduced several of the devices added to give 'variety' to the piano, such as the 'bassoon', which brought a strip of parchment into contact with the strings, producing a buzzing sound. In 1822 he perfected his double escapement action, and launched it at the Paris Exposition in the following year. This action, by restraining the hammer as it fell back from the first stroke, enabled players to achieve a faster repetition of a note. It was praised by the virtuoso Thalberg, and achieved great success though many manufacturers (notably Broadwood's friend in Paris, Pleyel) were sceptical.

The seal was set on Erard's success in 1829 when George IV bought an Erard grand (at first at Windsor, and later removed to Brighton) and subsequently gave Sebastien and Pierre Erard a Royal Warrant for pianoforte-making. The Warrant was renewed by William IV (as 'Harp and Pianoforte Maker in Ordinary') in 1833.

But the challenge seemed to be answered by the Broadwood sales figures. The company was dominant throughout the world, and Broadwood pianos were to be found in the most out-of-the-way places: a Broadwood grand was in the drawing-room of Sir Charles D'Oyley, opium agent and afterwards Commercial Resident at Patna, India, in 1824. As one commentator remarks: 'A Broadwood grand was so important to at least one Englishman serving his country in India that it was worth the expense of transporting it there and the considerable trouble of keeping it in playing condition to help create a corner of England in an out-post of empire.[18]

James Shudi was evidently considering export in some quantity to Russia; and the opera singer Madame Mara*, living in retirement in that country, even suggested that young Henry Fowler might be sent to start up a factory in St Petersburg (now Leningrad):

Reval, Apr 29 1825

As to your plan, I don't know what to advise, since the Duty for an English pianoforte has got up to 15 pounds sterling, which makes 338 roubles, besides other Custom House expenses; people are rather grown shy of them—they own their superiority over the Vienna instruments which are not lasting, but yet they shun the monetary expense . . . I often think of the pleasant day I passed in your House, when we went to the French theatre in the evening. If your young man would set up Instrument Maker himself at Petersburg it might answer, as I suppose the materials are cheaper there than in England, and the Duty would be saved.

G. E. Mara

In London, of course, Broadwoods remained dominant. When Weber came to London in the spring of 1826 a Broadwood cottage piano was ordered for his room at Sir George Smart's house in Great Portland Street, where it was used by the composer until his death there on 6 June.

---

* Gertrud Elisabeth Mara, née Schmeling (1749–1833) was an opera singer who first appeared in London in 1784, making a particular success in the Handel Commemoration at Westminster Abbey. She sang in London until 1791, finally retiring to Moscow in 1802.

Once again in the 1830s Britain was in political turmoil. The Great Reform Bill of 1832 had produced a bloodless revolution, but there were militant demonstrations up and down the country and the future was once again uncertain. James Shudi was now in his sixties and like his father before him was facing a period of upheaval and change; he began to feel that it was time for a younger generation to shoulder the burden. Now the eldest son of his second marriage was coming down from the university.

Henry Fowler Broadwood had been carefully educated. The public schools were now setting the pattern of English education for boys; while James Preston, twenty years earlier, had been set to the traditional eighteenth-century pattern of education, first with a clergyman who had boys to board, and then with tutors at home, Henry Fowler had been sent to Harrow at the age of twelve. However, he only spent three years there and was subsequently sent abroad, first to France and then to Germany. At Heidelberg he became a member of a student corps, and on his return was sent a book as 'an agreeable memory of our friends in Heidelberg who felt so sorry about your departure, and of the cheerful times passed in their company'.

Thackeray paints a picture of Rawdon Crawley (in *Vanity Fair*) which sounds like Henry Fowler at that time: 'A perfect and celebrated 'blood' or dandy-about-town . . . Boxing, rat-hunting, the fives' court, and four-in-hand driving were then the fashion of our British aristocracy; and he was adept in all these noble sciences.' Henry Fowler was later described[19] as 'very powerful physically, and (he) excelled in athletics, being a good oarsman, a fine shot, an expert sportsman, a great pedestrian, clever at single-stick, and an excellent boxer. In his youth fighting with one's fists was . . . fashionable . . . His trainer was the famous pugilist Ben Caunt, whose remains were interred with much solemnity close to those of Lord Byron in Hucknall Church, near Nottingham.'

After his exploits in Heidelberg Henry Fowler went up to St John's College, Oxford but he only spent two months there, before transferring to Trinity College, Cambridge. The reasons are unknown, but it may be that he had got into a sporting set from which his father wanted him removed. He did not take a degree at Cambridge; wealthy young men often did not.

On coming down from Cambridge he was put to work in the factory.

Life in the workshops was, of course, very different from the life he had been accustomed to at the University. Nevertheless, he enjoyed pianoforte making, and took the keenest interest in every detail of the work he could acquire. His activity and restlessness were remarkable. He would invariably run upstairs three steps at a time, and yet would stand before a piano for hours without uttering a word, intently thinking how he might improve it in certain particulars . . . He worked for some time at the bench, and then took instruction in tuning, in which branch of the pianoforte industry his father, James Broadwood, excelled.[20]

It was said of him in later life that Henry Fowler seemed to carry on two complementary existences, as pianoforte maker and as country squire and sportsman. In his twenties, this worried his father; even more it worried his Uncle Tom, who in the young man's absence on hunting, shooting and fishing holidays up and down the country felt that he must keep a closer eye on the business than ideally he would have wished. Tom's view of life was innately pessimistic. A careful man himself, he was worried by the extravagances of his high-living younger brother Henry as a courtier and politician. No doubt Tom saw Henry Fowler's sporting passions as presaging a spendthrift life like Henry's.

Nevertheless by 1834 James Shudi was confident enough in his son's grasp of the business to take his wife and daughters on a European tour, visiting Chamonix and Interlaken. Evidently young Henry Fowler's ambitions encompassed a rapid enlargement of the factory, for James Shudi wrote from Geneva on 24 September 1834:

As to increasing our shops by building, I must leave that to you & your Uncle. If the Order Book & the stock of instruments are the same as at the same time last year and we see no reason to expect an increase of sales, do nothing. If otherwise, begin to increase (by building or otherwise) your means of production *immediately*—& pay attention to old Forsyth's advice in so doing, as he is thoroughly a zealous, honest welljudging friend & servant. I cannot advise further at this distance. I have looked at all the Pianos I could get at since I have been abroad, but have learned nothing—they are all inferior things—& generally imitations of the English Pianos—but every town has its manufactory, which shows Pianos are in demand. I hope Russell & Darling [the foremen] continue satisfied with the new springs & touch of the Grands; if so, & with the care we take of the manufactory our Pianos will increase in sale. I am glad to perceive that money comes in well. After the long time we have been sowing & dressing, we have a right to expect a good and an increasing return, & if I mistake not, the next years will be more productive than the past, however satisfied we should be with them; and I flatter myself that your attention thereto will be amply rewarded.

Henry Fowler's attention received its first reward on 10 May 1836 when, a month before his twenty fifth birthday, his father and uncle took him into the partnership of John Broadwood & Sons. The older men retained two-fifths each, and gave him one-fifth. Henry Fowler Broadwood, the new generation, now had a stake in the business.

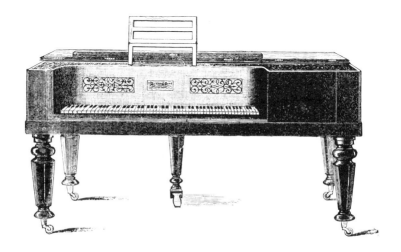

Chapter VI

The Years of Triumph and Challenge

1836–1857

*I*t is just seventy years ago since I first played in public upon a Broadwood Pianoforte. This was at Signor Lanza's concert at the Assembly Rooms, Blackheath, on June 23 1828. Since that period I have always been a faithful, devoted and enthusiastic Broadwoodite . . . I played on a Broadwood at the first Chamber concert ever given in this country (Concerti da Camera, as we called them) in 1835 and later on at the Philharmonic in 1850. Indeed I can safely aver that, except in Germany and Italy, my public performances have invariably been on Pianos manufactured by the illustrious house of Broadwood. In my own home too the name of Broadwood has always been honoured. As long ago as 1827 in my Father's house, Liszt and I, as boys, played Duetts together on a Broadwood; while the beautiful Grand Piano (No. 19493) which was generously presented to me some 35 or 36 years ago by Messrs John Broadwood and Sons, with that grace which has always characterised the dealings of the Firm, is still to me, at the conclusion of my Eighty Fourth year of age, a continual source of consolation and pleasure. Its tone is as delightful as ever, its singing powers as charming, and while its keys are always responsive and grateful to my touch, the cherished old instrument is still capable of discovering 'much eloquent music' in every fine gradation of tone. I am truly proud of my long friendship with the house of Broadwood.

Charles Salaman 1814–1901, *a London concert pianist, writing in the Visitors' Book of John Broadwood & Sons, 6 February 1898*

T he Broadwood piano was now supreme on the London concert platforms, as in the home. The firm was surely the largest maker of pianos in the world: in the last week of February 1836, 63 pianos were finished and 50 were sold—4 grands, 1 semi-grand, 6 cabinets or cottages, and 39 squares. The stock stood at 353 pianos; the rate of manufacture was over 3,000 pianos a year. The age of brilliant virtuosi on the piano had arrived, and in London they played Broadwoods.

When in the summer of 1837 the Paris piano maker Camille Pleyel came to London, bringing with him a notable young pianist, the latter played only once, at James Shudi Broadwood's house, 46 Bryanston Square. As Mendelssohn (who was in London at the time) noted in a letter: 'Chopin is said to have suddenly turned up here a fortnight ago; but he visited nobody and made no acquaintances. He played one evening beautifully at Broadwood's, and then hurried away again.'[1]

James Shudi introduced the young visitor from Paris to his wife and daughters as 'Mr Fritz', keeping up this pretence until after dinner when, sitting down at the piano and playing a few bars, the 27-year-old guest was instantly identified by Mrs Broadwood. The story rings true; it is in character with James Shudi's humour to play such a practical joke.

Chopin was a protégé of Pleyel, who had first launched him in Paris in the Pleyel hall (in a famous 1831 concert at which six pianists played six Pleyel pianos).

Pleyel's great rival in Paris was the house of Erard. The Erards had begun a fierce and two-pronged attack on the piano market. First, there were several technical innovations. The most important was the double-escapement action, developed with the concert pianist Henri Herz and, as the Herz–Erard action, widely adopted. One of Erard's workmen, Jean Henri Pape, patented several other inventions, notably the introduction of felt to replace leather for hammers. But the second line of Erard attack was publicity and promotion.

The last was a particular danger to Broadwood since the campaign was conducted with equal vehemence in Paris and London, as Erards had factories in both capitals. When in 1835 Pierre Erard petitioned the Privy Council in London for an extension of the 1821 double-escapement patent, the move was accompanied by the publication of a booklet listing 'a formidable parade of aristocratic support and artistic endorsement',[2] culminating in the purchase by George IV of an Erard grand, leading to a Royal Warrant. Broadwoods were furious.

In the summer of 1838 James Shudi was worried enough to write to Pleyel, who replied on 22 June:

My dear Mr Broadwood

... I thank you wholeheartedly for the interest you have shown, but I ask you to be completely reassured as to the strength of my house, which is always in full view of prosperity. The famous competitor that you mention [Erard] sells about two hundred pianos every year, and my house, without wishing to boast, sells eight hundred, but if one takes note of all the 'puffs' in the papers he is not only the principal maker in France but in the whole universe, and in a phrase (to use a very vulgar expression) he thinks himself the ultimate big noise* and the house of Broadwood is small beer beside him.

At all times, my dear Sir, there have been charlatans who have imposed themselves on the ignorant, but in the long run all these merchants of intrigue and lies will wear themselves out and truth will take their place.

Pleyel may well have been smarting because while Chopin was on his books, Erard had captured Liszt (although he later transferred his allegiance to Bosendorfer). Because they both felt threatened by this campaign of Erards, Broadwoods and Pleyel exchanged pianos for comparison: Broadwoods sent over an upright, and Pleyel responded with a bichord square of 6½ octaves in Brazilian rosewood.

It was in the pattern that Broadwoods should find their own virtuoso. The choice was particularly English; they chose the star pupil at the Royal Academy of Music, and in 1835 gave him a Broadwood grand. He was William Sterndale Bennett, and his friend J.W. Davison† remembered the day when he found Bennett in 'his comfortable study at the Academy, cheerfully lighted, warmed with a blazing fire, and with a splendid new Broadwood Grand just presented to him on the part of that munificent firm.'[3]

Sterndale Bennett was then eighteen. The son of the organist of Sheffield parish church, he had been brought up after the deaths of his parents by his grandfather John Bennett, who was a vicar choral at King's College, Cambridge. The boy became a chorister of King's, but showing remarkable musical precocity was sent at the age of nine to the Royal Academy of Music, where he became a pupil of Cipriani Potter. At first his practising was done 'in the school-room where the practice-pianos were kept, and used simultaneously. Order was maintained by an

* *Le Claqueur fini*
† James William Davison, music critic of *The Times*, 1846–1879.

136

ex-Sergeant of the Guards, whose favourite sentry-post was at the back of Bennett's cottage-piano, where he would stand motionless hour after hour looking over the boy's fingers.'[4] Under those conditions the young Sterndale Bennett managed to write five piano concertos, two of which he played at concerts of the Philharmonic Society. At seventeen he was discovered by Mendelssohn, who became a personal friend.

It was at an evening party in London in the spring of 1836 that Henry Fowler Broadwood overheard Thomas Attwood* lamenting that Sterndale Bennett could not afford to go to the Lower Rhine Musical Festival at Düsseldorf, where Mendelssohn was to conduct the first performance of his oratorio *St Paul*. Ever spontaneously generous, Henry Fowler said that of course the boy must go, and Broadwoods would pay. So Sterndale Bennett went, accompanied by his friend Davison (whose parents were wealthy). Mendelssohn encouraged them to attend the rehearsals as well as the performances of *St Paul*; early in the morning he would call on 'the lazy Englishmen', as he dubbed them, and after the Festival he made music with them, and played billiards.

Sterndale Bennett repaid Broadwood's kindness. When he played one of his piano concertos at the Gewandhaus in Leipzig on 17 January 1839, it was 'upon a fine piano expressly sent over by Messrs Broadwood, which piano was then to be retained by the firm of Breitkopf and Haertel, as a model to be followed in the manufacture of their own instruments.'[5]

Despite his precocious success, Sterndale Bennett found the early years after college difficult, since his music was academic and did not appeal to popular taste. In the spring of 1841 he was obliged to ask Henry Fowler for a loan of £20; Henry Fowler immediately sent him £30. It was a typically generous gesture.

Not surprisingly, these financial difficulties persuaded Sterndale Bennett to pursue the greater security of an academic career,† rather than the more risky life of an executant or composer. Nevertheless, he remained loyal to Broadwoods.

With Henry Fowler Broadwood installed in Great Pulteney Street, his father and uncle were able to indulge their pleasures as country gentlemen. Both had become figures of note in their respective counties. Thomas Broadwood was High Sheriff of Sussex in 1833; that December he dined with King William IV and Queen Adelaide at Brighton, noting

---

* Thomas Attwood (1765–1838), once Mozart's pupil, Mendelssohn's host in London, and organist of St Paul's.

† (Sir) William Sterndale Bennett (1816–1875), Professor of Music in the University of Cambridge (1856), Principal of the Royal Academy of Music (1866).

in his diary with pardonable pride that 'the King asked me to take wine with him twice during dinner which I considered a great honour'. James Shudi Broadwood emulated his younger brother, being 'pricked' as High Sheriff of Surrey in 1835.

Thomas Broadwood had political ambitions, and stood for Parliament that year, being defeated at Horsham by three votes—those, as he claimed, of his opponent, his opponent's father and his opponent's paid agent. Thomas's electoral ambitions brought about a difference of opinion between the brothers, one of the first of many. This was the decade when railways were striking dramatically through the English countryside. Landowners were worried about the effect that the railways would have on property values. James Shudi took legal advice on ways of defending the Lyne estate against the proposed Brighton Line. Henry Fowler obtained a lawyer's assurance that 'no railroad would be allowed to annoy a gentleman in the way of destroying his grounds in so unjustifiable a manner as I represented it was feared the Brighton line would annoy . . . ' However, he added: 'I see my Uncle Tom is a little annoyed about this shew of opposition, as he declares the railroad will increase the value of your property—and is sore afraid lest he should be confounded with you as an opposer of railroads—which might hurt him in the opinions of the Horsham electors . . .'

There were two elections in 1837, in May and July. Thomas stood for Horsham once again in July—'very foolishly', he confided to his diary— losing this time by only two votes. He had perhaps been emboldened by the success of his youngest brother, for Henry Broadwood was elected Member for Bridgwater in May, after several previous attempts and the expenditure locally of very large sums of money. Henry made determined efforts to persuade his eldest brother James Shudi to stand, forwarding to Henry Fowler a letter from the Tory leader Sir Henry Hardinge (later Viscount Hardinge, Governor-General of India) referring to James Shudi in flattering terms: 'I hear on all sides that he is in every respect of personal qualification a most fit man, & possessing as he does large Estates in the country there cannot be found a more desirable representative.'

Henry Fowler duly passed this on to his father, who was adamant that he would not stand himself, but left the field open for his son to make his own decision. But James Shudi never failed to make his own view crystal clear:

Sir H. Hardinge's letter *may* have been written at the request of my brother, to be forwarded to me. The leaders of the Party want votes

& they care little of the quality of the voters, of the ruin of health, peace of mind or fortune of those they may induce. But you are not one of those to be duped by such; but should you determine to sport the Patriot, it will be from conviction that you are serving the Country & not to & with the ruin of your self. I wish to avoid encouraging or discouraging you—that your decision should be entirely your own—& that no blame or reproach should attach to me.

To his brother Henry, James Shudi was more forthright, requesting him to 'stop this persecution' . . . 'I will do all I can for the Conservatives—but they have hurt themselves with their friends in this district by opposition to the new Poor Laws.'

There was a further reason why James Shudi was wary of his younger brother Henry. That was the affair of the Lion Brewery. Although this business concerned John Broadwood & Sons only through the involvement of its three partners, it was in this unfortunate débâcle that the seeds of family dissension were sown. It occupied the partners' time for over a decade and is in microcosm a pattern for the troubles that were later in the century to afflict the piano company, then unchallengeable in its productiveness of wealth and security.

Under the will of old John Broadwood his executors (James Shudi and Thomas) were required to hold young Henry's legacy of £20,000 during his minority, and then use it 'for placing him out to any business or profession he may be inclined to enter into as they shall think likely to be to his advantage'. In the event, by common agreement they bought him a partnership in the Lion Brewery in the City, at the same time as Thomas, as a personal investment, purchased the freehold from his friend Robert Goding.

Henry Broadwood was no brewer, and no businessman. He was a man-about-town, courtier and politician. But even substantial wealth, when spent lavishly, needs replenishment from time to time; and as Henry Broadwood ran through his fortune, he turned to his brother Thomas.

As during the following decade the Lion Brewery went from bad to worse, Henry Broadwood took on more and more commitments. He was elected to Parliament in 1837, and married Fanny Lowther two years later; that too may have been an investment for Thomas, whose accounts contain the entry: 'Lord Lowther's mortgage his House, his Bonds @ £800 per annum & principal money on the decease of the Earl of Lonsdale of £12,000.'

By 1846 Henry Fowler was drawn into the business of trying to help

Henry and the Lion Brewery; James Shudi, who was spending the spring with his wife and daughters at Bath, became wary of his brother Thomas's financial dealings and—in a letter that sadly presages the family disagreements of later years—wrote to his son:

> Perhaps it is a fault in me to look too far in the futurity—but I owe much to that fault—otherwise I should not be enjoying myself in one of the best houses, & be received amongst the best Society at Bath—or have the pleasure of seeing you & my other Children so well placed in the world, had I followed a desire I had some 30 years ago of retiring, content with the handsome fortune (as I then thought it) I had accumulated. The reduction of Interest—my increase of familly & other causes—would ere this have placed me in a very subordinate position than that we all now fill. This faculty of forethought is sometimes annoying—it makes me at the present uneasy at the thought—not improbable—that the love of money of mon oncle* may someday cause him to be unjust towards you & should he find you without funds to meet him—that he take advantage of the large share in our concern, to threaten to withdraw his Capital . . . I advise that in Pulteney Street Books may be kept, as usually done in all Partnerships—so that they may bear being examined in Court . . . and that you abstain from Building—or buying more materials than you can possibly avoid—but withdraw all you can so that you may have funds to meet any of the contingencies I dread—I hope erroneously—may at some future period occur.

(Henry Fowler took his father's advice over the books. Partnership Books were forthwith introduced at Great Pulteney Street, each partner retaining a set made up annually, each set being signed by each partner.)

The Lion Brewery continued to be a problem. Thomas Capel Broadwood, James Shudi's youngest son, who had been bought a partnership, was voted off the Board in 1847, emigrated to New Orleans, married the daughter of a wealthy lawyer, Mr Hennen, and founded a line of American Broadwoods.

Henry Broadwood remained afloat, and M.P. for Bridgwater, until 1852. He died in 1878. His son Arthur Broadwood (1867–1928) was a soldier. As an officer of the Scots Guards he served in the Sudan Expedition of 1885, and later rose to be Brigadier-General commanding

* Clearly, in the context, 'ton oncle', i.e. Thomas Broadwood.

the Royal Guards Reserve Regiment. He was a sporting friend of the Prince of Wales, later King Edward VII.

A decade earlier, James Shudi had been far from certain that his son Henry Fowler was going to turn out 'an active man of business'. In 1838, two years after he had been made a partner, he had written his father an enthusiastic letter advocating expansion of production; but he had written it from Scotland, where he was up for the shooting. His father wrote: 'Without you are inclined to devote yourself steadily & your attention seriously to the business, you had better not attempt to enlarge the sphere or alter or extend its present operations . . .' But he could not but admit that when *he* had been a young man, his father too had curbed his enthusiasm: 'My father was as little inclined as I now am, when I was at your age for pushing. I pushed on—and you know the result.'

As Henry Fowler progressed south from moor to moor his father and uncle directed him across to Liverpool, where one of the firm's best customers was complaining of a poor instrument. Thomas's letter illustrates the care they took in such instances:

> We have this moment received a letter and remittance from our very old friend & worthy merchant customer, Mr Rawdon, complaining that the Victoria GPF just sent his Brothers does not and will not stand in Tune played or not played on, although he has got an experienced Tuner to Tune it, & he must send it back *at once*. I think there is something unfair in the *experienced Tuner* & as he is so old & good a Customer & having sent us another order at the same Time, I have thought it best to send off directly Morison (not being able to spare Murray or Wilkie well) by the railroad to enquire into the case, & prevent its being returned if possible, & *satisfy Mr Rawdon we would not send him a bad instrument*; if you would call on him, it would be well, as he always has sworn by our House—everything goes on well here.
>   So in haste adieu Dear Harry
>   Ton oncle affecté
>   Thos. Broadwood

The French subscription—common in letters between James Shudi, Thomas and Henry Fowler—is a reflection of the cosmopolitanism of these men; fluent in French and German, they frequently slipped into French when topping and tailing letters among themselves.

James Shudi endorsed his brother's request in a letter to Henry Fowler from Lyne, which pointedly reflected on the amount of time the youngest partner was devoting to sport:

> If you can contrive to abstract some time from your pleasure, *I* would wish also you made that detour in your road home, to see our wholesale friends there and elicit their opinions as to our House, and their mode of doing business with others—& besides Liverpool is more worth your seeing than any place you have yet visited. [When back in London] you should remain at least a week, to deposit the fruits of your journey with my brother and Russell [the foreman] & arrange Murray's departure & inspect & give orders in the manufactory—as I think my brother will be pleased with this attention to the concern—he would, if you merely run through town on your return, be thinking pleasure was more your pursuit than business—and latterly he has taken a more active part in Pulteney Street, & seems more heavily engaged in it than I have known him do for years—and will probably be therefore more likely to notice any lack of attention on your part.
>
> I was a little surprised by a letter from my brother telling me you had sent up by Steamer 2 horses from Scotland—I hope you are not going to destroy your fair prospects in this world—by turning the 'Complete Sportsman'—I wish to see you enjoy shooting & hunting in moderation, as a secondary and very secondary pursuit—your principal object being to add to your fortune & to establish yourself well in the opinion of those whose good opinion is alone worth having (not the praise of the Sporting Man).

This paternal reprimand had its effect, for Henry Fowler went to Liverpool, and then spent some time at the factory. James Shudi was concerned to develop the retail trade. He wrote to Henry Fowler in September 1838:

> Tom . . . seems very desirous to push business—says he has given some orders to that end, & pleased Rothwell, Russell etc.—he thinks we have never sufficient stock—& probably he may have pleased these parties by ordering an increase of workmen (in giving them—the foremen—increase of power and consideration thereby)—but if . . . we have 23 weeks sale of finished instruments beforehand, all required is to have these or half of them put into such a state as that they could be sent out of the House at very short notice, & if the 2nd or last finishers cannot be brought to do this, all

that we should do by increasing our manufacture would be but to have 30 or 50 weeks sales in advance instead of 23 . . .

We want some rooms put apart entirely for our Retail friends— from which no instruments should be allowed to be selected by Ward, Russell or Murray for any of our Country friends, these instruments kept in order & as ready to be sent off as those in Purdies, Beales or any other Music Shops—so that no Retail friend should wait a moment. Our other rooms should also have assortments so nearly ready to supply our Country Wholesale friends as may be possible.

Evidently the old problem of sales lost through unavailability of stock was still pressing.

With the growth of Empire, markets were increasing world-wide. In 1837 Broadwoods shipped a cabinet upright (No. 6725) on the ship *Rhoda* to Launceston, Tasmania, for onward transmission to the Henty family in Swan River, Australia. Thomas Henty was a Sussex farmer who had emigrated a decade earlier with his 'labourers and servants, their stores and implements, their fruit-trees and their stock'. This Broadwood was later said to be the first piano ever in Victoria.[6]

But competition was becoming more fierce. Broadwoods having adopted brass studs similar to the Erard pattern (as most piano manufacturers were doing), Erards threatened legal action claiming infringement of their patent. On 28 August 1839 James Shudi wrote to his son at Great Pulteney Street:

I advise first that you speak to Russell (who I directed again to go to the Roll office & look at Erard's Patent) & question him whether the Patent claims the upright application or pull of the strings upwards (as he (Erard) I believe was the first so to do)—I took occasion to call on Stumpff, who having long worked with Old Erard, I thought might have answered some questions; but except that he told me that he had not remarked any brass bridge on his instruments, I learned nothing but his opinion that Erard might claim the invention of pulling upwards & the studs. If so—you must abandon using the studs—even on the belly bridge, & get your bearing on the brass bridge as heretofore . . . Russell can find out by some of our people, or the books, the time when I put some brass bridges on a few Square pianos—but the mode used was so different from this you have adopted, that you will gain little use by the enquiry, than to be able to assert that we used brass bridges years ago. Make enquiry thro' every person you can, who knows the old Makers, and you probably will learn that several have tried bridges with holes perforated as yours are, or something similar, that may serve you in your interview with Pierre Erard. If necessary look yourself at the Patent. After you have stirred in this matter and informed yourself sufficiently, come down here and see me before you call upon Erard. I told him you would probably be in town next week and would take an early opportunity of calling on him; so the latter end of next week will be early enough for your interview. My own opinion is that he can object to nothing but the studs.

The days were long gone when the piano-makers shared their inventions freely. Fifty years earlier John Broadwood had allowed his fellow-makers to adopt his development of the divided bridge without hindrance or the payment of any royalty. Erards were working in a cold commercial world; Broadwoods represented the market leader whom they were determined to bring down. They pressed on with a relentless use of the law and a flamboyant development of publicity. But the supremacy of Broadwoods endured still, and in April 1840 Thomas was able to report to James Shudi that the equity had risen from £191,000 to £207,000 over the year.

Nevertheless competition was increasing. Besides Erards, Stodarts and Kirkman (who had too belatedly followed Broadwoods into piano-making, by which time the junior firm in the eighteenth-century harpsichord market had become dominant), Thomas Tomkinson began making good pianos in the 1800s, Robert Wornum and Wilkinson & Co. a decade later.

The 1830s saw the emergence of several firms that were to make a challenge, such as John Strohmenger (1830), Collard & Collard (1832—the inheritors of Clementi & Co.), Allison & Allison (1837), William Challen (1838) and Charles Cadby (1839). In the 1840s came John Brinsmead, William Grover, John & James Hopkinson, together with more than two hundred other makers in the London area.[7] Many of these were one-man businesses; many, trained at Broadwoods, formed loosely-linked cooperatives, whereby one man would make the case, another would fit the soundboard, another the strings, and so on. Many worked in Stoke Newington, where it was said that every street had its piano factory.

The challenge was not limited to Britain, and did not arrive only in terms of quantity. In 1830 Jonas Chickering of Boston announced the invention of a solid iron frame for the grand piano, and patented the single-cast frame in 1843.

In the spring of 1839 Henry Fowler wrote a contrite note to his father: 'On quitting you at the close of the Season, I cannot do less than return you my hearty thanks for your continual kindness towards me, and for the forbearance with which you suffer sports—which occasionally, perhaps, interfere with your own pleasures.' Nevertheless he did keep up his sporting life, writing in the following summer to his Uncle Thomas: 'A fancy for travelling has come over me, which as I do not feel altogether well just now in London, I desire to gratify. My plan is to join some friends in the South of France, thence to Switzerland, where having got as much walking exercise as possible, I should return home by Paris and be back in England by the end of the first week in September. I can arrange matters in Pulteney Street so that all the work you & my father would have to do would be to sign the cheques on Saturdays.'

Thomas's irritation may be easily imagined. The managing director of the firm was planning to be out of the country for the summer, apparently and complacently leaving the factory to run itself. However, Henry Fowler's 'fancy for travelling' was not, on this occasion, abstract. It (or rather she) was feminine and vivacious, and her name was Juliana Maria Birch. She was living in the South of France with her friend and chaperone, a Mrs Deverell. On that visit, Henry Fowler proposed to Juliana Birch, and was accepted.

His fianceé followed him back to England. She was the daughter of Wyrley Birch of Wretham Hall, Norfolk, and they were married at Wretham Church on 3 November 1840. Possibly the matchmaker was Henry Fowler's closest Cambridge friend, Robert Pryor, who four years later was to marry Julia* Birch's sister Elizabeth. Robert Pryor was almost exactly Henry Fowler's contemporary in age, and shared his sporting interests. They were both descended from successful, wealthy trading families: Robert Pryor's father was Thomas Marlborough Pryor, a partner in the brewers Truman, Hanbury & Buxton.[8] The two families remained close. Robert Pryor was called to the Bar and became an equity draughtsman and conveyancer; but annually for most of their early lives he and Henry Fowler went fishing in Ireland together, or shared the costs of Scottish salmon rivers.

The responsibilities of marriage proved a sobering influence on 29-year-old Henry Fowler. It may also not have escaped his notice that his Uncle Tom had a son, that his young cousin (also Tom) was now nineteen, and that if he, Henry Fowler, did not take full control of the

* In general use, the name was shortened from 'Juliana'.

business the way would be clear for his cousin to take it.

At the end of his honeymoon, shortly before Christmas 1840, he wrote to Uncle Tom in terms that imply new resolutions, firmly taken:

> I can only return you my sincere thanks for so long wielding the labouring oar—and am now ready to take it from your hands and beg you will take that repose you must stand in such need of [Thomas was fifty four at this time]. I beg therefore that you will not think of coming up to town on account of the Pulteney Street business. After Xmas I shall be *quite* fixed in London—and shall devote all my energies to business.
>
> At the time of my marriage I promised Mrs Birch to bring her daughter to see her, if I could so manage it, about Xmas time; if therefore you be not quite worn out—but could write the cheques for two Saturdays about that time, I should for the last time tax your good nature. I shall make arrangements for selling my hunters and shall henceforward have no temptation to absent myself from London . . .
>
> I hope you will now between this & Xmas . . . rely on my presence in Pulteney St, & that you will kindly sign the cheques for the two Saturdays immediately following Xmas day; and in return I promise to be a good boy ever after.

When Henry Fowler joined his father and uncle in the partnership of John Broadwood & Sons in 1836, the older men had added to the partnership agreement a clause[9] empowering any partner to 'require that any son of his . . . may be admitted a partner . . . without any premium'. In September 1841 Thomas Broadwood nominated his son Thomas Jr, noting on a draft of the partnership deed: 'Tom decided to go into the business 1 Sept. I named the same to my partners on 10 Sept 1841.' Thomas Jr took no active part in the direction of the business (though after his father's death he became the largest shareholder), and in the late 1850s apparently suffered a debilitating illness. Subsequently he devoted himself to his passion for ocean racing (in June 1874 he won the Ocean Match of the Royal Harwich Yacht Club in his 60-ton cutter *Arethusa*). He died in 1881, leaving £424,000.

In 1843 James Shudi introduced his younger son, Walter Stewart Broadwood, as a partner. Walter Stewart was twenty four and had been working at Great Pulteney Street for a year since coming down from Cambridge (where he had been a Pensioner of Trinity, taking his degree in 1842). After the annual partnership meeting on 29 September that year he wrote to his father, in terms that have a certain historical irony: 'I hear from Henry [Fowler] that I am now made a partner in the firm, and I write to thank you for your kindness to me on this as well as on all other occasions. I trust that my conduct will always show that I am not unthankful.'

From old John Broadwood's retirement, in 1811, the shares in the partnership had been held equally by James Shudi and Thomas Broadwood. When he became a partner, Henry Fowler was given one-fifth, his father and uncle retaining two-fifths each. With two new partners, the division became more complex, the partnership being divided into twenty shares. James Shudi and Thomas retained seven each, Henry Fowler received four, and Thomas Jr and Walter Stewart received one each.

The social significance of the piano increased in the years following the marriage of young Queen Victoria to Prince Albert of Saxe-Coburg Gotha in February 1840. The young Queen's quiet domesticity set the fashion, in contrast to the more extravagant social pleasures of the years when her uncles set the royal pattern. 'Singing and playing the piano, and during the thirties and forties, upon the harp and the guitar, were approved feminine accomplishments. Gentlemen also sang and duets were in high favour, but play the piano gentlemen did not, that being considered a task only fit for ladies and professional musicians.'[10]

Prince Albert played the piano, and was a composer too; but then he was foreign, which no doubt accounted for it. He played upon his Broadwood square, making music often with a fellow-countryman who enjoyed great popularity in Britain—Mendelssohn. (At Great Pulteney Street the partners noticed that somehow Mendelssohn was always short of ready cash, and his main purpose in calling appeared to be to borrow a fiver.)[11]

The square was still the main selling line for Broadwoods. The majority of Broadwood pianos, including the grands, still had bichord stringing (two strings to the note). Some grands had been produced with trichord stringing—that made for Beethoven was a trichord—but this was unusual.

The challenge from other makers became more apparent during the 1840s. Broadwoods continued to hold a Royal Warrant for piano making throughout the reign of Queen Victoria; but so did Erards, and it was the Erard grand which now took pride of place in the Royal households. When Sigismond Thalberg, most popular of the touring pianists of the time, gave a concert at Blackheath in January 1840 he played an Erard grand. The general criticism made of Broadwood pianos was that their touch was heavy, and because of the bichord stringing the volume was less than that of their competitors.

Henry Fowler Broadwood was not the man to let such a challenge go by default. Settled now into domesticity himself, he also settled with enthusiasm into piano-making. Though he kept up his sporting pursuits, he spent some time in the Horseferry Road factory, constantly experimenting. It was said that he 'studied everything he could find bearing on the construction or history of the piano ever written in any language . . .' proving himself 'in every sense of the word a scientific pianoforte maker'.[12]

In 1842 he took out his first (and indeed only) patent related to the piano (No. 9245, dated 2 February 1842). It was an ingenious idea to help those learning the instrument. The lower part of the nameboard, immediately above the keys, was to revolve on a pivot. One side would be veneered to give the look of a conventional piano; at the pressure of a spring, this would swivel round to reveal a mock keyboard, painted with the name of each key, together with one octave of tonic sol-fa. He called it the 'Schoolroom Pianoforte, whereby the eye of a learner on such an instrument is more readily directed to the corresponding note of the gamut or scale, and whereby also I can turn the said gamut or scale away from view at pleasure'.

It was an early version of the cardboard learning aids that were to become popular many years later.

From 1843, stung by the success being enjoyed by Erards, he set out to produce something better. He consulted most of the leading technical experts of the day, including Theobald Boehm (1794–1881), the inventor of the modern keyed flute;[13] it seems that Henry Fowler's younger brother Walter Stewart was particularly interested in this correspondence, since he began to correspond with Boehm on his own behalf, and eventually himself wrote a treatise on the flute. Henry Fowler successfully developed a lighter touch for the grands. Then he turned his attention to the square, and by January 1846 had produced a square with a full iron frame.

The full iron frame had been applied to an upright by John Isaac Hawkins of Philadelphia in 1800. In 1825 Alpheus Babcock of Boston developed a full iron frame for the square piano. In 1840 Jonas Chickering, also of Boston, invented an effective single-cast iron frame for the grand, which he patented in 1843.

For the past twenty years Broadwoods had been using bracing bars of iron, set variously in parallel or diagonally. When in the mid-1840s

Henry Fowler Broadwood, as head of the greatest pianoforte makers in the world, was conducting experiments into the best way of improving the grand, an obscure country cabinet-maker in the Harz mountains of Central Germany was building a piano (it is said) in his kitchen in Seesen. He was Heinrich Engelhard Steinweg; and the piano he made was wooden-framed. It was not until his eldest son, Theodore Steinway (a trained engineer) began to study the capabilities of iron and steel in America that his firm's great breakthrough was achieved.

As Henry Fowler Broadwood studied the problem, and compared the various solutions being adopted to strengthen the grand with iron— either by additional bracing in the Broadwood fashion, or by the full iron frame adopted in America by Chickering—he did precisely what his grandfather John Broadwood had done.

As old John had put his problem to Tiberius Cavallo and Dr Gray, his grandson enlisted the help of the Bramah iron foundry, and of Dr William Pole. The Bramah factory, best known as locksmiths, was the creation of Joseph Bramah (1748–1814), whose inventions also included the beer-engine and the water-closet. With his colleague Henry Maudslay he perfected the hydraulic press.

Dr William Pole (1814–1900), a personal friend, was a remarkable polymath. He was both engineer and musician; Professor of Civil Engineering at University College, London, for seventeen years, Fellow of the Royal Society, an Oxford Doctor of Music and organist of a London church for thirty years, and an examiner for musical degrees at London University for eleven. His work on the philosophy of music (1879) is still read. He advised Broadwood on the drawing up of scales, and on the construction of an iron frame which was not a single casting, but a variety of different castings bolted together. This was built into a successful trichord concert grand by the late 1840s; and Henry Fowler was so proud of it that he later added to his entry in the Harrow School Register (from which it has been copied into many reference books): 'constructed first grand piano with frame entirely of iron, 1846'. It is an equivocal claim, since while it may be true of Britain, it is untrue world-wide, Chickering having already set the pattern for the American triumph.

Why did he not adopt the single casting? It seems that Pole advised against it. From his critical description of the pianos shown at the Great Exhibition of 1851,[14] he seems to have been sceptical of its prac-ticability. As Ehrlich remarks: 'It is a curious fact that Pole, despite his perceptive appraisal of the industry's present weaknesses and future opportunities, nevertheless shared his contemporaries' prejudice against the use of iron, and failed to appreciate the great contribution it could

149

The Broadwood factory in Horseferry Road, Westminster, 1842 *(Supplement to the Penny Magazine, April 1842)*

make to cheap mass production. The 'growing tendency to use too much metal', he argued, harmed tone and added to weight and cost.[15]

In 1842 John Broadwood & Sons were one of the twelve largest employers of labour in London. Three or four hundred men were employed at the Horseferry Road factory, and a further 150 at Great Pulteney Street. The numbers fluctuated with the seasons, for piano-making, like cabinet-making, remained a seasonal trade building up to the main period for purchasing in the autumn. Men were taken on as sales dictated (this irregularity of employment led many of them to start up one-man businesses: in hard times, however, some worked from week to week, pawning their tools on a Friday, selling a piano on a Saturday, and reclaiming the tools to start work again on Monday morning).

The Horseferry Road factory was regarded as a phenomenon. A contemporary description defines the four ranges of buildings between Horseferry Road and Holywell Street, each with three storeys, with a total workshop length of more than half a mile. Timber was brought in at one side of the factory, stored for upwards of two years to season in the courtyards, and then the almost finished instruments were carted out at the other side of the factory for despatch to the finishing shop and showroom at Great Pulteney Street. The east range of buildings contained the main wood store, and preparation of the rough woodwork—'bottom-making', the production of packing cases, and square case-making. In the far west range was the turner's shop for making legs, departments for making hammers and dampers, and the string section. In the range to the east of the central courtyard was a 'hot-room' for seasoning wood, with a steam-tank for bending (for example, the soundboard bridges). In that range worked the soundboard-makers and belly-men, case-makers for cabinet and cottage pianos, cleaners-off and polishers, and upstairs the key-makers and hammer-makers.

The square case-makers and belly-men were across the courtyard in the west central range, with the cabinet finishing shop, the glue room, rosewood store and veneer room. Finally, on the ground floor beside the Horseferry Road gate was the regulating and tuning department.

Five types of piano were made: grand, semi-grand, cabinet, cottage and square. The cabinet upright and square were declining in popularity, as the cottage upright increased; but the upright action was still imperfect. Broadwoods were making upwards of 2,500 pianos a year; and the journalist George Dodd learned that 'out of the eighty or ninety thousand pianofortes which have been made by this firm, there have been, to every hundred "squares", twenty-eight "grands", sixteen "cabinets", nine "cottage" and five "upright grands" and "semi-grands"; so that the "squares" constitute nearly two-thirds of the whole number'.

Broadwoods were thus geared to the production of a type of piano, the square, which was in a decline. The success of the square had been the foundation of the firm's prosperity; and many of the workmen had grown up with that instrument. 'The same workmen are seen year after year, occupying their old benches, using their old tools, coming to work and leaving work at the old hours, and seeming as if the old shop belonged to them and they to the shop. We noticed . . . that many of the workmen in the factory are elderly men who have occupied their present situation twenty, thirty, or forty years . . .'

Tradition was the keynote: the old ways were best. There were 3,800 separate pieces in a piano, and each one was separately fashioned from

Key-cutting

Cutting the frets for square pianos

Tuning a cabinet piano *(Supplement to the Penny Magazine, April 1842)*

the raw materials at Horseferry Road. The keys were cut by hand, the fretwork done by hand, and each intricate part of every action was fashioned by hand: 'many of the pieces are not more than a quarter of an inch square, some even less'.

The presence of a machine for turning legs was regarded as so remarkable that it merited special note by George Dodd;[16] and indeed the continued use of so much handwork, when mechanical woodworking machinery had been invented fifty years before, was regarded as a positive virtue: 'The pianoforte manufacture is one in which nothing but highly-skilled manual dexterity can make and adjust the numerous pieces of mechanism involved in it; and those workmen who possess this skill are not likely to be supplanted by any automatic machinery.'

Almost the only mention of metal in the construction of a piano, other than for the strings, is a passing reference that on opening a piano, 'especially a "grand", we shall see bars and rods and strengtheners of various kinds, placed in different directions . . . to resist the powerful strain'. This suggests that George Dodd's guide round the factory was more concerned to draw his attention to the woodworking than to the developments in metal.

This account does not mention another form of instrument made in the factory—the transposing piano. It had first been patented in 1801 (by Edward Ryley—Broadwoods bought his patent) for the square, and consisted of 'a false keyboard transposing semitone by semitone throughout the octave'. The purpose was, of course, to enable the pianist of modest gifts to play virtually every piece in the key of 'C'. Broadwoods made a square in this manner in 1808. Nearly forty years later, in 1845, the firm was making boudoir cottage pianos in two designs. In one, the strings and frame were suspended between two pivoted metal supporters, the keyboard and action remaining stationary. In the second, the strings and frame were mounted on wheels within a groove.

The 'patriarch of the establishment . . . not far from ninety years of age, who has seen out two or three generations of workmen' was old James Forsyth, foreman to John Broadwood thirty years earlier, still enjoying his free house and an honorarium of £20 a year (and to continue to enjoy them, and to keep an eye on the factory, for a further decade). The new generation was being brought up in this old tradition. In the 1840s the two sons of Daniel Giles Rose (the clerk who had witnessed John Broadwood's will in 1811) were 'senior workmen', George Thomas Rose by 1846 and Frederick Rose in 1847. A. J. Hipkins (who began to work for Broadwoods in 1840) achieved this status in 1849. The senior foreman, A. Russell, was well paid at £356 a year; other foremen could expect between £100 and £250 a year. To this was added an annual bonus, known as a 'present', given out at the discretion of the partners. This could be a substantial amount, and for special services could be more than a year's salary.

The wage of a skilled craftsman was between 28s and £2 a week. Getting a job at a prosperous firm like Broadwoods was a passport to security. It was an all-male society, of course; and so, as in all such closed societies, there were rigorous customs and disciplines among the workmen themselves which could be as stern as modern trade union practices.

Some of these are illustrated by a diary[17] that was kept by one of the workmen in the grand finishing shop during 1849–1850. Many of the brief entries are concerned with the convivialities that accompanied great events in a workman's life—his emergence from apprenticeship, transfer to a better job or departure from the firm.

There are also reminders of the sudden mortality from disease that was commonplace in mid-Victorian London: '25 April 1849, C. Stevenson died aged 20'; '12 August, J. Earl died with the cholera within 24 hours after being attacked by it'; '24 February 1850, C. Hunt died in his 21st year'.

When a newcomer joined a particular shop in the factory, it was the custom for the foreman to be tipped. Thus: 'J. Southwell came to Grand finishing—cost his master 10s.'; 'J. Ramsay Jr came to Grand finishing—his introduction cost his father 10s' and 'H. Dove placed under his brother—his introduction cost his brother 7s 6d'. Then, as now, the workmen held a draw on the Derby: 'Derby Club in the shop at 2s 6d per share'; and there were celebrations afterwards at which tempers might fray: 'Scruffy Senr. had some ale and beer in, when one of our *great men* came in and upset it because it was on his bench. Punishment: sent to Coventry'. He stayed 'in Coventry' for two weeks. His 'return' to social conversation a fortnight later is recorded, and he cannot have borne a grudge for he 'stood his country pot'.

Ostracism and fines were the means whereby the workmen maintained internal discipline among themselves. When one of them displeased his mates, they might convene a 'kangaroo court':

1850, Jan 3. Dispute among the men in the scraping shop about Thompson doing Cramp's work. He refused to make any allowance to them for it. They called a Court of the whole floor, when he was ordered to give up two [piano] cases, and fined 10s and the expenses of the Court for abusive language.

154

The 'Square Yard' in Bridle Lane behind Gt Pulteney St. *(John Broadwood & Sons Ltd)*

The men (as distinct from the foremen) were on piecework and thus the apportionment of work was of vital importance, and giving up payment for two piano cases a considerable fine in itself. This is reflected also in an entry which deals with what was apparently a production flow problem caused by a senior workman leaving:

1850, Jan 31. Mr R——[Russell, probably] in a consternation occasioned by he being acquainted that Mr John Allen leaving this place to go to Kirkman, Baker ordered to go to the ferry [Horseferry Road] to work; no work for him, work sent to him from the lane [Bridle Lane]. Mr R——16 cases behind hand in his supply of cases.

About once a month, or more often to celebrate notable events, groups of workmen would go out to dinner, sometimes to Chelsea or Kensington, occasionally down river to Erith or Gravesend:

1849, Aug. 10. Eighteen of us dined at Mr Balls, Lillie Arms, Old Brompton, at 2s 6d per head. Plain dinner, pasty, brandy and beer included, to celebrate T. Southwell being apprenticed to Mr Oborne. A very good dinner and very well served up. T. Murray and Mountain Senr. Chairman and Vice.

There was thus some degree of formality at these events, the Chairman being the senior person present and the Vice-Chairman (a practice still maintained in military messes) usually a younger man whose duty was to propose the Loyal Toast. Often they would be celebrating several events:

1850, Sept 20. Seventeen dined at Erith to celebrate the under-named circumstances, viz.

C. Darling coming of age	15s
T. Baker coming of age	15s
T. Baker launch	15s
H. Dove coming apprentice	15s
Schweegans coming apprentice	15s

Not surprisingly, the participants in these jollies could become emotional.

1850, Feb 11. John Allen washed out: 20 met, cost us 6½d. per head. Leave in the afternoon at Godwin's. Several great discoveries made. One in particular—Murray's mysterious cement of the soul. J. A. loved his bench mate better than his brother &c. Everybody's health drunk &c.

A week later, the diarist records sardonically: 'T. Dove moved round into the next shop to be loved like a brother.'

A workman's mug *(Photograph by the author)*

The beer-mugs provided for the workmen by the firm (See above) were well used on such occasions (the firm also gave tokens, as a bonus for good work, which could be exchanged for beer at the nearby tavern).

The anonymous workman also noted some of the minor mishaps that occurred in the factory:

1850, March 20. Dreadful accident. Poor Mike tripped up. He bit his tongue through and fainted away. Oh!
Nov 22. Donald Kerr fell downstairs and put his shoulder out.

In those days before the old-age pension, although firms like Broadwoods did provide a small pension for longer-serving workmen, an inability to continue working was often a prelude to poverty. The workmen rallied round on these occasions: 'On Tuesday evening October 27 it was unanimously resolved by the Friendly Musical Society that a raffle through the trade should take place for the benefit of A. Gow Senr., the oldest member of the Society, being from old age and affliction unable to follow his employment. The raffle will take place at the Adams Arms, Hampstead Street, Fitzroy Square on Monday 16 November at 8 o'clock in the evening. The highest thrower to have an Iron Mitre Plane. The lowest thrower to have a 5/8 Box and Toss. A shilling a member.' This illustrates, apart from goodheartedness, that there was a fellow-feeling throughout the craft, and not just within the company. There was mobility between the various piano-making companies of London, the craftsmen knew each other and shared a camaraderie that could ease bad times.

John Broadwood's predilection for reliable Scottish workmen continued as a tradition in the firm. There was always a workmen's dinner on St Andrew's Day (30 November). How this Scottish connection was maintained is shown in the career of Robert Moir. He was born in Laurencekirk, south of Aberdeen, in 1822, the son of a stone-mason. He himself was apprenticed to a cabinet-maker in Arbroath. There he watched the ships sailing for London, where his cousin Charles Trail already worked for Broadwoods. As soon as young Robert was out of apprenticeship, at the age of twenty three he took ship from Montrose for London and through his cousin's agency found work with Broadwoods in March 1845.

Moir began as a cabinet-finisher, and then after three years graduated to making music desks, pedal lyres, and finishing grands. 'It is an old-established axiom that where a Scotsman can insert his foot, there will he contrive to squeeze through the whole of his body.'[18] Certainly Robert Moir became a one-man employment agency. Two of his brothers and 'many acquaintances from his native village' joined him at Broadwoods: 'amongst those brought into the manufactory or office by him may be mentioned Messrs Thompson, Cross, Stuart, Main, Wishart, Fulton and others'.[19] He became a foreman in 1866, and was pensioned in 1890 after forty five years' service.

One of his contemporaries joined Broadwoods by another route. Edward Thomas Clayton was born in Bedford, where his father was clerk to a firm of timber merchants. Woodworking became young Edward's passion, and winning a school prize of £20 (a very large sum in those days) he invested the lot in a set of joiner's tools. Clayton came to London in 1831 when he was twenty four, and after some casual jobs became employed by Cubitt the builder in Grosvenor Road. He took lodgings in

New Street, Horseferry Road. His landlord was a Mr Day, who was an action-maker for Broadwoods in Bridle Lane, but who suffered from rheumatism and often had work sent to him to be done at home. Young Clayton would help him; and as a result, five years later he was taken into Broadwoods as a joiner. He worked on the bench for twenty five years, and earned the respect of his juniors because 'he never shirked his share of hard work, and in square case-making before the advent of machinery there was a precious deal of hard labour to get through'.[20]

The prevalence of hand-work well into the mid-century is confirmed by this anecdote.

Following the tradition of making gifts of pianos to distinguished musicians, Broadwoods sent a grand to Mendelssohn in Leipzig in the autumn of 1847. The composer had been on holiday in Switzerland in an attempt to throw off illness; and when with his family he returned to Leipzig in mid-September he 'found a new Grand piano, sent to him by Broadwoods, and this gave him great pleasure to play upon'.[21] In fact he defied his doctor's orders and 'played upon it for several hours'.[22] It was his last musical delight, for his sickness increased and he took to his bed, dying at the age of thirty eight on 4 November.

Once again in 1848 revolution and republicanism swept across Europe. Italy, Germany and France blazed with civil disorder. In Paris, Louis Philippe abdicated and fled to England, as did his prime minister Guizot, who (a personal friend of Henry Fowler Broadwood) was given shelter with his family at 46 Bryanston Square before taking a house in Pelham Crescent, Brompton.

Many Englishmen wondered whether the revolutionary fervour would cross the Channel. Thomas Carlyle gave 'our institutions, as they are called, aristocracy, Church, etc. five years'. James Shudi Broadwood, now aged sixty five and a man of wealth and property, looked upon these revolutionary stirrings so similar to those that had transformed France in 1789 when he was a 16-year-old; and he wrote this cool appraisal to his brother Thomas:

> I do not doubt . . . that should the operatives & the lower middle classes feel distress, that they will join [together] and try to make the more wealthy classes employ or feed them. I have long remarked the discontent of small capitalists at what they call the monopoly & oppression of the large capitalists & from the prevailing feeling now all over Europe, I suppose (should cotton mills & other large employers of men be stopped) that the Masters as well as the rich

farmholders & landed Men will be squeezed for their support as well as for the support of the State. And indeed to whom else can they apply? A war—if bloody, like a civil war—may check the wonderfull daily encreasing of our population (1000 per day)—but still the expence of that check must be paid by the People of Property—be it derived from Trade, or be it inherited.

The disturbances in France and in Germany all arise therefrom (that is) the struggle of the lower classes to better their condition, & from the Intelligence they have acquired, their modes of Combination by Trades & Clubs, they are far more formidable than those Classes were in the days of Jack Cade, the Jacqueries in France. And when on several occasions they rose against their Masters in the time of the Roman Emperors, on one occasion they succeeded and ruled all Gaul. But you & I cannot help this afflicting movement. We are in the ship & must sink or swim with it, except we choose to abandon it & take refuge in America or in some of our colonies. All we can do is support the Government, & not by opposition or democratic speeches give continuance to the Popular movements, & make ourselves as comfortable & (our Property) as secure as we can. Perhaps one way would be to divide our Property amongst our Children, making them more independent & ourselves less the object of envy or Pillage.

Despite these forebodings Britain weathered the political storms which rocked France. In Paris, there was street fighting that February; and as in 1789 and in 1830, musicians—particularly foreign-born musicians whose livelihood was in the fashionable Paris salons—looked to London. Charles Hallé, German-born, came to London that March, and Frédéric Chopin in April. Both looked for support to Broadwoods, and both received it.

Hallé was introduced to the London salons, such as that of Mrs Sartoris (Adelaide Kemble), by Moscheles and Henry Fowler; while in London he claimed to be the first to include a Beethoven piano Sonata in a public concert. He spent three months in London and then was invited to move to Manchester, which he made his home (and later founded the orchestra that bears his name). He regretted the friends he was obliged to abandon in London, in particular 'Henry Broadwood, that prince of pianoforte makers'.[23]

Chopin, on his arrival in April, took lodgings first at 10 Bentinck Street and then at 48 Dover Street: 'Here I am at last, settled in this whirlpool of London . . . Erard was charming, he sent me a piano. I have a

The Broadwood grand supplied to Chopin, 1848 *(John Broadwood & Sons Ltd)*

Broadwood and a Pleyel, which makes three, and yet I do not find time to play them. I have many visitors, and my days pass like lightning.'[24]

He went to hear Jenny Lind, the 'Swedish nightingale', sing *La Sonnambula* at Her Majesty's Theatre, and admired her talent, as she did his. But he was short of money, and therefore arranged to give two recitals in private houses—one for Mrs Sartoris at 99 Eaton Place, and the other at the Earl of Falmouth's home, 2 St James's Square. He did not play on the concert platform, preferring the intimacy of a limited audience. Once at Stafford House, the Duchess of Sutherland's, he played before Queen Victoria. Mrs Broadwood invited him to 'a small early party' at 46 Bryanston Square on 21 June.

The Broadwood in his lodgings was a grand, No. 17,093. Before the soirées he visited the showroom at Great Pulteney Street to try out the pianos; he paid for the hire with quantities of free tickets. For the soirées he used another Broadwood grand, No. 17,047 (see above).*

* This instrument is in the possession of John Broadwood & Sons Ltd.

Chopin was so weak that he had to be carried up the stairs. A. J. Hipkins, then a young clerk, recalled:

> He was ill, but only showed it painfully in his weakened breathing power; he could not walk upstairs; my father-in-law, Mr Black, and my wife's uncle, Mr Murray, carried him. He came to Broadwood through the recommendation and courtesy of the Pleyel House in Paris; he brought one of the Pleyel pianos with him, but only used it once . . . He immediately took to the Broadwood pianos, and after that occasion used them exclusively in England and Scotland.

The dour Scots who carried him upstairs were disconcerted by the contrast between his sickness and his almost feminine elegance; his hair 'beautifully curled', and pink gloves on his hands. Hipkins continued:

> He was frequently at Broadwoods: of middle height, with a pleasant face, a mass of fair curly hair like an angel, and agreeable manners. But he was something of a dandy, very particular about the cut and colour of his clothes. He was painstaking in the choice of the pianos he was to play upon anywhere, as he was in his dress, his gloves, his French; you cannot imagine a more perfect technique than he possessed! But he abhorred banging a piano; his *forte* was relative, not absolute; it was based upon his exquisite *pianos* and *pianissimos*— always a waving line, *crescendo* and *diminuendo* . . . He especially liked Broadwoods' Boudoir Cottage pianos of that date, two-stringed, but very sweet instruments, and he found pleasure in playing on them. He played Bach's 48 all his life long. 'I don't practise my own compositions,' he said to Von Lenz. 'When I am about to give a concert, I close my doors for a time and play Bach.'

On another occasion at Broadwoods Chopin met Frederick Beale, head of the music publishers Cramer, Beale & Co. in which Broadwoods had an interest. Chopin played Beale two new waltzes (in D flat and C sharp minor, Op. 64) which Beale thereupon bought for publication. Evidently this had been arranged by Henry Fowler. Chopin wrote of him:

> He is a very rich and highly cultivated man, whose father [James Shudi] left the estate and the factory to him and himself settled down in the country. He has the very best connections: he had Guizot and all his family staying with him; and is beloved everywhere. I met Lord Falmouth through him. To give you an idea of his British courtesy: one morning he called on me: I was tired, and

told him I had slept badly. At night I came back from Lady Somerset's, and found a new spring mattress and pillows on my bed . . . Mr Broadwood had sent it and my valet was told not to tell me.[25]

Henry Fowler's thoughtfulness was further displayed that autumn. Among Chopin's friends were two Scottish ladies whom he had met in Paris, Jane Stirling and her sister Mrs Erskine. In London that summer, they persuaded him to stay at their family home in Scotland. At Euston to catch the morning train north on Saturday 5 August, Chopin

found on the platform for Edinburgh a gentleman who introduced himself from Broadwood and gave me two tickets instead of one for seats in my compartment—the second one for the seat opposite, so that no one might be in my way. Beside that he arranged for a certain Mr Wood (an acquaintance of Broadwood's) to be in the same carriage. He knew me (having seen me in 1836 in Lipinski's in Frankfort!). He has music shops in Edinburgh and Glasgow. Broadwood was also kind enough to have Daniel [his valet] (who is better behaved than many gentlemen, and better looking than many Englishmen) seated in the same compartment, and so I covered the 407 English miles from London to Edinburgh via Birmingham and Carlisle in twelve hours by *express-train* (that is, a train with very few stops).[26]

Chopin stayed first at Calder House, near Edinburgh. He travelled down to Manchester to give a concert on 29 August, for which Broadwoods sent up the grand No. 17,047 that he had played at the London soirées. He was apprehensive that the hall was too big for his delicate style (it seated 1,200) and this seems to be borne out by the *Manchester Guardian* review:

Chopin . . . is very spare in frame, and there is an almost painful air of feebleness in his appearance and gait. This vanishes when he seats himself at the instrument, in which he seems for the time perfectly absorbed. Chopin's music and his style of performance partake of the same leading characteristics—refinement rather than vigour—subtile elaboration rather than simple comprehensiveness in composition—an elegant, rapid touch, rather than a firm, nervous grasp of the instrument. Both his compositions and his playing appeared to be the perfection of chamber music—fit to be associated with the most refined instrumental quartets and quartet-playing—but wanting breath and obviousness of design, and executive power, to be effective in a large concert hall.[27]

Returning to Scotland, though failing in health he was persuaded by Miss Stirling to visit more great houses. But he was happier in Edinburgh staying in the small house of a Polish-born doctor, Lyszczynski. His wife remembered that 'he would of an evening retire into an adjoining room, where an old Broadwood square piano of her childhood stood, and play upon it with evident pleasure'.

Chopin gave a recital in the Merchant Hall, Glasgow, on 27 September, and another in the Hopetoun Rooms, Edinburgh, on 4 October. Once again, Broadwoods sent a grand from London for the occasion (No. 17,001): it was afterwards sold locally for £30 above the list price (a Broadwood grand in rosewood then cost 155 guineas).

At the end of October Chopin, now seriously ill, returned to London, staying briefly at 4 St James's Street, where Henry Fowler was a regular visitor. On 16 November he was persuaded to play at a 'Grand Polish Ball and Concert' at the Guildhall. He played in a side room, and Francis Hueffer describes it: 'The people, hot from dancing, who went into the room where he played, were but little in the humour to pay attention, and anxious to return to their amusement. He was in the last stage of exhaustion, and the affair resulted in disappointment. His playing at such a place was a well-intentioned mistake.'[28]

Chopin had long been intending to return to Paris. The London fogs he found unendurable, and late in November 1848, accompanied by his valet Daniel and a Polish friend, Leonard Niedzwiecki, he took the train for Folkestone en route for Boulogne and Paris. Once again, Henry Fowler Broadwood had arranged for two facing seats to be booked, so that Chopin could put his feet up. During the train journey, he had great difficulty in breathing.

Broadwood received a present in gratitude from Chopin the following February, accompanied by an invitation to visit the composer in Paris. In a cheerfully good-humoured reply, Henry Fowler pleaded that he was too busy making pianos. He sent the good wishes of the Broadwood family 'for the restoration of your health'. In fact he was arranging for a special grand piano to be made for Chopin as a present—the first of his full iron frame grands. Tragically, Chopin never saw it. He grew weaker, and lingering through the summer, died in Paris early on the morning of 17 October at the age of thirty nine.

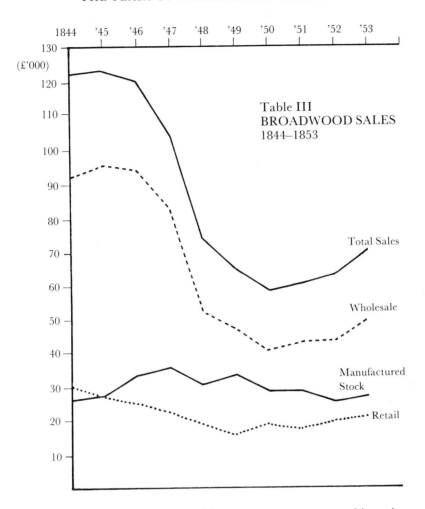

Table III
BROADWOOD SALES
1844–1853

Henry Fowler Broadwood was right to concentrate on making pianos in 1848. In public he continued to appear 'the prince of pianoforte makers', as Hallé called him: confident, masterful, the leader of the British piano trade. In private he must have been extremely worried. For from 1845 the sales of Broadwoods dramatically declined (see Table III)—from £123,942 in 1845 to £58,884 in 1850. This decline was due to the successful challenge by Pierre Erard's London factory, and to a lesser though significant extent by the emergence of French piano-makers led by Erards in Paris. The French challenge was made mainly in the export markets, as Ehrlich has pointed out: 'In 1850 France was producing fewer pianos than England, but the value of her exports was not markedly less and was growing vigorously. Between 1848 and 1857 it increased more than threefold, with flourishing markets throughout the world and particular concentration upon Belgium, the United States, Italy and Latin America.'[29]

Broadwoods' reliance on the square now began to look positively dangerous. The firm's best-selling line was going out of fashion. The grands, too, were being branded as old-fashioned; the need for the full iron frame grand was urgent. The firm was caught on two fronts, with an outdated model, the square, in the 'mass' market; and the late development of a modern grand, which took time to put into production, had allowed that market to be eroded by the competition.

The Great Exhibition, sponsored by Prince Albert, opened in London in May 1851. It was intended both as a demonstration of industrial development and an incentive (through the foreign exhibits) to try harder, particularly in design. Thirty-three British pianoforte manufacturers showed their wares at the exhibition in the Crystal Palace in Hyde Park. Many claimed 'new improvements'. These included Charles Cadby's 'new patent suspension principle' for mounting the soundboard by means of adjustable metal clips; Richard Hunt's 'tavola pianoforte', a pedestal table housing a piano, the keyboard of which was made accessible by spring bolts; John Champion Jones's twin upright, with keyboards both front and back; William Jenkins's 'expanding and collapsing pianoforte for gentlemen's yachts, the saloons of steam vessels, ladies' cabins etc'; Robert Addison's transposing piano in which the action, and not the keyboard, moved; and George H. Aggio's 'pianoforte fitted up in plate-glass case, and gold carvings, with embroidered curtain front'.

Other designs were more in the mainstream of development, and less bizarre. These included the well-established down-striking grand from Robert Wornum; and Pierre Orpheus Erard's 'new patent metal frames for pianofortes, designed to carry the principal part of the weight or pull of the wires, independent of the wood frame, with a new screw apparatus for tuning attached to the same; particularly adapted to extreme climates'.

Exhibitors wrote their own entries for the official catalogue,[30] prepared on a standard pro-forma. Pierre Erard used this as an opportunity for advertising; he described himself as 'Inventor, Designer and Manufacturer' (while Broadwoods put themselves down, simply, as 'Manufacturers'); and supplied a front drawing and side elevation of an upright designed to look like nothing so much as a miniature Gothic cathedral west-front, pinnacled and fretted with exotic abandon, and captioned: 'Erard's Elizabethan New Patent Grand Oblique Pianoforte'. Erard thus deliberately emphasised the introduction of overstringing ('Oblique').

The Broadwood entry in the official catalogue reads:

BROADWOOD, JOHN & SONS, *33 Gt. Pulteney Street*—
Manufacturers.
Four grand pianofortes, of different constructions:—
No. 1. In ebony case; 7 octaves, G to G; inlaid, carved, and gilt. Designed by E. M. Barry Esq.; inlaid by G. Watson; carved by J. Thomas; and gilt by G. J. Morant. Straight bracing.
No. 2. In amboyna case; 7 octaves, G to G; designed, carved and gilt by Mr. G.J. Morant. Diagonal bracing.
No. 3. In amboyna case; 7 octaves, G to G. Diagonal bracing.
No. 4. In walnut case, inlaid; 7 octaves, G to G. Inlaid by G. Watson. Straight bracing.

Broadwoods did not show the new grand with full iron frame, but relied on the established patterns with bracing bars, either straight or diagonal. It was Henry Fowler's decision to go for the reliability of tradition, rather than risk all on novelty; and who, looking at all those 'novelties' on show, can question his judgement? It was in character that he should give pride of place to a young man: for E. M. Barry was the 21-year-old son of the distinguished architect (Sir) Charles Barry, who a few years later was to rebuild the Houses of Parliament.

However, when the Gold ('Council' or 'Great') Medal for pianoforte manufacture was announced, it was given to Pierre Erard.

The system of judging at the Great Exhibition was complicated; but to understand how this humiliation for Broadwood came about, its hierarchical structure must be understood. First, at the lowest level, there was for each area of manufacture a 'special jury' consisting of men with technical qualification in that area.* Awards were made by the 'special jury' and passed up to a 'group jury' to be ratified or cancelled. The 'group jury' was made up of chairmen of 'special juries'. Finally, the awards ratified by 'group juries' were either ratified or cancelled by a Council, chaired by Prince Albert himself.

The 'special jury for musical instruments' recommended for Council Medals Broadwood, Collard and Erard. The 'group jury' rejected

---

* The 'special jury' for musical instruments was chaired by Sir Henry Bishop, Professor of Music at Oxford (composer of '*Home, Sweet Home*', and the first English musician to be knighted). Among other members were Sir George Smart, Thalberg, Sterndale Bennett, Cipriani Potter and Hector Berlioz.

Collard, but ratified Broadwood and Erard. Then the Council, with Prince Albert in the chair, rejected Broadwood and gave the single Council Medal to Erard.

Henry Fowler Broadwood was outraged. He was not a man for publicity, and in principle had not been in favour of the sort of public show that the Great Exhibition represented. But as a holder of the Royal Warrant for Pianoforte Manufacture, Broadwoods could hardly refuse to take part in an exhibition under the personal patronage of Prince Albert.

So the company had gone in. But to go in, and be short-listed for the first prize, only to be rejected at the supreme judging, was beyond bearing.

The members of the 'special jury'—including Henry Fowler's personal friends—felt equally strongly. Sir Henry Bishop and some of his fellow jurors (including Smart, Potter and Sterndale Bennett) drew up a protest which was sent to Prince Albert and subsequently printed and widely circulated.

Undue weight must have been attributed to misstatements made at the meeting of the Group jury, in the presence of many of the Chairmen, affecting Messrs. Broadwoods' claim as Improvers of the Pianoforte. The misstatements were upon remonstrance withdrawn; but it is a lamentable fact, that an injurious effect of such statements, positively put forth, can seldom be completely effaced by a retraction.

The Memorialising Jurors conclude by expressing their conviction that the House of Messrs. Broadwood has eminently fulfilled every single condition contained in the 'Instructions to the Juries', combining, in their Instruments, 'novelty of invention (of considerable importance and usefulness), perfection of workmanship, beauty of design, and superior quality of tone.'[31]

Despite this protest, and the private assurance to Henry Fowler by members of the 'special jury' that if they had been asked to recommend a single piano manufacturer for a Council Medal, Broadwoods would have received it, the Council decision remained on the record, and the Gold Medal with Erard.

Shortly after this disappointment, Henry Fowler Broadwood was assailed by a personal sadness. His father James Shudi Broadwood died at Lyne on 8 August 1851, at the age of seventy eight.

At the end of his life, James Shudi combined with his brother Thomas to make a fitting memorial to their distinguished father in the village of his boyhood, Oldhamstocks. In the summer of 1851 they paid for the rebuilding of the bell tower of Oldhamstocks church, and ordered a new bell from the Mears foundry in Whitechapel which it was specified must have 'a beautiful tone'. When it was delivered that September, it became a memorial to both John Broadwood and his eldest son.

The sons of a great man are not always, or indeed often, successful in their own right. James Shudi Broadwood was a devoted pupil of his father, and with his younger brother Thomas had developed their inheritance into a business of world-wide success, the admired example for piano makers. His humour, intelligence and goodness are illustrated by his letters; and it is due to him, and to Thomas Broadwood, that their name was synonymous throughout the Regency and the reigns of George IV and William IV for the British piano.

His personal estate was valued at £319,180. He used his wealth wisely and invested it shrewdly, particularly by the acquisition of the land around Lyne Farm to create one of the great estates of Surrey, well cultivated and with excellent shooting. He enjoyed country pursuits equally with investment, though that he did not despise (his son once threw back at him: 'You say, that the pursuit of riches is in itself interesting').

He endured his full share of human tragedy, in particular the early death of his first wife, and of James Preston, the son whom he clearly hoped would come into the business and be trained under his father's eye, as he himself had been. Henry Fowler, son of his middle age, was evidently born intractable.

James Shudi Broadwood was a great piano-maker; his expertise in tuning and acoustics was learnt by practical shop-floor experience. His sons and daughters were to do him honour in their lives, in the high noon of the British Raj (two of his grandsons, the Lyalls, were Governors of Indian Provinces). At his death, his brother Thomas and his four sons joined together to create a fitting memorial at Rusper, by the Lyne estate he had so much loved. He was buried in Rusper church; and in the next few years the Broadwood family rebuilt and enlarged the little Sussex church in his memory. The height of the tower was raised by 20 feet; timber came from Lyne, and Thomas Broadwood provided stone from his Holmbush estate. The church was re-dedicated in 1855.

The Gold Medal at the Great Exhibition having been snatched away from Broadwoods, Henry Fowler set himself to discover precisely what the difference was between his pianos and those of his rival Erard. He asked his friends to help in this analysis of the subjective qualities that make for a good piano tone. Among those friends was Charles Hallé in Manchester. Shortly before Christmas 1852 Hallé set up a recital at which he played first the Broadwood grand, and then the Erard. After Christmas he wrote to Henry Fowler (the original is in French; evidently Hallé was not yet wholly confident of his command of written English):

I have not kept my promise to write to you as to my impressions of the two pianos as soon as the concert was over; here we are already eight days later, and not a word. The fault is in part due to the festivities which have distracted me. However, I shall now make up for this and give you my observations, as well as those of the public which have been told me.

I played the first two pieces on your piano and the last two on Erards; and the first observation I made is that in the harmony of beauty and richness of tone there is no comparison, yours being far superior. I believe that the public unanimously shared my opinion. At least, everyone I have spoken to said the same thing, some even adding that the tone of the Erard piano, following yours, seemed at first utterly disagreeable. That question, it seems to me, has been totally resolved. Now as you have asked me to tell you frankly about the good qualities of the Erard, I shall obey you. This is what seemed to me to be the opinion of the public, as well as my own. First, as to the achievement of clarity in the very rapid passages, Erard undoubtedly has the advantage; does this happen because the tone is less rich and sonorous than yours, and is therefore more easily detached? I believe so.

I found further that the tone of the Erard is capable of a wider variety of shading—but this requires a longer explanation which I will do my best to give. I believe that the sum of the variations from *pp* to *ff*, if they could be measured would perhaps be as great in your pianos as those of Erard but the character of the variation (*'nuances'*) in Erards is rather different, and the effect is definite, in this way: in your pianos. the quality of the sound from the *pp* to the *ff* remains identically the same, that is to say, that whether you play loud or soft you hear—believe me—that it is always the same instrument, the same sonority. In the Erard pianos, on the other hand, the nature of the sound essentially changes according to the manner of attack; play *pp* and it is veiled, *ff* and it becomes loud and even strident; from this a larger variety of effects is certainly derived.

The difference in the quality of sound is sometimes so great between the *ff* and *pp*, that it seems to me impossible to believe that it is the same piano, without seeing it. This also makes certain effects much easier, for example all the effects of Thalberg (I speak from memory) and I must say that although now after a year I have only rarely played on an Erard, even at home, your piano was more tiring in the concert than the other, and as the touch is no harder—on the contrary—and the repetition is *at least* as good, I cannot myself explain this, other than by the greater effort that one makes to achieve the necessary variation of shading to make an effect on the public.

Could this be due to the action? I am not sure; but if you understand what I mean, I should like to have your opinion on this. In any case, do not take what I have said as more than an indication of what I would like to say; I shall be in London on the 5th February (Ella & I would ask you for a piano on that day) and then I can explain myself better; I believe—and I am utterly convinced of this—that if you could unite these qualities with those that your pianos already possess, you would produce a Phoenix that nothing could approach.

You see, dear Broadwood, that I have taken you at your word, and that I have spoken at length about the good qualities of your rival. You can easily hear them.

I have so often spoken of the good qualities of your piano that it is unnecessary for me to add anything else; I only repeat that the result of the test last Thursday was to announce, without a dissident voice, that your piano was superior to the other, particularly in beauty of tone. Finally I add that the other also had good qualities of which clarity is the primary one. I remain in complete accord with that verdict.

There are ambiguities in this letter. Obviously Hallé was making a determined effort not to offend his old friend and patron. But his recognition of the greater clarity of the Erard action, and of the 'greater effort' needed to achieve effects on the Broadwood, is not hidden.

Nevertheless, Henry Fowler had faced up to the challenge; and in 1851 the decline in sales had been halted; the turn-round seemed to have taken place, and in the two succeeding years increased sales were recorded (see Table III). But it was not to last. The market was flooded with cheap uprights, which began altogether to erode the sale of squares. Again in 1854 and 1855 total sales dropped menacingly. To counter this threat, Broadwoods contracted with a successful maker of uprights, John Reid, to supply uprights on an 'own name' basis (Reid produced 1,562 in four years). The cottage upright had now taken over completely from the cabinet upright, and the last of these made by Broadwoods, No. 8963, was sold in 1856.

The 420 Broadwood workmen streamed out of the Horseferry Road factory as usual at six o'clock on the evening of Tuesday, 12 August 1856. At about half past six, a passerby noticed smoke coming from the top floor of the central range of buildings, below the clock-tower. He raised the alarm; Mr Russell, the senior foreman who lived in a company house next door, dashed into the building with other local residents. He found that the fire had already caught a strong hold; but with assistance he brought up the factory's fire engine kept for such an eventuality, and coupled it up to the nearest of the twelve water-mains outlets provided through the buildings. Within a few minutes the fire had been contained, and it began to look as though the damage would be localised.

Then, at about 6.45, the water failed. The fire blazed up again, and soon the central range was an inferno. The London Fire Brigade, arriving on the scene, was powerless to prevent the flames from leaping the thirty feet to the ranges of buildings on either side; and by eight o'clock, as the *Illustrated London News* recorded: '. . . a vast body of flame rose high into the air, setting out in bold relief the fine architectural outlines of the New Palace [Barry's Palace of Westminster was then in building: Big Ben's clock tower was completed two years later] and the venerable Abbey, and attracting to the bridges and other elevated points of view myriads of curious spectators.'[32] Though the Fire Brigade was able to save the structure of the northernmost of the five ranges, this was only done by dousing it with water, which did further damage to the pianos.

During the fire, every handcart and trolley in the neighbourhood was brought into use to try and rescue the instruments. Some reached neighbouring warehouses, opened up for storage; but in the confusion there was of course no check on who was taking what, or where; so that after that night, not a few front rooms in Westminster and Pimlico could boast a Broadwood piano that had not been there before.

If pilferage accounted for some pianos, the fire took far more. Nearly a thousand instruments were lost—and, as serious a loss to the workmen, their tools of the trade, proudly garnered over the years, and their own possession. The tools of a senior workman might be worth £70, a year's wages. The next morning Henry Fowler and his workmen surveyed the appalling result. The first and most frustrating question was that of the failure of the domestic water supply. The water company was under contract to have the mains fully charged at six o'clock every evening; and yet at 6.45 that Tuesday night the supply failed. It is reported that 'the agents of the various insurance companies, on visiting the premises on Wednesday, expressed themselves very strongly upon this subject',[33] and we may well believe it.

On the following Saturday, Henry Fowler called the men to the factory shell and gave each workman a sovereign and each boy 10s from his own pocket. A fund was started to appeal to the 'nobility and gentry' to replace the workmen's tools, valued at between £3000 and £4000; within a few days £1200 had been raised.[34] Craftsmen at other piano firms also contributed in money or kind, as ironically Broadwoods' workmen had rallied round to keep Clementi and Collard going half a century before, after a similarly disastrous fire. Eventually the insurers paid out £14,168 to Broadwood, but the loss was far greater than that. All orders were eventually honoured, and the owners of Broadwood instruments that happened to be in the factory for repair or maintenance were provided with new pianos. Years later the family believed that the fire and its aftermath cost Henry Fowler some £50,000 personally.

Not much remained at Horseferry Road. About two hundred pianos were salvaged, and the stocks of pine and ebony which, being stored at the north end of the site, had escaped the fire. While Frederick Rose set to work planning the rebuilding, manufacture was concentrated in Soho and a factory was leased nearby in (appropriately-named) Phoenix Street so that many of the workmen could be re-employed. Strangely, it was at the same hour of the same evening, on the same day of the same month, that fire had destroyed the factory of Broadwoods' rival Kirkman, three years earlier.

Chapter VII

The Competitors Emerge

1857–1879

*A*lthough early starts in developing the method of invention had been made by the English, Scots, Dutch and French, from whom the Germans gained their earliest insights, it was the Germans who brought the method to perfection . . . By the third quarter of the century all the world acknowledged German supremacy in science, technology, and scholarship. To her university laboratories and seminars went the best students of America, the Continent, and England. The rapidity of German industrial development was one of the world's wonders and it was particularly notable in the industries dependent upon technology and engineering . . . How alien all this was to the England of the 1850s! By comparison, England then had nothing remotely deserving the name of a national system of education. Her universities were composed of undergraduate colleges. Her numerous original men of science were, except for a few trained on the Continent, usually brilliant amateurs. Scientifically trained technologists were rare . . . An unexpected result of the Great Exhibition of 1851, for example, was the recognition of the high quality of American technical enterprise by British engineers. They looked with astonishment upon three of America's mass-produced items which were soon to capture the English market: the sewing-machine, the revolver, and the mechanical reaper.

George Haines IV: *Technology and Liberal Education in 1859: Entering an Age of Crisis* (Indiana University Press), 1959

If there is an annus mirabilis *in pianoforte history it must be 1853, when Steinway (New York), Bechstein (Berlin) and Blüthner (Leipzig) all commenced business.*

Cyril Ehrlich: *The Piano, a History* (London, Dent), 1976

T he lease on the Horseferry Road premises was held not by the partners of the company, but by the Broadwood family, represented at this time by old Thomas Broadwood and his nephew, the Rev. John Broadwood. A week after the fire, old Tom, now in his seventieth year, wrote from his holiday home in Eastbourne to his nephew at Lyne:

> Referring to my letter to you about our Sad Calamity, I find on investigating our position as the landlords of the Horseferry Road premises, that their lease expires on the 25th December next, that they are bound by it to rebuild the workshops, which will be a great loss to them. At the time my brother [James Shudi] and myself took in Henry Fowler (his son) as a partner, with a small share, *as we had made the Business, he* thought we should have a higher rent for it *in consequence* (far beyond its then value) for 21 years, viz £1,200, for which term we granted the lease to him & any other partners that might come in, as Walter & Tom Jnr. did, & they have paid & will pay us that rent in full up to the end of their term, viz. Xmas next; but they are not bound to take another lease of us, if they can get cheaper premises to answer their present position in business; certainly no stranger will give us the same Rent, and if let to others, we may be a long time before we can find such safe Tenants and we may lose much by the premises remaining unlet (as we did for several years for part of them). Now as they want an immediate answer, as to what we shall expect them to give for a 7, 14 or 21 year renewal of their lease, to enable them to judge if they can take a fresh lease of us, or what they are to do (& they have to decide immediately)—Now finding this to be the case, I went to Mr Edwards & employed him to make a valuation for us of the *present* value of the premises, under all the circumstances of their being good & certain Tenants, giving us no trouble, or loss of Rent, or expence of agency &c, and he has written to me . . . My opinion is, that we had better at once offer to let them the premises at the price he names; it will put their mind at ease.

Edwards, the surveyor, had recommended that 'a moderate rent would be most advantageous to the lessors'. He set a price of £800 per annum for a 21-year lease, with a further £25 p.a. for vacant ground adjoining, and £25 p.a. each for five company houses on the site—a total of £950 p.a. The Rev. John, in his good-natured and gentle way, immediately approved the reduced rent.

Six months before the fire old Thomas Broadwood had formally retired from the partnership, handing over his remaining shares to his son Thomas Jr, who thus became the largest shareholder (with eight shares; Henry Fowler held seven and Walter Stewart five). But of the three partners, only Henry Fowler was executive, and involved in the day-to-day running of the business. Walter Stewart had chosen to leave, and young Thomas had never worked in Great Pulteney Street.

As in the planning of the rebuilding, Henry Fowler came to depend more and more upon the skills, knowledge and cooperation of the Rose brothers, he decided that they should be brought into the partnership. For some years George Rose had been in charge of the administrative and accounts office in Great Pulteney Street, and Henry Fowler left the detailed figurework entirely to him. At Horseferry Road, Frederick Rose was responsible for piano-making under the direction of Henry Fowler; and he was wholly in charge in those periods of the year when 'Mr Broadwood' was shooting or salmon-fishing in Scotland. In the winter of 1856, it was Frederick Rose who prepared the detailed plans for the new factory, and George Rose who organised the finance.

In March 1857, therefore, Henry Fowler proposed to his co-partners Thomas Jr and Walter Stewart that the Roses should be brought into the partnership 'in acknowledgement of their past services and as an inducement to increase their interest in the success of the said trade or business'; and each was given one-twentieth share in the partnership. They were thus distinctly minority partners, who together could be outvoted by any one of the Broadwoods.

At the same time the piano-maker John Reid, who having been making cottage uprights for Broadwoods in earlier years had evidently been taken into direct employment, was encouraged to buy himself into the partnership and provided with a one-tenth share. The partnership deed (in which Walter Stewart is, oddly, misspelt 'Stuart') instructs that 'the said John Reid, George Thomas Rose and Frederick Rose shall at all times . . . diligently employ themselves in the said trade or business and give their whole time and attention thereto but that the said Henry Fowler Broadwood, Thomas Broadwood and Walter Stuart Broadwood shall not be considered as any wise so to do . . .' and also that 'if John Reid, George Thomas Rose or Frederick Rose leaves, he will not set up as a piano manufacturer for 20 years or employ or refer to the name of Broadwood.' Despite this, the agreement only lasted for four years as far as Reid was concerned. He was repaid his capital, and left the partnership, in July 1861.

One of the casualties of the fire had been the Workmen's Library. This

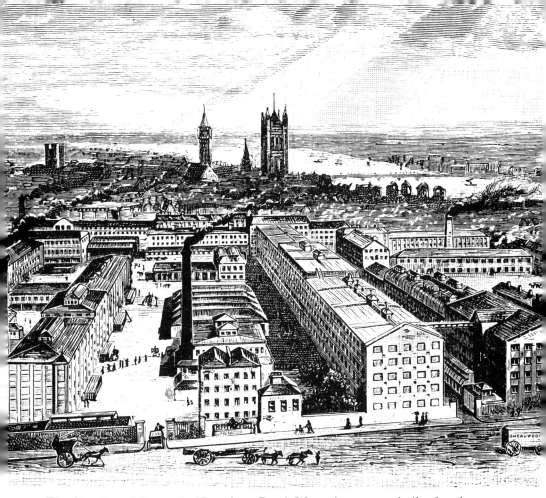

The Broadwood factory in Horseferry Road, Westminster, as rebuilt after the fire of 1856 (*John Broadwood & Sons Ltd*)

had been created in 1847 (four years before the first free public library, and a decade before the first such library in Westminster), based on a fund started by the Earl of Shaftesbury and Lord Brougham to encourage literacy among working men. The fund provided the first eighty books. After the fire, Broadwoods paid for the lost books to be replaced, and provided a free room for it, with gas lighting and a fire. A few years later the library held 4,000 volumes—a mixture of technical works, books on travel and adventure, and some popular novels (but very little music). By 1874 about 300 of the 700 employees belonged to the Library, paying 4d a month; and it was claimed that about one hundred books were taken out each day.

The new factory was re-created on the pattern of the old. In the light of future events this was unfortunate, since the old was out of date, and being overtaken in America and Germany by the introduction of modern machinery for wood-working. Broadwoods kept to the traditional craft-based principles. The firm was far from being alone in this: it was the general practice in wood-working.

During this period (1815–1855) Americans, with abundant cheap wood and a shortage of iron and skilled labour, developed a wide range of machines for sawing, planing, boring, mortising and tenoning, and introduced hundreds of special modifications for the manufacture of carriages, ploughs and furniture. In 1844 the Liverpool firm of William Furness began importing and patenting American machinery, but with little success. When G. L. Molesworth read a paper on 'The conversion of wood by machinery' to The Institute of Civil Engineers in 1857, he was charting virtually unknown territory in England. Resistance to the machine stemmed from a combination of mutually reinforcing circumstances—ingrained conservatism, the small size and limited market of the typical firm, and an abundance of skilled craftsmen throughout the country. Such conditions were pervasive wherever men worked with wood. Until the 1860s even cabinet making, despite large markets, 'could hardly be described as an industry'.[1]

The result was low productivity. As Ehrlich points out:

> Even Broadwood's elaborate division of labour achieved an annual productivity of only about seven pianos per man, no higher than that of small firms; indeed, one well-informed observer argued that it was considerably lower! Clearly there were few internal economies of scale. Moreover, production was very slow, tying up large capital sums in raw material and instruments on the long road to the ultimate buyer. The natural seasoning process required that wood be stored for several years (stocks equivalent to two years throughput were customary), and a grand piano remained 'in hand upwards of six months' before it was pronounced fit for the showroom.[2]

Gradually machinery was introduced, though belatedly; it was in February 1864 that Henry Fowler's daughter Bertha recorded in her diary: 'This morning we all went with Papa to Horseferry Road to choose one of the puppies to take to Lyne. Papa showed me the machine for fixing the little wooden pegs into the iron work of the pianos.' This implies, of course, that this machine was a novelty of which 'Papa' was particularly proud.

If Henry Fowler failed at this time to grasp the full import of mechanisation, it was certainly not due to any inattention to the business. In April 1860 he wrote a memorandum describing twenty four experimental instruments with new mechanism, stringing and bracing. 'The number and character of bracings, glueings, stuff thicknesses, at this period much exercised H. B.'s mind.'[3]

That spring he was also experimenting with different sizes of hammers, and wrote an instruction: 'The hammers of the Queen's instrument are covered as those of No. 76. Give orders to have all the grand hammers made similar to these. Let me know how the second of the short bichords with iron back-brace turns out, especially treble, tenor and bass.'

There is further evidence of his experimentation in a letter of June 1860: 'The sample of cloth you send me is of excellent texture, but the substance is too great to allow it to leave sufficient space for the wire to work through without an undue amount of breaking, so that exposure to the least damp would cause the centres to stick. I clothed several centres with it on Saturday, leaving them easy, and this morning I found them all sticking.'

All this work was being done against a backcloth of impending war. At Broadwood's, this meant the re-formation of the Volunteer Company. Sixty years and more earlier, James Shudi had led the Broadwood workmen in volunteering for military service to repel Napoleon's armies. In November 1854, at the time of the Crimean War, the men of Broadwoods had hired the Royal Soho Theatre and put on a concert to raise funds for 'the wives and children of our brave soldiers now fighting for their country in the East [the Crimea]'.

The threat in 1860 came again from France. The French Government had launched three new warships, 'ironclads', and Britain believed that this could only be the prelude to an attempted invasion by Napoleon III.

The Broadwood workmen were enrolled as No. 8 Company of the St John's Division of the Queen's (Westminster) Rifle Volunteers. The company was in existence for some twenty five years, eventually becoming the F (Broadwood) Company of the 13th Middlesex (Queen's Westminster) Volunteers. During that time, the company's strength varied from about 70 to 100 men. In 1860 once again a musical launching was organised, at a Grand Concert at the Hanover Square Rooms on 23 January, with a 'band' of workmen brought together for the occasion. After this, a wind instrument class was formed, and in April 1860 they brought in a tutor and conductor—Mr Sullivan, Instructor of Music at the Military School of Music, Kneller Hall. When the band marched out at the head of the Broadwood Volunteers, Sullivan's sixteen-year-old son played the bass drum.

Young Sullivan was already indebted to Broadwoods—a debt that he was to repay loyally throughout his distinguished life.* Two years earlier, Henry Fowler Broadwood contributed generously to the boy's musical training, as his teacher Sir George Smart confirmed:

George T Smart to H F Broadwood, 26 June 1858

My dear Sir

I beg to acknowledge the receipt of your Draft of this date for Thirty Pounds, being your most liberal donation to A. S. Sullivan, the present Mendelssohn Scholar, towards the payment of his expenses at the Conservatoire at Leipsic; I hope he will ever prove grateful for the kindness you have evinced towards him.

The Broadwood band was so good that it attracted the attention of a contemporary composer of band music—ironically a Frenchman, M. Favarger—who wrote a march for it, dedicating it to Captain [George] Rose, and presenting the band with the score. In 1861 some younger Broadwood employees formed a drum-and-fife band, directed first by Drum-Major West of the 1st Battalion, Scots Fusiliers, and later by Drum-Major Loomes of the Coldstream Guards. The band went from strength to strength, and by 1862 was able to fill the St James's Hall for a concert patronised by Earl Grosvenor (later Duke of Westminster) with half a dozen leading soloists, among them Arthur Sullivan and Charles Hallé.

The elder Sullivan died in 1864, and his son presented the Broadwood band with his practice-books, which were bound by the firm into twenty volumes. The band turned out to play for many special events, such as (in 1863) the opening of the Pimlico Literary and Scientific Institution. The band was allowed free use of a room at Horseferry Road for practice, and there was a scheme whereby the bandsmen could borrow money from the company to buy instruments. From 1862 the band gave annual concerts, usually in March, at the Pimlico Concert Rooms, and under the management of one of the clerks, A. J. Hipkins, these were not only artistically successful, but also made a profit. Some of the profit went to underwrite an Annual Dinner in July, a function usually held at Southend and attended by about one hundred of the bandsmen, their families and supporters.

* Sir Arthur Sullivan (1842–1900), composer, and collaborator with W. S. Gilbert in the Savoy Operas.

For some years the band had a somewhat ambiguous character, being both a civilian orchestra and a military band (in January 1868, after Irish outrages in London, the band led 400 workmen in a march from Broadwoods to Westminster Hall, where they all signed on as special constables).

In 1885 the band finally gave up its military role and, as 'the Broadwood Orchestral Band', gave a concert at the Westminster Town Hall on 6 March. The conductor was Charles Doust, bandmaster of the Queen's Westminster Volunteers, but the composition of the 'orchestral band' was altogether more pacific—12 violins, 2 violas, 3 cellos, 2 double basses, 2 flutes, 1 oboe, 2 clarinets, 1 bassoon, 2 cornets, 1 trombone, 1 euphonium and 1 kettle drum. If this suggests a flowering of executant skills among the Broadwood workmen, they did not tax themselves (at least on that occasion) with avant-garde music. The principal item was the *Valse Vénetienne* by that popular Victorian composer, Waldteufel and perhaps the effort at becoming 'orchestral' was too demanding, for there is no record that the band ever performed again.

In July 1860 Henry Fowler Broadwood sent to the factory an order which marked the beginning of the end of an era: 'Discontinue all Squares which are not made solid for the tropics, and reckon on a sale of these a third less than last year. Reckon on making in the year (so many more) cottage-grands. Add these to the number of solid squares and then see how many workmen these Indian instruments will keep well employed. Recollect that all will have to have Grand actions. Turn over any really good men to other jobs and reduce the Indian instrument men to just the number you can keep in employ at good wages.'[4]

The square piano was being defeated by the cheap upright, and this was an acknowledgement of what had already become apparent in the sales. The factory was to continue making squares for a further six years, though only of the solid-cased (i.e. unveneered) variety. The last square, (No. 64,161) was made in 1866.

This truly represented a major watershed in the history of the firm. For it was on the square that the prosperity of the company had been founded, eighty years before. The upright, which was supplanting it, was implicitly cheap, and the majority were still being made in England with the old-fashioned and unreliable 'sticker' action. It was Henry Fowler's decision to adhere to quality; and so he set the company to concentrate on the grand, while developing a quality upright 'with the grand action'.

Thomas Broadwood died at Holmbush in 1861, in his seventy fifth year. His partnership with his elder half-brother James Shudi had created an internationally respected business from the foundations laid

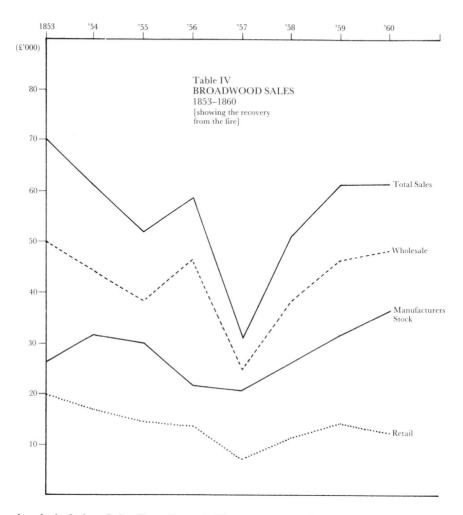

Table IV
BROADWOOD SALES
1853–1860
[showing the recovery
from the fire]

Total Sales

Wholesale

Manufacturers
Stock

Retail

by their father John Broadwood. He was an excellent foil to his brother. James Shudi was imaginative and forward-looking, while Thomas was meticulous and careful. He managed the firm's finances with precision— and also his own; he built up a personal fortune, and kept it.* He would thoroughly have approved the modern fashion of giving business management into the hands of accountants, for he was the accountant in

---

* His personal estate was valued at £350,000. Apart from bequests to his family and servants, he left £100 each to the Royal Society of Female Musicians and to the Sussex County Hospital, Brighton. One of the sons of his second marriage was to be a famous soldier: Robert George Broadwood commanded the cavalry at Omdurman, fought with distinction in the Boer War, and as a Lieutenant-General died of wounds in 1917, much loved and respected.

A square piano by John Broadwood, 1774. The nameboard is walnut, inlaid in
boxwood and harewood with floral sprays, boxwood and harewood stringing
and mahogany crossbanding, inscribed on a boxwood plaque *Johannes Broadwood
Londini fecit 1774*. The case is mahogany, with two hand levers controlling forte
stops above and below middle C. This piano, now restored and in the possession
of the author, must be one of the earliest surviving Broadwood pianos *(Photo:
David Thorpe)*

James Shudi Broadwood (1772–1851). The eldest son of John Broadwood, who with his brother Thomas headed the company in its period of greatest expansion. This watercolour, which catches his light-hearted humour, was done about 1820 *(The Broadwood Trust) (Photo: Graham Miller)*

Left The 1796 Broadwood grand designed by Thomas Sheraton, with Wedgwood medallions, for the Marquis du Godoy. This piano, now owned by Mrs Florence C Chambers, is at present in the Museum of Fine Arts, Boston *(Photo: Arthur Vitols, Helga Photo Studios)*

Thomas Broadwood (1786–1861). John Broadwood's second surviving son (of his second marriage) who was business manager of the company, but who as a young man arranged for a grand to be given to Beethoven. The artist is unknown *(Formerly in the possession of Miss Elizabeth Broadwood, his direct descendant, the portrait is now in the Colt Clavier Collection) (Photo: Photographic Records Ltd)*

essence. His carefulness over money, which became a family legend, did no harm to the partnership while he was a leader of it. Though no romantic, he was capable in his younger days of imaginative gestures, as when he gave Beethoven a piano. In historical terms it looks like a provident piece of public relations; but at the time, he was making the gift to a composer who, though widely respected, was far from the pinnacle of general admiration that he has since enjoyed. Thomas Broadwood ensured the solid financial base of John Broadwood & Sons in its period of greatest expansion.

A second International Exhibition was held in London in 1862, in the buildings newly erected in South Kensington as a centre for science and the arts. The celebrations were muted since the instigator of the Great Exhibition, Prince Albert, had died in the previous December and Queen Victoria had withdrawn into the deep mourning and seclusion from which she was not to emerge for many years.

The 1862 Exhibition was more satisfactory for Broadwoods than the 1851 had been, since this time they were awarded a Gold Medal, and the musical jury reported that Broadwoods 'stand, without controversy, at the head of the Pianoforte Makers who exhibit on the present occasion'. In this year, too, Henry Fowler reversed the practice of previous generations and published two booklets. One[5] in the guise of a catalogue to his firm's exhibits; the other[6] was a more personal memoir of the history of the company, based on notes made by his father James Shudi, thirty years earlier. To compile the former, a search had been made through the firm's ledgers to establish the dates on which famous virtuosi had 'either used our instruments exclusively, or played upon them in public occasionally'. Of the sixty seven names, many are now forgotten; but the list contains some impressive customers (with the dates on which they first appear in the Broadwood books):

J. L. Dussek	26 March 1791
J. N. Hummel	13 June 1791
Joseph Haydn	26 September 1791
Dr Burney	6 February 1792
Samuel Wesley (the elder)	5 October 1792
Muzio Clementi	13 October 1792
J. B. Cramer	February 1793
Von Esch	13 June 1794
Ignace Pleyel	30 June 1796
Luigi Cherubini	2 March 1815
Ignace Moscheles	30 June 1821

C. M. von Weber	3 March 1826
Franz Liszt	4 October 1826
Henry Litolff	29 October 1830
Carl Czerny	14 April 1837
Robert Schumann	22 April 1840
Felix Mendelssohn	16 May 1844
Frédéric Chopin	27 April 1848
Charles Hallé	20 May 1848
Madame (Clara) Schumann	29 April 1857

The catalogue also recorded that 'from the beginning of 1780 to the end of 1861, our House has manufactured 124,048 Pianofortes, 75,700 of which have been made since 1826. Of the total number, no less than 27,479 were Grand Pianofortes. That these Grand Pianofortes are endowed with a power of resistance, formerly neither attained nor believed to be attainable, combined with a durability at one time regarded as scarcely less utopian, may be gathered . . . The Grand Pianoforte, indeed, may, at this present period, be said to have attained the *maximum* of power.'

This meticulous searching through the records to produce eminent names and detailed statistics was the work of A. J. Hipkins. Born in Westminster, he joined Broadwoods as a clerk at the age of fourteen in 1840. Every modern historian of the pianoforte or the harpsichord owes much to his scrupulous research a century or more ago. This present story would not be possible in such detail had Hipkins not examined and annotated many records that have subsequently been lost.

The catalogue contains one other significant pointer to the future. A detailed description of the grand is prefaced by this introduction:

The Pianoforte appears usually in three forms, called respectively the SQUARE, the GRAND, and the UPRIGHT . . . The *Square* form was formerly very common, but is now fast becoming obsolete; very few being made at the present day, except for India, where they are found to stand the climate better than any other kind. The *Grand* and *Upright* forms are those now most commonly made. The Grand form is reserved for instruments of the first class; the Upright is made in vast numbers for more general use.
It is our object here to give a description . . . of the construction of the best class of instrument—the *Grand*; and, therefore, we shall omit all further mention of the two other kinds.

This was the conventional wisdom of 1862. Broadwoods made the best, and the best was the grand. The upright was cheap, and often shoddy and unreliable.

And yet . . . On the back cover of the Official Catalogue of the Fine Art Department of the 1867 Exhibition Chappell's from their 'New Rooms at 50 Bond Street' advertised 'Pianofortes of every description by Broadwood, Collard, Erard &c for sale or hire'.

Though pride of place was given to 'Chappell & Co's Ten-Guinea Pianoforte', a miniature upright only 2 ft 6½ ins wide and 3 ft 3½ ins high, the most expensive instrument advertised was 'Chappell's Foreign Model Cottage [Upright]' at 50 guineas: a tri-chord of seven octaves. 'Chappell's English model' was cheaper, at 35 guineas in rosewood or 40 guineas in walnut. 'To amateurs preferring the pure English tone of the Broadwood and Collard quality, the English model will be found the most perfectly satisfactory instrument at a moderate price. The action is of the same simple description as the above makers, and therefore especially adapted to the country, where the more complicated actions are objectionable to the tuners.'

The foreign invasion had begun. But it would be wrong to suppose that Henry Fowler was complacent. To the 1862 Exhibition he went day after day first thing in the morning and 'himself tried every one of the hundreds of pianos gathered together within the building'.[7] Nor did he ignore the challenge of the upright. Robert Wornum had invented an improved upright action that bettered the unreliable 'sticker'. The French manufacturers took it up, and it thus became known as the 'French action'. But while the French manufacturers all bought their actions in from a single great action-maker, Herrburger-Schwander—Henry Fowler chose to have the actions made at Horseferry Road.

Above all, he argued the case for quality control, writing to the Roses in October 1863: 'I feel sure that if we attend to our trade and to the details of construction we shall continue a good business. This will take constant, unremitting attention in all departments, and economy must be more esteemed than hitherto. Of a good article much is expected, and people expect super-excellence. What will pass as a fair article will not do to put our name upon.'[8]

He came to rely heavily upon Hipkins's judgement. writing in the same year: 'I should feel obliged if you would desire Hipkins to look over the instruments for Milan and Madrid, and desire that, under no circumstances, they be sent away until he passes them.'[9]

Henry Fowler wrote these instructions, of course, because he was not at the factory himself. His presence, though intently commanding, was intermittent.

At the Piano, by James McNeill Whistler, 1859 *(Louise Taft Semple Bequest, the Taft Museum, Cincinnati)*

In 1863 Broadwoods launched two new ranges of instruments: the Royal boudoir grands, 7 ft 6 ins long and of 6⅞ octaves (they were made 7 octaves in 1866) and cottage grands (which were 6⅞ octaves until 1878). These improved the sales figures, which showed a steady increase for the following three years.

In January 1864 the Rev. John Broadwood, eldest son of James Shudi, died at Lyne. A quiet, kindly scholar, he is best remembered as a collector of folk songs (an interest that he passed on to his youngest niece, Lucy). Inheriting the Lyne estate under the trust established by his father, the Rev. John and his wife Charlotte, who were childless, had encouraged Henry Fowler and Julia to use the estate as a country home for their large family. Now, in his fifties, Henry Fowler became the master of Lyne. The Rev. John's widow Charlotte moved out, and on 29 April Henry Fowler's daughter Bertha, just eighteen, recorded in her diary: 'Today we all moved down to Lyne. I do hope the children will get to love the dear old place as much as we elder ones have always done.'

Henry Fowler was now a Victorian *paterfamilias*, with nine surviving children.* Eight daughters had been born before the first longed-for son, to inherit the business. Henry Fowler's interest in history was shared by his wife and elder daughters. It had, in fact, been inculcated by his mother: for Margaret Schaw Stewart—like other expatriates, born abroad, who return to their homeland—was intensely interested in her Scottish ancestry, and up to her death in 1849 conducted detailed correspondence with her Stewart and Murray relations. The Broadwood daughters traced the family back to Scotland and Switzerland. When the two sons were born in the 1850s they were both given the name of their great-grandfather in its Swiss form—Tschudi.

Henry Fowler was an instinctive builder. In 1853 he had extended the Bryanston Square house (at a cost of £724 10s) to accommodate his growing family. Now, with the family's eager help, he planned to enlarge Lyne. There were family conclaves. Bertha, no inconsiderable artist, drew plans of what they wanted. These were then presented to the architect Richard Armstrong (who said, unsurprisingly, that he thought them very professional). The builders moved in during February 1865, and had finished by January 1866. The result was a solid Victorian country house, enlarged from James Shudi's Regency villa, the modest corner turret raised by a further storey to form a miniature castellated tower looking over the surrounding parkland. In red brick trimmed with white stone, it was a comfortable family house rather than an architectural masterpiece. On the ground floor the three main rooms— drawing room, library and dining room—led from an airy central hall lit by a skylight which illuminated the best of Henry Fowler's increasing collection of fine paintings.

The library, with its floor-to-ceiling bookcases housing leather-bound classics, was particularly fine. But throughout, the woodwork was of the most excellent quality. The timber came from the estate, and the workmanship from the factory. The best of Broadwoods' craftsmen worked on it, and Henry Fowler paid the firm £843 17s 6d for their services, most of it labour costs. In all, the rebuilding of Lyne cost £3,444

---

* Katherine Margaret (22), Edith Juliana (19), Bertha Marion (18), Mary Stewart (14), Evelyn Charlotte (12), Amy Murray (11), James Henry Tschudi (9), Henry John Tschudi (8), Lucy Etheldred (5). Two other daughters died in the London cholera epidemic of 1849: Augusta Barbara (aged 6) and Henrietta Jemima (aged 1½).

The improvements in medicine within one century, leading to a decline in child mortality, are illustrated by this family. John Broadwood had ten children of his two marriages between 1771 and 1793, of whom four survived to adult life. James Shudi Broadwood, his son, had sixteen children of his two marriages between 1798–1822, of whom ten survived to adult life. Henry Fowler, once married, had eleven children between 1841 and 1858, of whom nine survived.

Henry Fowler Broadwood, aged 50 *(The Broadwood Trust)*

19s 3½d. To celebrate its completion, Charles Hallé Jr painted a portrait of the master of the house.

A rather grander London house seemed called for, and 46 Bryanston Square was put on the market in 1866 (at £6,000); a house in Mayfair was purchased—8, St George's Street. Despite that, from this point Henry Fowler and his family regarded Lyne as their principal home. The family would go up to London for the Season, and to Scotland (where they rented The Pavilion, Melrose) for the autumn. Henry Fowler had grown up at Lyne, and he loved it profoundly. He was a benevolent landlord; and indeed his agent complained that the tied houses on the estate came to be occupied by elderly servants and farm-workers because 'Mr Broadwood' refused to turn them out. It was benevolent, but it made it

Lyne House, Surrey, as rebuilt by Henry Fowler Broadwood, 1864 *(The Broadwood Trust)*

hard for the agent to recruit young men for the estate if he could not offer them accommodation.

There was no doubt at Great Pulteney Street or Horseferry Road who was the head of the firm. It was 'Mr Broadwood'.

His instructions continued to reach the Rose brothers, George and Frederick, in a steady stream from Lyne or Melrose. Brimful of ideas as ever, Henry Fowler poured them into ears that gradually became unreceptive, preoccupied as their owners were with the day-to-day management of the business and the factory. In 1870 George Rose noted the financial results of the previous five years. In 1865 the company was valued on paper at £175,065. In 1870 its value was £175,391. The profits in those five years had averaged £20,865 a year. The sums withdrawn by the partners had averaged £20,800. No profit had been ploughed back into the business. As partners, though with minor shares, the Roses were aware of this.

Had there been anyone to challenge him, Henry Fowler could have claimed with some justification that he was making good the personal losses he had incurred during the fire and the rebuilding of the factory. The insurance companies had paid but Henry Fowler reckoned that the business had cost him personally more then £50,000, and it seems probable. No similar claim could have been made by Thomas Broadwood Jr or Walter Stewart Broadwood.

Nevertheless, the Broadwood grand remained respected in Europe, and that reputation was confirmed at the Paris Exhibition of 1867, when the first Gold Medal was awarded to Broadwoods (and was presented to Henry Fowler personally by the Emperor Napoleon III). The second and third Medals went to Steinway and Chickering, both of whom showed full iron-framed grands, the Steinway overstrung. With a typically lavish gesture, Henry Fowler had paid for 117 of his workmen to travel to Paris for the Exhibition, lodging them in wooden huts on the site. When the award became known at Horseferry Road, the men drew up a congratulatory address, bearing fifty eight names—the name of one man from each department. It is a reminder of the scale of the enterprise, and also of the fact that Broadwoods still made every part themselves, requiring fifty eight divisions of work.

Not all commentators at Paris were so impressed by the Broadwood grand compared with the American models. One leading musical journalist called it a 'souvenir des travaux passés'. The jury report, written by François Fétis, the Director of the Brussels Conservatoire, commended the powerful tone resulting from more solid construction and heavier strings than were found in European instruments; the American pianos achieved a sonority to fill the largest concert hall, and the Steinway in particular was described as the ideal piano for concert room and parlour.[10]

Henry Fowler must have seen that danger signal clearly before him but, reassured perhaps by the Gold Medal, he regarded it as directed towards cheaper competition rather than towards his craftsman-built instruments.

Some clue to his attitude of mind is given in a correspondence that year with a former employee, Andrew Oborne, who had emigrated to the United States in 1858 and was now working for Chickerings in New York. Oborne had made what he regarded as certain improvements to the 'English action' used by Chickering. He sent models to London, clearly hoping that Henry Fowler would either buy the rights to the improvements or enable him to take out a British patent. Henry Fowler's reply, technically detailed, indicated his ready willingness to experiment, but at the same time his fundamental belief in the superiority of his own designs.

Having a case of a Concert Iron Grand ready for stringing I shall put to it an action copied from your No 1 Model, adapting the key to our underdampers. I see no other way of trying the action fairly. The instrument will go out to concerts and we shall soon hear from

Professors whether they find either touch or tone improved. I have in the same way tried Erards' and other actions, of course without drawing the Professors' attention to the circumstances, but I have always hitherto had to fall back on what we best understood—the old action with the proportions enlarged to suit modern requirements. You shall be fully informed of the result—and I will take care your action shall have a fair trial.

As to the Chickering & Steinway cast iron frame—the preliminary objection in this country would be the difficulty of getting the *quality* of casting. We prefer wrought Iron for string plates, and for bars of Grands of the *largest* kind.

Henry Fowler may have been right in his scepticism of the British ironworks, and the new steel (the Bessemer process of steel-making was patented in 1856). Similar doubts were common among British engineers, and a historian of the iron and steel industry has commented[11] that this 'despairing view' was not banished until foreign makers had demonstrated, using British inventions and British technology, that the material was reliable. There were financial handicaps, such as tariffs and taxation, which militated against the British industry, but not to an extent that explains its decline.

To a large extent the crisis of the British iron and steel industry is the crisis of all capital goods industries in the great industrial nations which have reached the limits of their national and international expansion, though this crisis will come sooner in the older and most industrialised countries, of which Great Britain was the first. This crisis reacts on the industry inasmuch as by threatening profitability it weakens the incentive to boldness, the readiness to modernise, and tends to make the industry run to shelter rather than seek to strengthen itself[12].

It is scarcely necessary to draw the parallel with Broadwoods in the late nineteenth century.

As the great steelworks of Pittsburgh and the Ruhr began to dominate iron and steel markets, a son of the Steinway family made a study of them. He was well equipped to do so, for Theodore Steinway was a trained engineer and scientist, and also a personal friend of Hermann von Helmholtz, the Berlin physicist who devised the theory of overtones.[13] Theodore Steinway went from Germany to join the family business in New York in 1865, just about the time that Henry Fowler was doubtfully experimenting with casting.

Steinways can be taken as an example of the classic theory of the economic historian, 'the advantage of a late start'. That alone might not have been overwhelming had there been at Broadwoods someone with the technical training of an engineer, capable of harnessing to tradition the relevant aspects of the new technology. But there was not. Henry Fowler's strongly held belief was that the way forward lay—in that revealing phrase of his—with 'the old action with the proportions enlarged to suit modern requirements'.

He sent Oborne a copy of Broadwoods' exhibition catalogue, with its detailed technical data; Oborne thought that 'the gratuitous publicity of so much practical information & experimental result would seem rather startling here, in view of the secrecy with which such matters are generally guarded'.

But it was ever Henry Fowler's way. There were times when a sense of industrial security would incline him to be wary, saying 'It is as well that we should keep *this* experiment to ourselves'. But more often, and generally when taking visitors round the factory, his enthusiasm and self-confidence and pride in his historic family firm led him to show off every detail. If his lieutenants objected, he would say: 'Let them copy; when they do what we are doing now, we shall be ahead with something else.'

This ebullience was also characteristic of his business dealings, as when at the time of the Franco–Prussian War in 1870 when the demand for Broadwood pianos outstripped the productive capacity of the factory, Henry Fowler bought in a dozen French and a dozen German grands for re-sale, unafraid to be seen dealing in rival products. When a decade later Anton Rubinstein made his last visit to England and expressed a wish to play Becker grands from St Petersburg, Henry Fowler agreed that the four Russian grands should be unpacked and regulated at Horseferry Road; and he detailed his best tuner to accompany them during Rubinstein's tour.

The interruption to pianoforte production in Europe during the Franco–Prussian War did benefit Broadwoods commercially; sales increased to a new peak in 1872 and declined only marginally during the following six years. But it was a false dawn.

When the centenary of Beethoven's birth was celebrated at a Festival at Bonn in August 1871, Charles Hallé played two piano works—the Pianoforte Fantasia with Chorus, and the 'Emperor' Concerto. Appropriately, considering the associations of both Beethoven and Hallé with the company, a Broadwood concert grand was specially sent over from Great Pulteney Street. Although the orchestra does not seem to have been adequately rehearsed—the *Guardian* reported that in the

Pianoforte Fantasia 'there seemed to be among the wood and brass a general ignorance of the work; and the mistakes which occurred at the rehearsal . . . also occurred at the concert', Hallé was particularly praised in the Concerto. 'Mr Hallé played the solo part with extraordinary neatness, finish and poetry, and was, at the conclusion of the Rondo, recalled to the platform with enthusiasm.'[14]

One further curiosity emerged from Broadwoods in 1871. This was the Pedalier concert grand—a grand to which a four-octave pedalboard (similar to an organ pedalboard) had been attached. It was agreed that for some years, organists had attached pedalboards to pianos for the purposes of practice; but this was claimed to be the first time the device had successfully been produced to give a first quality performance.

The *Musical World* was ecstatic:

For a pianoforte with pedals which should be as playable as the keys the musical world has long waited, and many have been the efforts to produce the desired thing. 'J. S. Bach,' says an authority, 'had in his possession a *Cembalo con Pedale*, and wrote for it several admirable compositions, among which may be cited the *Passacaile* in C minor . . . The 'Pedalier Grand Pianoforte' of our world-renowned English firm was put to test on Thursday week in the Hanover Square Rooms, M. Delaborde being the experimenter . . . The new instrument proved a complete success.[15]

If the musical world, as distinct from the *Musical World*, had long been waiting for this instrument, it showed no great interest in its arrival. The Pedalier grand pianoforte disappeared as rapidly as it had appeared (although not before a correspondent had pointed out that Erards had produced a similar sort of thing a decade earlier). The theory was that the pianoforte repertoire would be enlarged to exploit the instrument, a perfect example of the fallacy that composers follow instrument-makers rather than *vice versa*. Meanwhile, it was said, the music of Bach (then little played in concert) would be resuscitated. The Pedalier was a historical oddity, and its development bears all the signs of the historical enthusiasm (and, it should be said, knowledge) of A. J. Hipkins, who was becoming recognised as a leading historian of keyboard instruments: from 1878 he was to contribute the relevant sections to Grove's *Dictionary of Music and Musicians*.

Nevertheless, some critics noted the power of the Pedalier; and power, particularly that made possible by the heavier stringing and larger hammers associated with the cast-iron frame, was becoming an admired quality in the instrument. Executants were appearing who could apply the necessary muscle. They were lionised in society (see page 204), and fashionable hostesses would hire a fashionable grand for the occasion. Broadwoods were leaders in this hiring trade.

The vehemence of some pianists did not please all ears; and the *Figaro* made this comment on a recital by Hans von Bülow* at St James's Hall in November 1873: Dr Bülow's thumping was magnificent; he treated his piano as mercilessly as though he had been using gentle arguments to his *épouse heureuse*, and so greatly exerted himself that an indignant connoisseur in the stalls feelingly exclaimed: "If I were Broadwood, I would not allow it!"'

With the public reputation of his pianos high, and with a steady demand bringing profits to the company of over £30,000 a year up to 1878 (Table V), Henry Fowler could have been forgiven for seeing no real reason for apprehension. True, Steinways opened a London showroom in 1877, and were importing increasing numbers of their solid frame grands. True, the German piano manufacturers were increasing their inroads on the British market. But a greater threat at this time seemed to come from plagiarism: in 1877 Broadwoods took a Manchester firm to court—they had been buying up old pianos, stencilling them 'Broadwood', and selling them as genuine. It was a tribute to the continuing commercial value of the name.

Yet there were profound sadnesses in Henry Fowler's life in that decade. In July 1874 he received the news of the death in India of his eldest daughter and first-born child, Katherine Margaret Craster. She had married, in 1862, Edmund Craster, heir of a good Northumberland family, and a member of the Bengal Civil Service. From Bangapore she had written back to Lyne vivid letters about her life and growing family. She was musical, too, was proud of her Broadwood piano and knew what would please Papa: 'Tell my father that I can tune my pianoforte easily now. I did so some three weeks ago, & it is in fair tune still, notwithstanding the extraordinary variations in the temperature.' Now, at thirty three, she was dead. It was a severe blow to Henry Fowler, to whom she had been particularly close.

At about the same time, it became necessary to plan the careers of the two sons, James and Harry. Both, as befitted the sons of a man of wealth and position, had been sent to Eton. Both were to go to Cambridge—

* Hans Guido von Bülow (1830–1894), pupil of Liszt and later a noted conductor of Wagner.

James to Trinity, his father's college, in 1873; Harry to Jesus College, two years later. But it became apparent that neither was attracted to the idea of joining the business. Their school friends were young aristocrats; and both James and Harry had been brought up as the sons of a country gentleman. The background with which they were familiar was Lyne or Melrose, and not Great Pulteney Street or the noise and dirt of Horseferry Road.

It was hardly their fault if they had grown up with the ideal of the 'gentleman amateur'. It was the fashion among their friends to despise 'trade'. A gentleman did not engage himself in technical matters.

The snobbery of late Victorian and Edwardian England was deep and damaging. Above all, the *nouveaux riches* who had made their money in the dark satanic mills by hard work were looked down on.*

So it was agreed that James would read for the Bar. At Cambridge he was something of a sportsman, a 'wet bob', rowing No. 3 in the Third Trinity second boat. He took his degree in 1877, became a member of Lincoln's Inn, and was called to the Bar in 1882. He did not practise, but spent most of his time at Lyne, overseeing the family estate.

Harry took his degree in 1879. On coming down, he was put to work in Great Pulteney Street. Once again there was a 'Mr Broadwood' regularly on the premises. For gentle, shy, stammering Harry, it was a torment.

---

* A classic story circulated particularly about Broadwoods, and is told by Jonathan Gathorne-Hardy in his *The Public School Phenomenon* (Hodder & Stoughton, 1977); though this must refer to the Thomas Broadwood branch of the family who had returned to live in Scotland:

> New money, money from what was loosely termed 'trade', was despised. I was brought up on a story about my great-grandmother, Lady Glasgow. The Broadwoods had come to the neighbourhood. After a while (they were extremely rich) Lady Glasgow said that although they were in 'trade', they must be asked to stay. But instructions were given that absolutely no one was to mention the word 'piano'. That would be in extremely poor taste. The weekend went very well. Finally, the farewells came, the embraces. At last my great-grandmother went to the window and turned with uplifted arms sadly. 'I'm afraid, Mrs Broadwood, the time has come to part,' she said. 'Your piano's at the door.'

Yet another reflection of this attitude is to be found in William Dale's *Tschudi the Harpsichord Maker* (Constable, 1913), where he remarks: 'We must dismiss from our minds modern ideas concerning business, and rest assured that no social stigma was attached to the fact that Shudi was, after all, only a craftsman, nay, even a mechanic, who lived at his shop. Everything indicates that he mingled on equal terms with the famous people of his day.'

'Only a craftsman, nay, even a mechanic'! This of the founder of a multi-million pound business, based on skill . . . It is a historical cliché now to regard Victorian snobbery as one root cause of Britain's failures in technology and industry during the century that followed; but seldom can it have been as clearly illustrated as in these quotations.

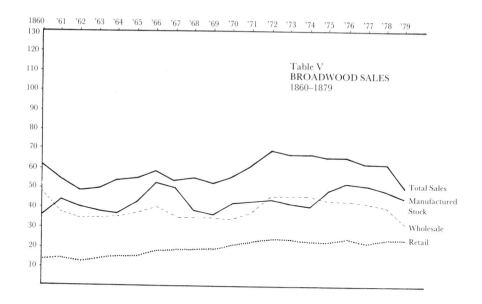

Table V
BROADWOOD SALES
1860–1879

Total Sales
Manufactured Stock
Wholesale
Retail

It can have been no less embarrassing for the Rose brothers, who for forty and more years had devoted themselves to working day by day for the company, to have the 'boss's son' thrust into their midst, fresh from Eton and Cambridge, with no experience either of business or of piano-making.

Indeed, to the working world of London—the piano teachers, wholesalers and retailers—'Broadwoods' meant George Rose, who held court at Great Pulteney Street. One of the clerks wrote of him: 'Mr Rose . . . was a popular man with the Professors & Gentry, and out a great deal in Society, always wore a coat lined with satin, he being the Messrs. Broadwood to everyone at 33 on business.' The Rose brothers had a particular link with the musical establishment of London through their friendship with the Macfarren brothers,* who were pillars of it.

As young men, Frederick Rose and Walter Macfarren shared a house. The Roses, the Blacks and Alfred Hipkins were the familiar faces always to be found by callers at Great Pulteney Street. On notable occasions they would throw parties on behalf of the firm, with George Rose as host. In a note to Rose at the end of 1869, for example, the pianist Pauer apologised

---

* (Sir) George Macfarren (1813–1887), composer and teacher, for many years a Professor at the Royal Academy of Music, and from 1876 its Principal; and his brother Walter Macfarren (1826–1905), pianist and composer, and a Professor of Piano at the Royal Academy of Music from 1846 to 1903.

Henry John Tschudi Broadwood,
c. 1872 *(The Broadwood Trust)*

James Henry Tschudi Broadwood,
c. 1872 *(The Broadwood Trust)*

that he might be 'too busy to wish in the New Year with you, Mr Black
Senr and Jr, and Mr Hipkins'.

When in 1874 Walter Macfarren applied to Broadwoods for a
subscription towards the rebuilding fund of the Royal Academy of
Music, it was to George Rose that he wrote; and it was George Rose who
replied, eliciting the acknowledgement from Macfarren:

> My dear Rose,
> The munificent subscription of your old house . . . is another
> example of the alacrity with which 'J. Broadwood & Sons' have ever
> been forward in the van when any good or useful work had to be
> accomplished.

Inevitably, therefore, at Great Pulteney Street and Horseferry Road
Henry Fowler Broadwood became 'the old man', revered and respected

on those rare occasions when, usually unannounced, his carriage would roll up to the door and he would tour his empire.

Greeting the older workmen by name, he would try out a dozen or so pianos chosen at random. He would take a piece of chalk and mark poor notes with an 'x'. Summoning the foremen, he would issue a stream of detailed instructions, climb back into his carriage, and depart. When he had gone, the workmen would rub off the marks and send the pianos out.

Once, his instructions rebounded. He had issued a general order, very properly, that nothing should ever be placed on the lid of a grand. One summer, a clerk walked into the showroom and to his horror noticed a white panama hat on the lid of the nearest grand. He picked it up and flung it across the showroom—where it narrowly missed 'Mr Broadwood', whose hat it was.

So in the autumn of 1879 his younger son was to work in the business. Henry Broadwood, aged twenty three, entered nervously into the company of piano-making professionals. A new generation of the family took up its inheritance.

Chapter VIII

The Partnership Breaks Up

1879–1901

*T*he proportions and balance of the Victorian industrial state, as it had stood in the middle of the nineteenth century, were destroyed by the agricultural depression of the years 1873–1900 . . . Farming and the land apart, the years after 1880 saw the beginnings of new and sweeping changes in the field of manufacturing technique. The foundations of Victorian industrial success had lain in the national priority in the exploitation of steam, iron and coal. The time at last arrived, with the growing industrialisation of the West, when the main advantages to be derived from having been first in the use of these slipped away. About the same time, in the 1880s and 1890s, the signs appeared of new and momentous scientific applications, which had to do mainly with electricity, the internal combustion engine and the application of industrial chemistry.

W. H. B. Court: *A Concise Economic History of Britain from 1750 to Recent Times*, (Cambridge University Press, 1954)

Michael . . . began to rip the wires out of the Broadwood grand . . .

The cart reached Cannon Street without disaster; and Mr Brown's piano was speedily and cleverly got on board.

'Well, sir,' said the leading porter, smiling as he mentally reckoned up a handful of loose silver, 'that's a mortal heavy piano.'

'It's the richness of the tone,' returned Michael, as he drove away.

Robert Louis Stevenson and Lloyd Osborne, *The Wrong Box*, 1889

In its high noon the British Empire was astonishing in its grandeur. That high noon lasted from the symbolic accession of Queen Victoria as Empress of India, in 1877, to the old Queen's death in 1901. It was followed by the golden afternoon of the Edwardian age. But while it lasted, this Empire on which the sun never set was sustained by its colonial territories, by the wealth flowing into Britain along the arteries of trade, by unmatched military strength and by the Royal Navy guarding the trade routes on the world's oceans. Danger signals were appearing, particularly in Africa (where the Zulu War was fought in 1879, and Kruger declared his Boer Republic in 1880). Gordon died at Khartoum in 1885, and the might of Britain failed to save him. At home, Irish Home Rule was a matter of political contention, as it had been for 200 years and was to continue to be for at least a century more.

Nevertheless, in Britain there was the self-confidence founded on wealth, power and success. It was a self-confidence and assurance to be seen in all levels of society; and it was in 1878 that the word 'jingo-ism' was coined to define the idea that British must be best.

Broadwoods were well placed to be pianoforte-makers to this glorious age. A *Punch* cartoon of 1879 (see page 204) vividly defines the fashionable society of that time: the women elegantly gowned, bejewelled and coiffed, the men uniform in white tie and tails, for an evening party. Broadwoods did not hold the Royal Warrant as a formality; in 1873 they hired grands to the Prince of Wales at Marlborough House and to the Duke of Edinburgh at Clarence House, and in 1874–1876, at Queen Victoria's behest, they restored a Broadwood grand of the same pattern as Beethoven's, which had been supplied in 1817 to Princess Charlotte of Wales, the daughter of George IV. In 1881 they made a grand with brass ornamentation by Wertheimer to the commission of the Duke of Edinburgh. Henry Fowler Broadwood, now 70 himself went to Clarence House to regulate the instrument, and while he was doing so, 'the Duke entered the room and had a long conversation with the venerable piano maker in regard to the accomplishments of certain schemes concerning the Royal College of Music'.[1]

It was one of the last practical duties performed for the firm by Henry Fowler; for in that year, having attained his three-score years and ten, he effectively retired to Lyne (though still remaining a partner, and keeping in touch with Great Pulteney Street and Horseferry Road in a steady stream of correspondence). That year also Thomas Broadwood Jr died. He left £424,000. His shares in the partnership were bequeathed for division among the remaining partners, which meant that there was no immediate shortage of capital.

'Mrs Lyon Hunter' has hired a Broadwood grand and asked her friends round –
and the visiting virtuoso will not play. *(Punch, 8 November 1879)*

The Broadwood name was now famous world-wide. Rudyard Kipling
may have believed (as he wrote in The Song of the Banjo') that 'you
couldn't pack a Broadwood half a mile', in the sense of 'put on a pack-
horse'; but Kipling was profoundly wrong. The company was
meticulously careful about its export packing. Pianos were first wrapped
in tin-foil, then packed rigidly in braced wooden packing-cases. In that
way, they travelled many thousands of miles.

No. 977, a No. 15 model in mahogany, was shipped on the *Dorunda* to
Mr Alex Allen 400 miles up-country in Madras. 'The first box we opened
was the piano which was nicely packed & when taken out of the case and
put up in our drawing room looked just as it came out of the shop, and in
wonderfully good tune; all the people who have called think it splendid.'

Some pianos had still more dramatic journeys. No. 44452, a No. 7
model mahogany cottage piano, was sold to Messrs Miller & Sons of 179
Piccadilly, and then despatched on the *Abernyte* to G. P. Pearce in
Auckland, New Zealand. Mrs Anna Elizabeth Still wrote from
Netheravon Vicarage six years later, in 1882, to describe its travels, after
its arrival in Auckland. 'Thence in a small schooner to Norfolk Island,

where it remained for more than a year in a hot climate, without being tuned. It was then repacked by inexperienced hands, put on board a small schooner again and taken back to Auckland where it was once more unshipped and put on board a sailing vessel and brought to England. Since then it has moved three times—twice in Wiltshire and once to Cheshire. In perfect condition and nothing could be more sweet or true than its tone and touch.'

From Tientsin, China, Miss Ann Michie wrote in 1886 to thank Broadwoods for the safe arrival of her piano—another No. 7 model, No. 58818, this time in rosewood, which had been shipped on the *Ravenna* through Shanghai. Another Broadwood cottage piano sailed round the world with the Royal Navy. In 1890 Mrs Thornton, widow of Captain Thornton R.N., recorded its journey:

> The little cottage piano was chosen for me by Mr John Parry about 1860, and we had it at Southsea till we went to Greenwich (Royal Naval College). We only had it for the year 1873 at Greenwich, as I went over to France and Captain Thornton took it to China with him in H.M.S. Modeste. When Sir George Nares was appointed to command the Arctic Expedition,* my husband was offered the command of the *Challenger*: then in China (Sir George's ship), and of course the little piano was transferred to her from the *Modeste*; and my husband told me one curious fact, that when in the tropics, it went perfectly dumb, and on coming into a cooler climate the sound returned, and in perfect tone and tune. At the same time his violincello (in the tropics) fell actually to pieces, and was repaired by the ship's carpenter. It is needless to say that this Warrant Officer is as good as a thorough cabinet maker.

Perhaps the most formidable journey of a Broadwood piano in the heyday of Empire was that endured by the little pianino that in 1880 travelled up-country in Colombia, South America, to adorn the Ladies School directed there by two English ladies, Miss Blagborne and Mrs McKennan. Mary Blagborne wrote to Broadwoods on 7 October 1880:

> From Honda, the head of the Magellan navigation, such packages have to be brought up by a gang of men, generally indians. These rascals are in the habit, it now appears, & in this case followed their custom, of taking the pianos out of the wooden case as soon as

---

* The then Captain Nares naturally took a Broadwood pianette on that expedition 'for the entertainment of the crew of H.M.S. *Discovery*'.

A Broadwood grand supplied to Archbishop Benson, 1884. Colt Clavier Collection *(Photo: Photographic Records Ltd)*

out of sight of the people who forward them [in this instance, Mr F Stacey, the English consul at Savanilla] and carrying them up in the bare tin [tin-foil], and the box alongside, in order to save weight in the main package.

The pianos thus exposed without proper defence for many hours daily for perhaps a fortnight to the rays of a vertical sun, with alternations of tropical rains, usually arrive here in a sad state of damage. The scoundrels put the piano back in its case on arrival at the beginning of the cart road at this end of the journey and nothing shows signs of meddling until delivery has occurred.

In this instance, a traveller passing saw what they had done, protested, and gave information. Fortunately, owing to the care and skill of your packing, no serious injury has occurred.

Export sales were not only to the expatriate British. As Harry Broadwood told a journalist in 1890:

We have recently despatched a Grand to a wealthy African native, in the interior of Africa; another instrument has recently gone to a part of the Wild West, the chief inhabitants of which are Red Indians. And our trade with India is very large. One of the most extraordinary scenes witnessed in this house was when the celebrated Prime Minister and Commander-in-Chief of Nepal, General S. Jung Bahadur &c &c came to choose an instrument. He had with him his whole suite, in their gorgeous costumes, blazing with jewels. The Court musician, who represented the entire musical department of the Court, tried the pianos with one finger and made the choice. I believe the only man in the General's household who could play any European instrument was his brother, whose capacity extended to playing the first part of 'Rousseau's Dream' on the flute. When a 'Grand Concert' had been secured, it was paid for at once in gold, and while the money was counted on the desk, the whole suite stood round with drawn swords.[2]

The immense solidity of the standard Broadwood grand of the last quarter of the nineteenth century is well described by the singer (Sir) George Henschel. He arrived in London in 1877 as a young man, and having met Walter Broadwood at the Düsseldorf Music Festival two years earlier, took up an invitation to visit Great Pulteney Street. There he found

three adjoining old houses . . . These houses, from cellar to top story, were filled with pianos large and small, and I was struck not only by their quantity and variety, but particularly by the size and appearance of the 'Concert Grands', which seemed to me longer than and altogether different from any I had ever seen before. Nearly all of these were built of oak, coated, like old violins, with a fine golden varnish which retained the colour and the grain of the wood. The joints of the keyboard cases were hidden by bands of

207

33 Great Pulteney Street, doorway (*John Broadwood & Sons Ltd*)

polished brass, fastened by innumerable little brass screws, and the lid was joined to the piano by finely designed massive brass hinges stretching almost across its whole width. These instruments are seen no longer, at least not in this country, and I wonder what can have become of them, as they seemed to be made to last for ever. May be they have found their way into parts of the vast empire across the seas, there, in the durability and strength of which the wood they are made of is the emblem, to bear witness to the staunch solidity of the Mother country.[3]

The 'special' grand designed for the Duke of Edinburgh was one among several completed at this time. In 1878 Broadwoods made a 'Byzantine' grand for the Royal Academician, (Sir) Lawrence Alma Tadema. This amazing instrument was designed for a room in his house—Townsend House, Regent's Park. The room and the piano case were designed by Alma Tadema and executed by G. E. Fox, who was the interior designer at Windsor Castle. The case was on columnar legs of rosewood and ivory, and was inlaid with ebony, tortoiseshell, mother-of-pearl, mahogany, gilding, brass and ivory. The frieze round the edge of the case was inspired by decoration in the church of St Sophia at Constantinople. The inside lid was left comparatively plain, so that Alma Tadema could pin sheets of parchment to it upon which distinguished visitors were invited to sign their names (see page 210).*[4]

When the painter Edward Burne-Jones married in 1860, his aunt gave him a little upright piano. It was by Priestly of Berners Street, and was left plain so that he could paint it, decorating it with a frieze of Pre-Raphaelite women.

But it aroused in Burne-Jones an interest in the piano and its decoration which he communicated to his friend William Morris and Morris's pupil Kate Faulkner. The heaviness of Victorian furniture, and particularly the high gloss Victorian grand with its pie-crust decoration and ugly bulbous legs, jarred on the Pre-Raphaelites' concern with delicacy of form and beauty of expression. In 1878, therefore, Burne-Jones ordered from Broadwood a grand to be built to his own design. He first redesigned the shape of the case, returning to the old harpsichord pattern on a trestle stand. He chose the shape to conform to the line of the strings, believing that he was making form follow function. It was a logical idea, except that it worked only in relation to the outdated straight stringing of the Broadwood (overstringing led to the bulbous tail of, for example, the Steinway). He designed the curve for the bent-side by drawing it freehand on a large sheet of paper in the Broadwood house in Golden Square;[5] and when the curve was compared with the early Broadwood grands, based on the harpsichord shape, it was found to be almost exact. The case was stained a plain olive-green, and on the keyboard the accidentals were stained a green-blue.

A year later, Burne-Jones was commissioned by his friend and business adviser William Graham M.P. to design another grand, for the wedding of Graham's daughter Frances. Once again he adopted the harpsichord shape.

The exterior is sombre, with brown, buff and grey-green details on a deep olive-green stained background. The theme is from Dante's *Vita Nuova*; the roundels along the sides tell the story of Orpheus and Eurydice.[6] The case was painted by the artist's pupils but Burne-Jones himself painted the lid and the details, among them the rose-petals sprinkled on the gilded interior ironwork and soundboard. It is said that

---

* The Alma Tadema piano was destroyed in an air raid during the 1939–45 war.

The 'Alma Tadema' Broadwood grand, 1879 *(The Graphic, 16 August 1879)*

Burne-Jones was inspired by a Van der Meulen painting inside a Ruckers harpsichord of the seventeenth century.[7]

The inside lid is amazing. Mother Earth sits among vines, surrounded by cherubs. The figure of Mother Earth is strange, since the face of a young girl is placed incongruously on the rounded body of a fecund woman; and some of the dusky cherubs, with their pointed ears, Afro haircuts and wicked grins, are distinctly evil. It is said that Burne-Jones, then a married man in his forties, was deeply in love with Frances Graham; and while he was glad at her wedding, he was irritated that she had married another middle-aged man. Certainly the face of Pluto on one roundel, which is said to be a self-portrait of Burne-Jones, is looking peculiarly ill-tempered.[8]

Both the Burne-Jones and the Alma Tadema grands were displayed at the Inventions Exhibition in London in 1885. The young critic of *The Dramatic Review* (George Bernard Shaw) wrote:

THE PARTNERSHIP BREAKS UP

There are two pianofortes in the gallery . . . One of them has been painted by Mr Burne-Jones. The other, the property of Mr Alma Tadema, who designed it, is a stable, massive structure of polished oak, brass, and ivory, with well-proportioned but mechanical lines and curves . . . The bench is a far more humane piece of furniture than the piano, which suggests an expensive American "casket" (coffin). It is difficult to contemplate it for five minutes without looking about for a heavy woodchopper. On the other hand, a musician could live with the instrument painted by Mr Burne-Jones, and like it better every day. Visitors who have not their thinking apparatus ready are disagreeably affected by it at first; but those who know enough to consider that a pianoforte should be taken seriously will come back to have another and another look at it. It is the instrument best worth looking at in the Exhibition, the Stradivarius fiddles and the Rucker's harpsichords not excepted. (19 September 1885)

In 1880 Kate Faulkner was commissioned to decorate a piano, and consulted Burne-Jones, who replied:

Georgie has shown me Mr M's* letter, and I write to explain at more length about it. I have been wanting for years to reform pianos, since they are as it were the very altar of homes, and a second hearth to people, and so hideous to behold mostly that with a fiery rosewood piece of ugliness it is hardly worth while to mend things, since one such blot would and does destroy a whole house full of beautiful things. People won't pay much to have it beautified, but I have a little mended the mere shape of the grand piano, and feel as if one might start a new industry in painting them—or rather a revived industry—only it is important that people should not be frightened at the outset and think that nothing can be done under two or three hundred pounds. I should like Broadwood to be venturesome and have a few of the better shape made on speculation, some only stained, not always green, sometimes other colours, and then a few with here and there an ornament well designed and painted, and at least one covered with ornament, and presently we should see if people would have them or not . . . It would be nice if a man could go to Broadwood and say that he had

* Muir Mackenzie; the piano was made for his wife Amy, another daughter of William Graham, and later passed to their daughter Dorothea, wife of the concert pianist Mark Hambourg. It is now in the Birmingham City Museum and Art Gallery.

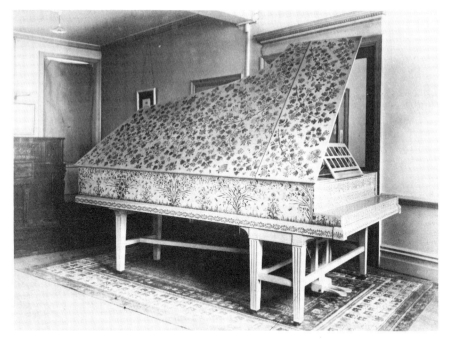

The Emir of Kabul's grand by Broadwood, c.1882 *(The Broadwood Trust)*

even so poor a sum as £20 to be added to the cost of the instrument in order to make its colour lovely, and sometimes a duke would come who would give £1000. So have no fear—Morris & I will come to your help if you are the least puzzled.[9]

A series of ornate Broadwood grands followed Kate Faulkner's completion of this commission. In 1883 Alexander Ionides ordered one for his home in Holland Park. This was in silver on Celadon green. A few years later, Philip Webb collaborated with Kate Faulkner to decorate a Broadwood for W.K. D'Arcy with a pattern of vines and geometrical motifs. One more was done by Kate Faulkner to a Burne-Jones design for the Emir of Kabul; a pattern of spring flowers in silver was worked on a ground of 'granulated Rose du Barry'.

Other artists and architects followed the fashion. Alfred Waterhouse decorated a grand with floral patterns in boxwood and mother-of-pearl. T.G. Jackson designed an ebonised case inlaid with pearwood, satin-wood and mother-of-pearl, interspersed with painted cartouches of musical quotations; the inside lid was vermilion and covered with laurel boughs, gilded on gesso (the medium is plaster, moulded on wood and

Grand by Alfred Waterhouse (architect of Manchester Town Hall). c.1880, in basswood, with mahogany underframe and inlaid ornament in boxwood *(Victoria and Albert Museum)*.

painted).[10] For the Czar of Russia, Broadwoods made a grand in white enamel, gilded 'in the Byzantine style'.*

On completion, these 'artistic pianofortes' were shown off at evening parties at Great Pulteney Street. They kept the company name before fashionable society, and other special commissions resulted: in 1886 (Sir) Henry Irving ordered a grand in inlaid satinwood. In 1893 Broadwoods supplied an upright to 'Dr Conan Doyle, the clever writer of detective stories'.[11] The sheer volume of past production meant that Broadwoods were in use throughout the country: in Malvern, a local choirmaster, Edward Elgar, used a Broadwood square as his domestic instrument.†

These designs were beautiful; but they did not sell. This concentration on artistic decoration was the despair of at least one man in the factory—George Daniel Rose. He could see that for such extravagances to be

---

* The Orpheus piano is still owned by descendants of William Graham. The first Kate Faulkner is in the Birmingham City Museum and Art Gallery; the second, in the Victoria and Albert Museum.

† Now in the possession of John Broadwood & Sons

economically viable, there must be a strong base formed from stock lines that sold. It was not there.

Twenty years later (in a discussion following a paper by William Dale to the Society of Arts) George Rose put the view of a practical piano-maker. His words then give some clue to the nature of the debate that must have raged at Broadwoods at this time.

> Mr Dale had asked: Why is the pianoforte externally the thing we see it (he said)? The simple answer to that was that the pianoforte was what the makers found they were able to sell. If the pianoforte maker were to work upon the lines Mr Dale had suggested, he would be utterly unable to pay his way . . . It was very difficult indeed for the manufacturers to carry out the ideas which Mr Dale and the Chairman [the architect, T.G. Jackson] had so ably put before them. If their clients could only be educated, the manufacturers would be only too glad to make what they knew to be things of beauty . . . It was strange that the instrument Mr Jackson had designed . . . had absolutely never been copied. The reason, surely, was not far to seek. Though we were constantly talking about education in art, as in other things, the public were not yet able to appreciate always what was really beautiful. It was no use asking why the piano was always made of rosewood, and polished like a boot. It was simply because the public wanted it, and would not buy it if it were made of anything else. All his life he had had before him the beautiful examples Mr Dale had shown, and many others, yet he had found it impossible to get the ordinary customer to accept them. There is a discerning class of people, but the ordinary client would say—'Yes, it is very nice, indeed', but would pass good design by. One direction in which improvement might well be made was in that of simplicity. Personally he thought the proportions and the lines of a pianoforte were more important than any other attributes of the design.[12]

The 'artistic pianofortes', therefore, were no technical advance; in fact, they were a retrogression, being based on the harpsichord shape, with straight stringing. However, in 1888 the firm made a major step forward. A patent was taken out in the name of Henry John Tschudi Broadwood (No. 1231) for 'improvements in the metal frame for pianofortes'.

> In place of the metal framing used generally in the manufacture of Pianofortes I use a plate or framing consisting of a single plate of mild steel, the edges of which are formed into a flange or flanges

whereby the necessary strength and rigidity are imparted to the whole. The said flange or flanges may be formed on either or both sides of the said plate or framing and may be continued round the plate or framing. Frames constructed according to this invention possess the advantage of great lightness. This my invention is applicable to both horizontal and upright pianofortes.

The patent was immediately assigned to John Broadwood & Sons. It was the beginning of what was to be the mainspring of the firm for the next decade—the 'barless' piano, and in particular the 'barless concert grand'. Straight stringing rather than overstringing was, however, continued. Though the patent was taken out in the name of Harry Broadwood, the technical ingenuity of the idea suggests that some of the development work may have been done by a young man who had gone through a complete apprenticeship in piano manufacture in both Germany and France—George Daniel Rose. The son of Frederick Rose, he was working at Horseferry Road from at least 1885.* George Daniel Rose was to figure largely in the company's affairs, as the one executive with practical experience of European developments in the piano.

Ranged against him, George Rose had the immense and unchallengeable historical knowledge and experience of Alfred James Hipkins. Hipkins, Fellow of the Society of Antiquaries, was now great in years and reputation. He was the touchstone on whose opinion Henry Fowler Broadwood had relied; his was the judgment that must be satisfied before any special piano could be sent out. He was the British authority on the history of the piano, author of the relevant articles in the *Encyclopaedia Britannica* and in Grove's *Dictionary of Music and Musicians*. He lectured widely, and was an expert on musical pitch.

It can be claimed of Hipkins that he more than any other man was responsible for the revival of 'ancient instruments'. A fine executant himself, he virtually re-introduced the clavichord, giving many admired performances of Bach's Chromatic Fantasia on it. He was also noted for his re-introduction of the Goldberg Variations, which he first played on a double-manual harpsichord in 1892. Hipkins began a trend that paved the way for his rival Arnold Dolmetsch, who built his first harpsichord in 1896.

Hipkins was also a meticulous historian of the Broadwood family and company. However, as a recent piano historian has noted, his publications 'are greatly admired and have influenced the his-

---

* He appears in 1885 as 'Lieut. G. D. Rose' in the annual report of the Broadwood Volunteer Company, whose Captain he became in the following year.

G.D. Rose *(The British and Colonial Piano Journal, April 1906)*

toriography of the piano in England down to the present day, but their prejudice against technical progress was unacceptable even to knowledgeable contemporaries'.[13] Within the company, though he was never a partner, the white-bearded Hipkins in his dark room in Great Pulteney Street was the repository of knowledge and of the law.

A fellow-musician has left this picture of him:

> I honestly believe a gentler, kinder, sweeter man than Alfred James Hipkins never lived. Nor a more modest one. For who, seeing him in his office at the Broadwoods', whose rare privilege it was to profit by his faithful and devoted services for more than threescore of years . . . could have suspected in the simple, silent man the learned author of several standard books on various branches of the science and history of music, and an unrivalled authority on old keyboard instruments, on which he himself was a most accomplished and graceful performer, and of which he possessed several fine specimens? To leave the giddy world and repair to the delightful home of the Hipkinses in Warwick Gardens, there, in the genial company of mutual friends upon a Sunday afternoon to partake of

A.J. Hipkins *(The Broadwood Trust)*

the spirit of simplicity, love, and harmony prevailing in the little household, consisting of father and mother and daughter and son, to listen to and join in the lively conversation from which anything approaching gossip was ever absent, to see the look of supreme content and happiness in our dear host's face as, after a week's toil, he would sit down before his beloved harpsichord or clavichord and play us a Bach or Scarlatti in masterly fashion, has been among the purest joys of my life. Dear Hipkins![14]

Any innovation therefore had to run the gauntlet of Hipkins's immeasurable experience and knowledge. Of his devotion to the firm and the family there can be do doubt; his whole life was given over to the greatness of Broadwood, and he was particularly proud that through his mother's family, the Grants of Rothiemoon, he shared Scottish origins with the Broadwood family.[15] There is no doubt, either, that he had thought long and seriously about the two questions of overstringing and the single-cast iron frame. Both are dealt with in some detail in his book on the history of the pianoforte (1896). He mentions that a suggestion for overstringing came from Theobald Boehm, the improver of the flute, in a letter to Walter Stewart Broadwood; Boehm claimed to have suggested it to a London piano-maker in 1831. That maker (Gerock and Wolf of Cornhill) was against it 'because it disturbed the action and cost more'. Hipkins also described and illustrated the full iron frame as introduced in America by Chickering and Steinway. He noted, correctly, that 'in upright pianos the single casting has become universal . . . and overstringing prevails in the larger upright instruments of America and Germany'.

Why, then, did he reject these innovations? He gives no clue to the refusal of overstringing; but of the iron frame he says: 'The tendency to be feared is that pianoforte making may become mechanical from the fixity implied by systems of casting, but owing to the tighter straining of the strings, in combination with the influence exerted by masses of iron in large castings, there is obtained in the pianoforte a more *sostente* or singing tone, and the instrument stands longer in tune'.[16]

Throughout the 1880s, therefore, Broadwoods refused to adopt overstringing; and it was not until 1888 that the 'barless' piano was patented, with a metal plate in a single casting of very expensive mild or cast steel. Hipkins considered that 'it is an ideal construction, and the musical instrument thus produced is of singular beauty and equality of tone'.[17]

In April 1886 the Abbé Liszt, visiting London for the last time, played a Broadwood grand at a reception in his honour at the Grosvenor Gallery, and wrote a note commending the piano's character. Liszt always was generous with his testimonials; and it may be noted that George Bernard Shaw was asserting at about the same time (*The Dramatic Review*, 25 July 1885) that 'the old-fashioned English piano is not . . . likely to maintain itself on the concert platform against the much richer and more powerful instruments made on the American system'.

By 1895 the firm had overcome its prejudice against advertising and published a lavish 'Album of Artistic Pianofortes'. The tone is set by the preface, where it is claimed that 'It will at least be evident, that the responsibility of making no pianos save those which are truly works of art, is fully realised by The reader's most obedient servants, John Broadwood & Sons'. The Album lists six basic grands, and six uprights. The short (6 ft 3 ins) grand was available in rosewood, walnut or ebonised; or in a 'decorated' form in Adam or Louis XV style in Spanish mahogany, satinwood, rosewood or mahogany. 'Inlaid scrolls and trophies, and the standards (or twin-columns) are rounded and prettily carved'. The boudoir grand (7 ft 1 in.) was available in rosewood, burr walnut or mahogany. The semi-grand (7 ft 3 ins) was in rosewood, burr walnut or

Oak grand by Broadwood, c.1890

black wood. The drawing room concert grand was 7 ft 9 ins, the concert grand 8 ft 6 ins, and the 'barless' concert grand was also offered.

As many styles of upright were available as grands. The number of homes with drawing rooms, large enough to house a 7 ft 9 ins grand was already declining. A new market had opened up for the bijou upright:

> Customers who live in residential flats with artistically furnished rooms of small size have often-times raised an objection that pianofortes of good tone occupy too much space. The extreme portability of this class of piano has rendered it in request, not only by purchasers living in residential flats many storeys above ground—where a lift is seldom provided of sufficient strength to bear the weight of so heavy an instrument as a full-sized piano—but by military officers on foreign service constantly moving from one station to another, to whom every extra inch in height or extra pound in weight is of consideration.

Nevertheless the bijou was offered in Chippendale or Adam style, either in satinwood or Spanish mahogany, 'tastefully inlaid'; also

219

'blackwood or solid mahogany for tropical climates'. A morning-room piano had been 'supplied to HRH The Duke of York on board H.M.S. *Melampus*'; it seems improbable that he often played it, for the future King George V said in later years that he spent much of his time on *Melampus* being seasick.

The upright grand was available as standard in a variety of woods, and even with 'almost invisible electrical connections fitted to the candle brackets at a slight extra cost'. Electricity was now replacing gas for domestic lighting. One oddity in this album is the Japanese upright:

> The external appearance of this Piano is quaint to a degree. At a time when the attention of Europe is drawn by War to the Far East, Japanese fashions and industrial artwork have become endued with absorbing interest. The casing is of Andaman Redwood or Padouk . . . The surface is here stained a subdued violet black, or brown-black, according to the tint of the panels, being finished off dull, with the grain or pores of the wood left open. The panels are embellished with skilfully manipulated reliefs of coloured ivory, mother-of-pearl, and metal, executed by an accomplished native artist in Osaka, Japan.

The Pianette was a miniature piano: 'For Chambers, Schools, Barrack-rooms, House-boats, Shooting Lodges and Yachts. It has been transported on camel-back across sandy deserts or on the heads of coolies through rugged wilds in tropical parts, on the other hand it has well withstood the rigours of an Arctic winter, as when an instrument was taken to the far North in the British Polar expedition of 1875 by Captain Nares for the entertainment of the crew of H.M.S. *Discovery*.'

The Album included testimonials from Lord Tennyson—'The pianoforte is an excellent one and has kept in marvellously good tune. It was used as an accompaniment to Herr Joachim on this last day (after six weeks' use without being tuned) and approved by him'; from Richard Wagner—'The tone of the Broadwood pianofortes reminds me of the character of the old Cremona violins'; and Franz Liszt—'No Pianofortes last so well as those of Broadwood'.

Considering the extraordinary variety of styles on offer, it is scarcely surprising that the *Timber Trades Journal* could remark that 'The Broadwoods put by their wood as carefully as the Apician lays down his best brands of wine. This Thames wharf offers therefore an unique object-lesson in dendrology. Inside, we were brought face to face with fallen giants from the tropical jungle, from the silent Australian bush, from the dense backwoods of the Wild West, and from the stately and historic wealds of England . . . Messrs Broadwood probably possess the largest and finest stock of rosewood belonging to any one firm in the world.'

Despite this grandiose public image, Broadwoods were in difficulties that year. The challenge came mainly from the development of high-quality upright pianos, and by the exploitation of the cheaper upright in Britain. Simultaneously, the market in which Broadwoods had been supreme—the domestic grand in the homes of landed gentry and professional classes throughout the country—became impoverished by the agricultural slump in the last two decades of the century.

At home, a number of firms arose in Britain making cheaper uprights, notably that of John Brinsmead & Son which, founded in 1837, was by 1890 manufacturing about one thousand pianos a year, most of them uprights.[18] Brinsmeads accompanied their growth with a massive campaign of publicity and promotion. There were also considerable numbers of one-man businesses turning out uprights that were often shoddy as well as cheap; but it was the '"medium class" manufacturers, as they were called in the trade, [who] grew to increasing importance. Unhampered and unassisted by such legacies of the past as an ageing skilled-labour force, commitment to old designs and techniques, superfluous capital or a famous name, [they] built up a steady trade in modern upright instruments'.[19]

The market grew with the introduction of hire purchase—known as the 'Three Year System'—from 1878, though for many years it was the subject of litigation to establish the rights of ownership in hired instruments.

A no less dangerous challenge came in the 1880s from the German manufacturers, particularly Bechstein and Blüthner. By adopting the 'American' iron frame and also overstringing, the Germans began to export in increasing quantity to Britain and what had hitherto been a British export market, Australia. The value of U.K. imports of musical instruments from Germany rose from about £600,000 in 1875 to well over £1 million in 1891.[20] This was achieved by efficient and economical production (including, for example, the centralisation of action-making) allied to intelligent marketing techniques—well-briefed salesmen, multilingual catalogues and reliable delivery.

The response in Britain was complacent. A British Government Blue Book of reports from H.M. Consulates (1885) notes that

The pianoforte makers have bitter complaints to urge against the

Tariff of the United States, but they do not speak of benefits received from their own. A very eminent and successful German manufacturer informs me that, in his opinion, good German pianos stand very much on the level of Broadwoods and Collards, being, on the whole, as sonorous, mellow and durable. The equality is for instruments of all sizes . . . Some time since, the Germans had been walking away from our makers in the way of improvement, but we had now caught up the lost ground.[21]

Broadwoods gave evidence, and in reply to the question: 'Are German pianos and uprights, as sold in England, cheaper (and how much so) than English pianos of equivalent make as to goodness and appearance?' they said:

German pianos are no longer cheaper in England than English pianofortes. Some ten years ago, when the former came into the home and colonial British market, they met with great favour, being louder and cheaper, and interfered seriously with home-made instruments. But gradually the English makers improved their pianofortes so much, that there are unmistakeable signs that they are rapidly recovering lost ground, and will very probably once more beat the Germans in the market, being superior to them for tone, design and workmanship, and durability, and equally low in price. This reply applies mainly to what are called second and third-rate pianofortes. The first-class English houses are still unapproached by the Germans, where the desiderata sought are those qualities of tone and finish which are essential in a perfect musical instrument . . . The German pianofortes are generally inferior in variety and beauty of design to the English.[22]

At the top end of the market, the increasingly important showcase of the concert platform, Broadwoods were also under challenge. The Steinway iron frame and overstrung concert grand was coming to rival the Broadwood; and, once Steinways had opened their Hamburg factory in the early 1880s and so were able to reduce transport costs in Europe, Broadwoods were no longer able to undercut them in price (both sold in London for £300).

There was some consolation, and prestige, to be gained from the Gold Medal awarded to Broadwood at the International Inventions Exhibition of 1885. But Gold Medals did not necessarily impress the market.

222

Symptomatic was the loss between 1880 and 1900, almost by default, of the Australian market. The Germans launched their export attack at the Melbourne Exhibtion of 1882, when forty three German makers took part. The older British firms, Broadwood among them, did not show. One importer said that 'Broadwood, Erard and Collard think it beneath their dignity to solicit business'.[23] The consequence was that while in 1880 Australians were spending at least ten times as much on English as on German pianos, by 1900 the pattern was exactly reversed in a vastly expanded market.[24]

Yet Broadwoods had earlier put some effort into the Australian market. In 1873 they sent out a grand for a tour by the popular concert pianist Arabella Goddard*, who was a friend of Henry Fowler Broadwood: as the *Sydney Morning Herald* reported:

The public of Sydney have narrowly escaped a great disappointment. Up till 10 o'clock this morning it was extremely probable that Madame Arabella Goddard's concert would have to be postponed. The concert iron grand piano sent out by Messrs. Broadwood & Sons for her use in Sydney arrived last week by the *Aviemore*; but owing to the weather, the ship was unable to discharge. Fortunately, there was a change this morning, and by extraordinary exertions the instrument, which is priced in Broadwood's list at 280 guineas, was found and landed. All the arrangements for the concert are therefore perfect.

In 1890, in an effort to recover the ground lost in Australia, Broadwoods financed a coast-to-coast tour of that country by Sir Charles and Lady Hallé. It was launched at a musical reception in Great Pulteney Street in April, which proved perilously popular: too many invitations were sent out, the streets of Soho came to a standstill with traffic, and many guests could not get into the house.

The Australian tour, taking in Geelong, Melbourne, Ballarat, and Sydney, was a personal success for Hallé, who cheerfully acquiesced in some business promotion; as he noted in his journal in Melbourne that August: 'Mr Rose [Algernon Rose, who was acting as concert-master] was waiting to conduct me to the branch establishment of Broadwood's here, which was to be inaugurated yesterday. There I found thirty to forty musicians, writers and friends assembled, and a large array of bottles of

* Arabella Goddard (1836–1922), concert pianist, and friend of Sterndale Bennett, whose piano concerto she often performed. She attracted considerable audiences at the Crystal Palace and the Monday Popular Concerts, and in 1859 married J. W. Davison.

champagne. Speeches were made, healths drunk, and prosperity wished to the new establishment, which indeed promises well . . .'[25]

Rose's comments on German pianos in Australia, when he returned, were supercilious. They were 'very pretentious in appearance, very cheap in price, and uncommonly shoddy in quality'.[26] However, they were selling.

The Hallé tour was said to have cost £10,000. It did not recoup its cost in sales.

Within the partnership, and indeed the family, there was discord. The 1880s proved to be a lull before the storm. During that decade, Henry Fowler saw both his sons marry. In 1884 James, the elder, married Evelyn (Eve) Fuller-Maitland, daughter of one of Henry Fowler's closest friends; Harry, the younger, in 1886 married Ada, the daughter of a Surrey neighbour, Admiral Sir Leopold Heath. Ada was to take the keenest interest in the company and its workforce. In 1890, for example, she organised an immense Christmas party at Westminster Town Hall for a thousand children of Broadwood workmen. She also regularly gave away the prizes to the Broadwood Rowing Club, which was started in 1892.

But then the tragedies began. On an evening in July 1888 Henry Fowler Broadwood, then in his seventies but still active, went to close the curtains in the drawing room at Lyne. He pulled them as vigorously as ever; inadvertently he dislodged the heavy wooden curtain-pole. Falling, it struck his head. He was concussed, and for some days it seemed that he would be permanently paralysed. Though after a time he recovered his mental faculties, most of the remaining years of his life were spent in a wheel-chair. He was cared for by his wife Julia; and from the time of his accident his eldest unmarried daughter, Bertha, dealt with those business affairs that still needed his attention.

Bertha had long been the 'manager' in the Lyne household. Vitally energetic, she had created her own life, and a very full life it was. At the time of the agricultural depression, she had studied everything she could find on the rights of land-owners, corresponded with people in a similar predicament all over Europe, and wrote numerous articles, closely argued, which were published.

She was concerned, too about the responsibilities of land-owners, and rallied the wealthy wives of rural Surrey to organise, and pay for, nurses and home helps to look after the poor in rural districts. Her organisation became known as the 'Holt–Ockley System', was taken up throughout Britain, and became one of the first provisions of a district nursing

Presentation of prizes to the Broadwood Rowing Club, 1892 *(The Illustrated Sporting and Dramatic News, 26 November 1892)*

system. Bertha travelled all over the country, lecturing women's groups, recruiting nurses and setting up homes for them.*

In the same month that Henry Fowler fell ill, the elder of the Rose brothers, George Thomas Rose, wrote expressing a wish to retire at Michaelmas 1889 from, as he put it, 'those duties which I have for so many years (half a century) continuously discharged'. That was agreed. But Henry Fowler's illness had an impact in another quarter. In Malvern, Walter Stewart Broadwood heard of his elder brother's illness, and was much disturbed. He remembered that in 1880 and 1881, certain amendments had been made to the Articles of Agreement of the partnership, to establish that if any partner died or left the partnership, he should be entitled to receive from the partners succeeding to his shares

---

* Bertha Broadwood's organisation of a 'home help' provident nursing system with some eight hundred cottage nurses, 4 per cent of whom were certified midwives, has been described as 'very largely a one-woman achievement and no inconsiderable one'. Though the Holt-Ockley system was strongly opposed by the Queen's Institute as unprofessional, Mary Stocks's judgement is that the nurses 'fulfilled a need and brought comfort to many poor homes' (*see* Mary Stocks, *A Hundred Years of District Nursing*, Allen & Unwin, London, 1960).

'the amount standing to the credit of the partners so dying or ceasing to be a member of the firm'; and the second amendment added that 'the firm shall be primarily responsible to the partner who shall cease to be a member of the firm . . . or to the executors'.

The purpose of these clauses (to which the Rose brothers objected at the time, though Walter Stewart accepted them) was to ensure that the daughters of Henry Fowler and Walter Stewart could obtain any monies bequeathed to them, that might be tied up in the firm; for it was axiomatic that daughters would not wish to leave their capital in the firm.

But much had changed in ten years. The profits had dropped from over £30,000 p.a. in the early 1880s to £16,000 in 1888. Walter was worried that on Henry Fowler's death the company might collapse, and he be responsible for paying legacies owing to Henry Fowler's six daughters living, as the surviving partner. He formally notified Great Pulteney Street of his intention to retire from the partnership.

The other partners at this time consisted of Henry Fowler, his son Harry, and the two Rose brothers, George Thomas and Frederick. In Henry Fowler's absence, Harry Broadwood and the Rose brothers took the valuation of the company in the way it had always been done; and they reckoned that Walter Broadwood was entitled to £56,000 and George Rose to £15,000. This produced an immediate shortage of capital. To provide cash, it was agreed that Henry Fowler would authorise his elder son James to obtain mortgages on the Lyne estate, put £30,000 into the company, and become a partner.

An approach was made privately to Walter Stewart Broadwood to postpone payment. He was invited to Lyne to discuss the matter, but refused to go. He intimated that unless he were paid over the seven years established by the partnership agreement, he would sue the partners for the last farthing. The partnership was thenceforward required to pay £6,000 to Walter Stewart Broadwood* and George T. Rose for each of the following seven lean years.

A son, Stewart Henry Tschudi, was born to Ada and Harry Broadwood in 1888: a second son, Leopold Alfred Tschudi, was to follow in 1890. But tragedy struck the family yet again when in 1889 Eve (James's wife) died at Malvern a few days after giving birth to her third child and only son (he was christened Evelyn Henry Tschudi Broadwood).

In December 1891 Harry wrote to Bertha that yet another £30,000 was

---

* Walter Stewart Broadwood died in 1898, leaving a personal estate of £143,332.

needed in the business 'as we are hampered in every way in pushing an increased demand for good cheap instruments as well as expensive ones, and without proper machinery and money to buy wood when it is going cheap, we can not make nearly the profits in any class of instruments as we used to ten years ago'.

The family then began to sound out relatives and friends to try and find a new source of capital. They approached the Pryor family. Robert Pryor had been Henry Fowler's best friend at Trinity College, Cambridge, and had shared many sporting holidays with his brother-in-law, both having married daughters of Wyrley Birch. He was a wealthy barrister (his mother was a daughter of the banker, Samuel Hoare). His eldest son, Marlborough Pryor, had been a merchant in South America and was now chairman of the Sun Insurance Company, and the Sun Life Assurance Society. Of Robert Pryor's other sons, the third, Selwyn, had been a contemporary of James Broadwood at Eton and Cambridge. The fourth son, Francis, was a Lloyd's underwriter. The Pryors examined the firm's books and decided not to come in. But Marlborough Pryor kept a watching brief.

By January 1893 it began to seem that the firm must be wound up. The capital to keep it going had now risen to £35,000. Marlborough Pryor was approached again. Again he refused. The next door neighbour of the Broadwoods at Lyne was a Mr Harben, deputy chairman of the Prudential Assurance Company. He was interested in taking an option on part of the Lyne estate. With James's concurrence, Bertha put this to her father. Old Henry Fowler vetoed it: 'I will *not*,' he said. 'James may do what he pleases presently.'

Bertha, now so deeply involved in the affairs of John Broadwood & Sons, began to be critical of the firm's management, and in particular of her younger brother Harry. She wrote a tough letter to her sister Lucy, already becoming well-known as a collector of folk songs. It elicited the following reply, which with some accuracy describes the predicament of the company and its managers at this time:

I think you are mistaken in thinking that H. [Harry] and others do not realise the grave state of affairs . . . H. and Ada often said to me that if matters came to the worst we all should suffer. I repeat that it seems extraordinary that *all* the partners (not H. in particular) did not a year ago make a formal statement of affairs, & some great effort.

As to new machinery, that was *absolutely necessary*, for the reason that Father & the other elder partners had not, with their old &

227

inefficient machines, kept up a *quarter* enough stock of pianos; people applied, could get no pianos, & went elsewhere. *This year* for the first time the proper & necessary stock has been turned out, & that is at the cost of workmen doing extra hours every day last year for months. One cannot tell poor Father that it is owing to the inferiority of the pianos which were made during the latter years of his time, and the persistence in most extravagant ways of carrying on business, & the objection to walking with the times, that lost client after client to the house of J. B. This is *absolutely true*, & it is just as true that *now*, as Mr G. Rose said to me the other day (& also Mr Hipkins), 'Whereas for years we had to deal with complaints we *now* get the highest praise'.

Father has not been told (*and is not to be . . .*) that important alterations (one* which is universal, but which he always refused to adopt) have already brought us pianists who hitherto declined to play on our instruments. It should have been adopted years ago, & is certainly right. I add a few other improvements which I know are due to H.

A full and orderly ledger system (not used before).

A formation of a company of tuners, who absorb practically the whole tuning business of London etc.—the firm makes some 1,000s by this arrangement.

Institution of telephones & other modern arrangements, thereby doing away with a staff of expensive messengers & thereby saving time.

Saving largely in fuel, etc.

Incalculable improvement in artistic quality of instruments.

These I consider weigh very heavy in the balance.

H. readily confesses that what they want is a man of *business* in the firm. He will certainly never be one himself, any more (or less) than our Father, of whom Uncle Tom told me our grandfather said: 'He is an excellent piano-maker but a shocking man of business.'

It seems to me *the* point—and a very important one—to place before Mr Upton [the Estate solicitor] or Robert Dobbs, and to impress on Father when the time comes is this: That the Firm is now

---

* Overstringing. However, not all authorities would consider Henry Fowler to be wrong: 'Thanks to this compacter arrangement of the strings, the over-strung Piano is shorter than the old type. At the same time—if the pedal is raised—the close proximity of the strings increases the wealth of overtones, and therefore the volume of sound. The tone of the over-strung Piano has not, however, the limpidity of the older instruments.'—Karl Geiringer.

The outdoor tuners' trip to Brighton, 1897 *(John Broadwood & Sons Ltd)*

suffering for the mistakes of years ago, i.e. for the mistakes of the elder partners.

Had they been *ordinarily* prudent, and had they stored up reasonably against a rainy day, the younger partners of today would not be in such a plight at present. Not a penny put by for machinery, for emergencies!

Therefore it is for the elder partners to make reparation. Two of the elders have retired but Father is still able to do something. The elders have had all the cream and the youngers all the skim milk and sorrow.

As H. is not business-like he should all the more have been put through the account-work as a youth, as a preparation. He never was, & was never enlightened as to the workings at all. Cuthbert Heath, I remember hearing once, was instructed from a small boy upwards with a view to his calling, & began at Lloyds as filler of ink-

The Ockley cricket team and supporters, 1880. (Back row, third from left) Cuthbert Heath; (to his left) Harry Broadwood. (Front row, second from left) James Broadwood.

pots & book-keeper. If H. had had that training it would have been good indeed . . . As an artistic inventor he is, as Mr Hipkins said to me more than once, 'A most remarkable pianoforte maker'.

Cuthbert Heath was Harry's brother-in-law. The Heaths were neighbours of the Broadwoods in Surrey; Admiral Sir Leopold Heath, ADC to Queen Victoria, had been one of the most distinguished of naval officers (and beachmaster at the Crimea landings). The Heath children and the Broadwood children had grown up together. Cuthbert had always been a rather isolated boy, because of chronic deafness. His brothers followed their father into the Royal Navy, but Cuthbert, after Brighton College and a period in Bonn, had been put to work in the City as a clerk.

There—perhaps compensating for his 'failure' to be healthy as a boy—he was already laying the foundations of an immense success in the world of insurance. At this time, in fact, he was preparing to launch his own company, C. E. Heath & Co, which he did in 1894. He was thus the most materially successful of the generation of the younger Broadwoods; wealthy, a man of substance, in his mid-thirties. The Broadwoods were very well aware of him, since he took part in family holidays, and had been to stay with the Dobbs in Ireland.

Having read Lucy's letter, Bertha wrote her brother Harry a letter more notable for its briskness than its encouragement:

No doubt your work is very similar to Father's between 1838 and 1870. He found elders' arrangements antiquated and worked away very hard to secure a fortune for himself and his children (being 2nd son remember). Then in 1856 his younger children's fortunes were 'burnt up'* as he expressed it, & had to be remade! Of course neither he nor any of the elders 15 years ago foresaw the present competition and diminution of trade. Nor I suppose had you sufficiently acquainted yourself with the accounts to warn them that you were all partly living upon capital.

Pray don't pity yourself for having to work hard, it's far better & safer for mind & body than want of occupation. Your business may not be exactly what you would have chosen, but it has its advantages . . . Not to use is to lose powers whether of muscle, mind, or position . . .

There was a good deal of the cold-bath cure-all about Bertha. Harry was stung into a reply which describes some of the changes in the firm, and in business life in Victorian England:

My mother and you write as if you thought that in endorsing cheques I had to sign my own name . . . It is entirely in Mr Fred Rose's department to open letters & endorse cheques, & George Rose & I come to his aid at this season of the year, when one opens the letters & the others endorse . . . By the time you have finished 200 cheques your hand will be tired and your brain will not be as fresh as when you started.

You compare the business now with what it was between 1838 and 1870; there is no comparison; in the first place we had not a tithe of the tunings, no one thought of writing a cheque under £5, there were no 'postal orders', & people used to come in to pay their accounts in cash. When I first came here in '79 I have seen as many

* In the fire at Horseferry Road.

William Cary Dobbs, *c.* 1895 *(Lucy Broadwood collection)*

as twenty people waiting to pay their accounts at the same time. Nowadays it is very rare for anyone to come in person. My father in the memory of Fred Rose never did any office work at all. It was done by Mr Rose's father & another cashier with a clerk or two. My father always looked after the instruments & left the writing to other people . . .

On the day that Harry wrote that letter, Bertha was making two arrangements. The first was to obtain her father's signature on a document that would release a further £35,000 to the firm, in the name of her brother James, who became a partner. The second was to introduce into the company the son of her legal adviser and brother-in-law Robert Dobbs as an executive partner. Educated at Winchester, William Cary Dobbs had done well at Cambridge: tipped as a Wrangler, he had come eighth in the Mathematical Tripos. Bertha called him 'the most competent of my father's grown-up grandsons'. Neither James nor Harry Broadwood was much attracted by this development.

Henry Fowler Broadwood died at Lyne on 8 July 1893, aged eighty two. He was carried to his rest in the family vault in Rusper church with

King George IV's Broadwood grand. This 'elegant grand' with its brass trim
was sent to Brighton Pavilion on 21 December 1821 *(Colt Clavier Collection)*
(Photo: Meier, Thun, Bern, Switzerland)

an escort of farmworkers and gamekeepers from the estate which he had so loved. It was a fitting tribute to a fine sportsman, and it was recalled that until his accident, and well into his seventies, he could bring down a rocketing pheasant, and would wade into Scottish salmon-rivers up to his waist and land a struggling thirty-pounder that a younger man would fail to master.

His generosity was extreme. Indeed, he carried generosity to a fault. Having grown up in a situation of very substantial wealth, he enjoyed it in every way he could, and encouraged others to enjoy it. Building, creating, expanding, he was amazing in his self-confidence.

For the high years of Victorian prosperity he was 'Mr Broadwood'. The firm was him. He ruled it autocratically, and his word was law. He was immensely and completely proud of it—of its history, its traditions and its standards. The *Music Trades Review* called him 'one of the most conscientious and profoundly scientific of pianoforte makers'.

Yet he misjudged the two great innovations in piano construction in his time: the introduction of the single-casting iron frame, and of overstringing. There were good reasons for his decisions, and many in his position might have made the same choices. Unfortunately they were wrong.

It was merciful that Henry Fowler did not live to see an advertisement published two months later in the *Scotsman*. It quoted a conversation between Queen Victoria and an Italian concert pianist: 'After the concert, Her Majesty conversed cordially with Signor Buonamici, and asked him what instrument he preferred. Signor Buonamici replied that he preferred the Bechstein piano, and Her Majesty said that she held the same opinion.'[27]

It was still more merciful that Henry Fowler did not live to see a concert programme of the following year (1894) in which Sir Charles Hallé, whom Henry Fowler had helped as a young man, was quoted in these terms: 'I corroborate with pleasure Liszt's, Rubinstein's and Bülow's expressions of admiration for the Bechstein Pianos. I have now so frequently preferred to use the excellent Grands for my concerts that I cannot help acknowledging gratefully their splendid qualities. Their beautiful singing tone in the greatest forte as well as in the most delicate pianissimo is always noble, and capable of the most refined expression.'

When Henry Fowler Broadwood's will was published in the following November, there was astonishment when his personal estate was only £71,407. It was pointed out that his cousin Thomas Broadwood Jr had left £424,000 thirteen years earlier. Rumours began to circulate about the firm; and there was even public criticism of the pianos.

The *Pall Mall Gazette* commented: 'We do not suggest that there was anything wrong with the Broadwood grand upon which Fanny Davies played, but every now and then the strangest discordant jingling noises fluttered, as it were, about the body of the music; and, as far as we could judge, the jangle came from the piano itself.[28] In contrast, the critic of *The Times* found space in several notices to commend 'the fine Broadwood grand'; but then, he was Fuller-Maitland, James Broadwood's brother-in-law.

The firm was in a battle, and the music critics recognised the fact. George Bernard Shaw, the critic of *The World*, wrote (25 February 1891):

It is no longer true of the Broadwoods, as it was twelve years ago, that they had fallen so far behind the time as to make their then monopoly of the concert platform a nuisance to themselves, to the public, and to the artists, upon whose gratitude they had strong and perfectly honorable claims. The monopoly is now broken down; the full force of the competition of Steinway, Erard, Bechstein, and Pleyel has been brought to bear on them; and the result is that they have enormously increased the power of their instruments without sacrificing the artistic individuality and homogeneity of tone which always distinguished their pianofortes from the massive overstrung machines which first put them out of countenance.

However, the physical force now being exerted in concert performances was such that things could go wrong, as Shaw recorded at a recital by Adeline de Lara at the Crystal Palace two months later (*The World*, 29 April 1891); 'The particular Broadwood in question so resented her handling that it ruptured a hammer and stopped the performance. When, after much disconsolate contemplation of the interior of the instrument by everybody in the neighbourhood, she consented to proceed with one note dumb, the maimed member extemporized a castanet and tambourine accompaniment by clattering and jingling among the strings.'

In the months that followed Henry Fowler Broadwood's death, Bertha discussed the position with her unmarried sisters Amy and Lucy. Each was entitled to £8,000 under their father's will. Under Bertha's leadership, they agreed that they would leave their inheritance in the company. On 1 December 1893, an agreement was signed empowering James and Harry Broadwood to introduce to the partnership William Cary Dobbs, with effect from 27 September 1894 (the end of the next financial year).

Henry Fowler's widow, Julia, moved out of Lyne, which was let from February 1894. Never, in the four years that remained to her, is she known to have uttered a word of complaint or blame for the events that had clouded her last years. When she died, she was remembered as a kindly, gentle and forgiving old lady, far more concerned for her children and grandchildren than about herself.

Within the factory, there was urgent action to modernise the instruments; to introduce an iron frame in addition to the costly barless steel frame, and to bring in overstringing. In February 1896 Broadwoods sent round a circular to all dealers announcing two new models of upright 'with overstrung scale'. The pianette 'now has the full iron frame'. And there was an announcement of 'an overstrung Grand which we are introducing, 6 ft 4 ins in length, which has been pronounced by many competent judges to be the finest short Grand ever offered to the public'. An iron frame concert grand followed, and was first used in public (No. 44752) at a concert in the St James's Hall on 26 February 1897.

These new instruments were certainly effective. One of them greatly impressed Bernard Shaw, who heard it played by Fanny Davies at the Hindhead Hall and wrote in the local newspaper (*The Farnham, Haslemere and Hindhead Herald*, 17 December 1898):

> Such a piano! When its clangour first burst on my ears, I wondered what new maker had astonished the world. Judge of my surprise when, standing up to look at the instrument, I saw it bore the familiar name of Broadwood. When I shook the dust of musical criticism from my feet in 1894, I certainly did not think that the world would stand still on that account; time and change, I knew, would pursue their accustomed revolutionary work. But one thing I knew to be impossible, and that was that Broadwoods would ever overstring their pianos. Yet, after four years, here was an overstrung Broadwood, beside which the modest and retiring Steinway grand of the previous concert would have been 'banged into dumbness'. They even tell me that this uproarious instrument is not the latest Broadwood achievement, which is barless, and audible for miles in reasonable weather.

Throughout the 1890s Broadwoods remained in touch with the artist-craftsmen of the day. Following the tradition revived by Ruskin, William Morris and Burne-Jones, the Arts and Crafts movement actively attempted to improve the standards of industrial design. Burne-Jones had 'improved' the grand; the architect Hugh Baillie Scott* in 1896

* M. H. Baillie Scott (1865–1945), domestic architect.

The 'Manxman' upright by Baillie Scott. This example has a case of ebonised wood with roundeli of pewter, carved wood flowers and marquetry with stained ivory embellishments *(Victoria and Albert Museum)*.

produced a most unusual design for the upright. The upper part of the piano was encased in a cupboard-like frame with folding doors at the front, which opened to reveal keyboard, music-desk and candle-holders. The original was of oak, stained green (in the William Morris fashion), and the heavy iron hinges were a feature of the design. It was named the 'Manxman' (Baillie Scott came from the Isle of Man). Versions of the same design were produced by Broadwoods for various artists, notably

236

A detail from the front door of the 'Manxman'.

C. R. Ashbee.† One of Ashbee's designs was in Spanish mahogany with satinwood panels, the interior lined with white holly; another was of mahogany with black and white patterned inlay; yet a third was of light oak, its decoration derived from the heavy beaten ironwork of the hinges (the last commissioned for Peter Jones, the store owner).

When Ashbee married in 1898, he gave his wife as a wedding present a Broadwood grand of his own unusual design. It is a 'square piano' in a literal sense, since the whole immense and extremely heavy case of light oak is square. The top is divided into two halves, which prop open from the middle line. The beaten iron hinges are each four feet long, bearing the 'bee' image that Ashbee usually applied to his work. The interior is veneered in sycamore, painted and stained in shades of apple green, blue and lilac, with Art Nouveau illustrations of young women playing instruments in fronded groves. The accidentals of the keyboard are of wood, stained dark brown; the iron frame is most unusual, since it is not a single casting but made of several castings, painted apple green and assembled with immense nuts and bolts left in natural metal.

The piano (see Plate 13) is now at Toynbee Hall, London where

† C. R. Ashbee (1863–1942), architect and director of the Guild of Handicrafts.

Ashbee was a supporter of the universities' settlement. The design was copied at least once, in 1902 by T. Middleton Shawcross with painting by F. C. Varley.

In the summer of 1901 when the commission collecting items for an exhibition of English decorative art to be held in Budapest the following year asked Broadwoods to supply two uprights 'designed by well-known artists upon the lines of the new school of decorative design', they naturally asked 'Mr H. B. Scott and Mr C. R. Ashbee' to provide them. Another young architect was similarly commissioned to provide piano cases. (Sir) Edwin Lutyens was making his name by the country houses he was building in Surrey, Sussex and Berkshire. In these houses Lutyens was an exponent of 'total design'; he would design not only the houses, but the furniture to go into them—including the piano. In 1900 he designed for Broadwoods a grand in a case of panelled oak which won the Gold Medal at the Paris Exhibition that year (see Plate 12) and was subsequently displayed at Great Pulteney Street in March 1901. Lutyens thereafter designed several more Broadwoods for the houses he was then building.

When in January 1898 the Incorporated Society of Musicians held its annual conference in London, the members toured the factory in Horseferry Road. A booklet produced for the occasion noted the modern changes: 'A visit to the Westminster manufactory by one who was there, say, ten years ago, will show what remarkable changes have of late taken place in the method of production. Whereas at one time the pianoforte maker was exclusively a cabinet-maker, nowadays—when certain grand pianos have to withstand an aggregate tension of over 30 tons—he is, to a great extent, an engineer.'

The musicians went on to Great Pulteney Street, where Walter Macfarren eulogised the greatness of Broadwoods: 'Where now, I should like to ask, is the house of Silbermann, which made harpsichords for Frederick the Great—like this firm? Where now is the firm of Stein of Augsburg, which made instruments for Mozart—like this firm? Where now are the once great firms of Stodart, Southwell, Tomkinson, and the special rival of Broadwood, Kirkman? They have all vanished into thin air, and, to use the words of the poet, 'left not a wrack behind'. Yet we find the house of John Broadwood & Sons still enduring, and, fresh and vigorous, throwing out new blossoms . . . ' Fine words: but for at least one or two of those who heard them, unendurably bitter. For they knew (as the City suspected) that the company was on a financial knife-edge, and within an ace of following those other great names into oblivion. The position was held for a further two years. But in 1900 the partnership of

John Broadwood & Sons, most eminent of piano-makers, turned in a loss on the year's trading.

'When does the Horseferry Road lease expire?'

The question was posed in a letter from Bertha Broadwood to Frederick Rose at Great Pulteney Street, dated 8 January 1893. The plain fact was that the great manufactory in Horseferry Road was leased from the Duchy of Westminster for a fixed term, and was valueless beyond the term of the lease.

The lease expired at Lady Day (25 March) 1902; and it is one of the many bizarre features of this story that although throughout most of the last decade of the nineteenth century the partners were aware that the lease had an established term, the future site of the business was still being debated at midsummer 1901.

The introduction of Willie Dobbs into the factory in 1894 was not happy. It could hardly have been otherwise. Aged twenty three, just down from Trinity College, Cambridge, with no knowledge of the techniques of pianoforte manufacture and no experience of business, he was somehow expected (by his aunt) to restore a situation that was becoming more critical month by month. No hierarchy was established; he was to be 'manager', yet was not designated 'managing director'. Inevitably, decisions needing a knowledge of piano-making continued to be made by Harry Broadwood and George Rose.

Further, it was unfortunate that Willie Dobbs was not a gregarious or easily convivial man. Of his serious-mindedness there can be no doubt, but to his fellow partners and to the workmen he seemed aloof, cold and forbidding. He made appraisals of ways of improving procedures, decided how he wanted things changed, and then ordered that they be done, without detailed explanations and without giving reasons. This quickly built up resentment, as when he devised a new method of cutting veneer which he surmised would result in less waste than the old method. He told George Rose what he wanted done; and Rose ordered one of the veneer cutters to do it, but without full explanation. The result was a botched job, and the waste of nearly £1,000 worth of expensive veneer.

Time rolled inexorably on. Harry Broadwood, George Rose and Willie Dobbs all agreed on the need to introduce overstringing, and an iron frame grand; and these innovations had some effect, so that in 1897 the profits had apparently been turned up and in that year were £8,590. There was still a need for more working capital; and so in 1898 a young Etonian was taken on, initially as assistant to Alfred Hipkins as head of

Leonard Bevan, 1893 *(Eton College photograph)*

the showroom, and impresario of Broadwood concerts. He was Leonard Bevan; and he joined the firm with the option, within a few years, of buying a share and becoming a partner. Bevan proved an enthusiastic and popular member of the staff. Gregarious, amiable and knowledgeable about music, he was backed by very substantial funds. He was the son (in old age) of Francis Bevan, of Trent Park, Hertfordshire— High Sheriff of Hertfordshire in 1899, a Lieutenant for the City of London, and Chairman of Barclays. He was overflowing with bright ideas for the development of the business—so many, in fact, that the partners began to feel that he was presuming somewhat on his wealth and importance. He was treated more warily after the gossip reached the Broadwood family that one of the Bevans had said in a London club that they were just waiting until Broadwoods crashed, after which they would pick up the firm cheap for young Leonard. The family became still more apprehensive when it was learned that one of the financial backers behind Bevan was his Hertfordshire neighbour, Marlborough Pryor.

The question of a site became urgent. Early in 1898 the last hope for a renewal of the lease in Horseferry Road faded when the Westminster Estate named a figure that made it wholly impracticable to consider remaining. That summer, Willie Dobbs toured piano factories in Britain and North America. When he returned, the partners began desperately to look for somewhere to move. The Roses favoured Surrey, and sites were examined at Sutton and Mitcham. Bertha Broadwood suggested Edmonton (sensibly, as ever, because this was near where most of the workmen lived). The greatest problem, of course, was the want of capital.

Willie Dobbs wrote to Bertha Broadwood in May 1898: 'I think probably it will require about £40,000 to get new buildings etc. I do not think that this year the partners can save any money, & I cannot say what may happen in the next three years. Saving depends to a certain extent on the partners themselves. Mr Rose does not, I am sure, know more than anyone else what amount of money Beavan [sic] would wish to invest. But I should think it would be much better that means should be found of raising all, quite independently of him. When that has been done the firm will be able to let him in as a favour.'

By the end of 1898 the partners had agreed on a site, and Dobbs called a meeting of the workmen at Horseferry Road at the end of the working day on Monday, 28 November.

Four of the five partners were present that evening: Harry Broadwood, Frederick Rose and George Rose, and Willie Dobbs. The only absentee was James Broadwood, who was ill. Willie Dobbs told the workmen that it had been decided that the factory should move 'where the atmosphere is clearer than London'.

The place we have decided upon is the town of Bedford . . . A county town of some 35,000 inhabitants situated fifty miles from London, and taking an hour to reach from town . . . It has gravel soil, a fine river for boating and plenty of room for cricket, football and everything that is conducive to the health, happiness and welfare of our workmen [cheers]. There is another point; it has the best schools in England. That, no doubt, will appeal more to the older ones here tonight.

We shall have our pianos better and cheaper. The surroundings will be cleaner and moreover we hope to secure a large and increasing trade . . .

Old Frederick Rose spoke next, saying that he had 'the arrangement of the factory when it was rebuilt nearly 45 years ago'. George Rose followed, and said:

The moving of the factory has been the desire of my heart ever since I came of age. I have long been convinced that Westminster is not the place in which to make good and clean pianos. You cannot keep your hands nor even your aprons clean, let alone your work [Hear, hear and laughter].

[Mr Dobbs: 'Nor your lungs'].

When I was working in Paris some years ago I saw a piano which had been standing in the workshop for fourteen days. There was then not enough dust upon it to show a finger-mark. I contrasted that with the conditions here and thought, 'Good God, how can we make pianos in such a place?' Nothing would induce me to live in London and I am convinced that the decision we have come to is a good one.

Then Harry Broadwood, stammering slightly on one of his very rare appearances at a public meeting, added his imprimatur: 'Gentlemen: I thank you for the attention you have given to what has been said. I endorse every word. I am not a speaker, but feel I must stand up, if only to say these few words.'

The next morning, George Rose called the clerks at Great Pulteney Street together, and told them. His remark that 'nothing would induce him to live in London' was perhaps unfortunate, since most of the workmen *did* live in London, in the Islington-Stoke Newington square mile that was the traditional home of piano-making, or in the area of Victoria around the Broadwood works. Many of the skilled workmen were disinclined to move. The proposal did not appeal to them, and it began to look as though there would be an acute shortage of skilled manpower if the move were carried through. Nevertheless, a site at Bedford had been bought (for £4,000) and the company began to build up wood stocks there, and run them down in London.

To counteract the manpower problem, the firm recruited six young apprentices in Bedford, and brought them to London on the understanding that they would go back home with the firm. They were known in the factory as 'the Bedford boys'.

One of them was Dennis Carrier, who wrote some years later:

A well-known pianoforte manufacturer whose lease in London was to expire in two years time decided to build a new factory in my town, and let it be known that they would select half a dozen boys from my school to go to London as apprentices, and spend the first two years at the London factory in lieu of premium. I was one of the six chosen, and on October 16th 1899 with my tin trunk packed, I went to London and started work the next day. They were long hours and hard work, but I was intensely interested and loved this kind of work.

The first two years were uneventful, and I managed to keep myself in humble digs on 14s a week. Two events stand out in my memory in those far off days—one was a series of organ recitals at St Margaret's Westminster by Edwin H. Le Mare on Saturday evenings, and a free ticket from my firm to the Sunday afternoon Orchestral Concerts at the Albert Hall. These never failed to thrill me.

Then the blow fell. The firm announced that they had given up the idea of moving to my native town and had bought a factory in the East End of London.[29]

The decision was taken after long and bitter debates among the partners, who had begun to blame each other for settling on so out-of-the-way a place as Bedford. In particular, the Roses blamed Willie Dobbs. The Roses declared that unless plans for a new factory were limited to a cost of £20,000 they would retire from the partnership (Willie Dobbs envisaged spending £40,000). Dobbs was certainly tactless on occasion: once he issued an arbitrary dictat that, forthwith, no Broadwood employee was to take commissions on the sale of pianos. This cut across established custom and practice in the trade, and was bitterly resented.

In an effort to reconcile the differences in the partnership, a 'Shareholders' Board' was established, with Bertha Broadwood a member of it. Her commanding figure would sweep (usually late) into the Board Room at Great Pulteney Street and she would deposit her large handbag on the table where, as often as not, it would burst open and water biscuits (of which she carried a store for emergencies) would roll across the polished mahogany.[30]

Bertha's forthrightness was not popular. Her comment that 'economy is abhorrent to the British man's mind: he unfortunately despises details' did not endear her. Schemes for saving the firm were drawn up and canvassed by the partners, their sisters and their cousins and their aunts. By this stage, with Horseferry Road due to close in less than two years and with no decision taken on a new site, even the members of the family were communicating only through their solicitors.

In her scheme for the reconstruction of the company, Bertha Broadwood chose as preferred chairman a family friend, Robert Seton (a barrister, shortly to become Recorder of Devizes). Among her list of potential directors were her sister Lucy, and a Surrey neighbour, just thirty, who was beginning to make his name as a composer—Ralph Vaughan Williams.

By May 1900, however, the Pryors were arguing that Willie Dobbs must leave the firm. At this time there was general agreement on only one fact: that the assets would fetch no more than 10s in the £ and that the capital of John Broadwood & Sons was worth no more than £100,000 instead of the £200,000 which had been the accepted valuation only a decade earlier.

Bertha was adamant that Dobbs would not be jettisoned, and with her sisters' agreement she played her trump card. The sisters would withdraw their £24,000 unless Dobbs was retained.

Equally firmly, she declined to accept Harry Broadwood's proposal (through his solicitor) that the firm should be wound up. As 1900 drew to a close, therefore, with the partnership recording a loss, there was a situation of stalemate.

The loss was on a turnover of between £65,000 and £75,000 a year; and 1,689 instruments had been made in the previous year (455 grands, 1,232 uprights and 2 organs). There may have been some reassurance, too, in the fact that Broadwoods' predicament was shared by the other two oldest piano-makers in Britain: Kirkman had been wound up in 1897, and Collard & Collard was suffering from precisely the same pressures.

What had caused the débâcle was obvious. The market for Broadwoods' quality grands had disappeared. The company had not been able to answer the challenge of quality German uprights, either in Britain or in its traditional export markets, such as Australia. The business was still being run on lavish old-fashioned lines; despite the decline in production, it was over-manned. An accountant surveying the firm in 1901 noted that 'all parts of pianos . . . are manufactured in the firm's shops, with the exception . . . of about one third of the grand piano keys which are now being purchased from Germany'. This was a major factor in the company's inability to challenge the German importers on price, since the production of parts in Germany was now largely standardised and centralised.

There were efforts to end some of the more generous practices of earlier years. In January 1900 a letter went out from Great Pulteney Street to all those who in the past had been lent grand pianos for provincial concerts, with Broadwoods paying all transport and maintenance costs as a promotional exercise. In future, the firm would charge for such hirings. But such palliatives did not cure the disastrous profit record (Table VI).

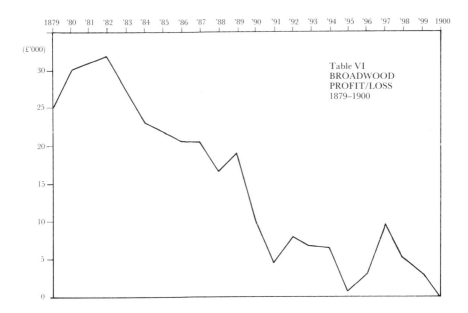

Table VI
BROADWOOD
PROFIT/LOSS
1879–1900

By March 1901 Cuthbert Heath had taken the initiative, and proposed that the partnership should be wound up and replaced by a limited company, recapitalised from the City. With classical tact and timing he set out to persuade the family, and in particular Bertha Broadwood. He so far succeeded that in March, Bertha wrote to Robert Dobbs of Heath's plan: 'He has secured a good man, musical, good taste, and bred to business at Lloyds, to bring in capital which will enable us to be independent of others, if needs be.'

The 'good man' was William Henry Perry Leslie. He was the son of Henry Leslie, a noted Welsh composer and conductor, particularly of amateur choirs. William Leslie had gone into Lloyds (as a partner in Godwin & Leslie) but had continued his father's interest in amateur music-making. He was also a member of the Council of the Royal College of Music, and later, Master of the Musicians' Company.

Heath had also recruited another man of musical taste with capital— William Hugh Spottiswoode, a director of the Queen's Printer, Eyre & Spottiswoode. Son of William Spottiswoode, a distinguished President of the Royal Society, Hugh Spottiswoode was himself a polymath; mathematician, physicist and linguist, he was also an enthusiastic amateur musician and a director of the Royal Academy of Music.

At Cuthbert Heath's urging, the partners commissioned Edwin Waterhouse to prepare an actuarial survey of the firm. After only a day or two, he produced a preliminary report urging 'the necessity of providing accommodation for the manufacturing business of the firm after this time next year'.

His full report, received a month later, was devastating. In part, it said:

There would not appear to be any reason but want of good management why a firm having the name and position of Messrs. Broadwood should not earn a fair manufacturing profit on such work as passed through their hands last year. I am asked to point out why the profits of the business in the recent past have been of such an unsatisfactory character . . . The impression conveyed to my mind is that of late the business has needed a strong control intent on the manufacture of an article which will be the best of its kind technically, and of a form to meet the ever varying public taste. It seems to be admitted that the inventive power of the late Mr Henry F. Broadwood maintained the reputation of the firm at a very high level and that the position it attained under [his] management enabled large profits to be made for some time after his abilities to direct its policy had to some extent declined, and even after what may be considered a wrong direction was given to the methods of construction. Just when high competition arose from foreign houses, notwithstanding the natural prejudice in favour of English manufactures, the firm was not in a position to hold its own and to maintain its reputation. It has had to go to much expense in making-good work which had been turned out during a period of admitted inferiority of workmanship. By doing this it has probably saved its good name and prevented its following some of its English competitors affected by similar circumstances into comparative disrepute.

In my letter of 15th ult. I pointed out the very crucial position into which the firm seems to have brought itself by want of foresight in arranging for the change which must take place within a year from now in the site of the factory. An opportunity is forced on the firm for the complete reorganisation of its workshops, a matter involving great labour and expense, but fraught with great possibilities for the future in the way of facilitating and cheapening its operations. The necessity for the change had been before the partners for years and yet with the exception of the purchase of the land at Bedford, a proceeding to my mind of doubtful expediency, nothing has been done practically towards the preparation of the necessary shops and machinery . . .

Cuthbert Eden Heath, by Sir William Orpen *(C. E. Heath & Co Ltd)*

In these days of high artistic designs, a firm such as that of Messrs. Broadwood must be ever seeking to meet the public taste by changes in the external construction of their instruments, taking care, of course, at the same time that the internal construction is more than able to hold its own against all competition.

To do this class of business effectively and profitably the most close and harmonious relations must exist between the factory and the selling department . . .

There is a class of customer to whom price is of no object if an article unique in character and perfect in technical excellence can be procured. There should consequently be a fair profit on such work, while the reputation gained by such sales ought to give an impetus generally to the sale of less expensive instruments such as required by the wholesale trade.

247

On 22 March Cuthbert Heath wrote to Bertha Broadwood in the country, evidently for the eyes of her brother James, who was staying with her.

It seems to me that there are three courses open.

1st The present arrangement with fresh capital added.

2nd Dissenting partners to be paid out by the remainder and fresh partners to come in.

3rd A sale of the whole bag of tricks for what it will fetch.

No 1 is what is preferable but I am beginning to fear impossible. No 2 is possible but the ease with which it can be effected depends entirely on the amount of partners' capital which will have to be replaced (in either of the cases, a Company would have to be formed).

One of the points I think James should consider is what, if he elects to go out, he would take for his shares or whether he would leave at least the mortgage money in if it is properly secured. Personally I wish to goodness both W. Dobbs and Rose would go if the thing is to perpetually revolve round their two interests apart from those of the Broadwoods as a whole.

It was another gentle intimation that Willie Dobbs would have to go.

Even now at this last minute to midnight Bertha Broadwood was still casting around for support. She drafted a letter of introduction from Willie Dobbs to Lord Kelvin. 'My brother and the bearer of this note, our nephew William Dobbs, want to get into their business some gentleman, by preference Scotch, of practical engineering & scientific knowledge, so as to keep abreast of the science of *sound* and *metals*.

'I venture to hope that you may be able to indicate to my nephew some such gentleman, or how one may best be heard of.'

History is full of 'if onlys'. William Thompson, Lord Kelvin, was at this time seventy six, full of honours and distinctions (the following year, he became one of the founding members of the Order of Merit). Among the greatest mathematicians and physicists of his age, he had registered fifty six patents for developments of electricity. A leading academic, he was also a partner in the firm of Kelvin & White of Glasgow, which was the main industrial outlet for the development and application of his inventions. He had been an engineer for the laying of the Atlantic cables in 1857–1858, and subsequently for cable-laying across the oceans of the world. He had invented a mariner's compass, a navigational sounding machine and many electrical measuring instruments.

He was also musical. A founder of the Cambridge University Musical Society, he had played the french horn in its inaugural concert (no great challenge, perhaps, to one who had matriculated in the University of Glasgow at the age of ten, and become second Wrangler in the Mathematical Tripos at Cambridge at twenty).

Considering the impact of electronics on musical instruments in the past century, it is tempting to wonder what changes and developments might have been accelerated had Henry Fowler attracted William Thompson's interest in the 1860s (when Theodore Steinway was talking to just such imaginative minds in the physical sciences).

The Waterhouse report clearly defined the problems. The most serious, of course, was the want of a factory. A site was found in Bow, East London, and Heath wrote to James Broadwood in April: 'The offer is not open very long. Mr Waterhouse is right in saying that the possession of a factory makes a large difference in the value of the assets and if this particular factory is found to be suitable, it seems to me that whatever the final arrangement as to shares etc. is to be it could be better to seize the present opportunity rather than risk losing it. I am told that only a small deposit is wanted (£3,000 or so) and that no more will be wanted till Xmas.'

The deposit was paid. By June, Heath and Leslie had interviewed most of the partners and senior staff. For a few weeks they hoped, as Heath wrote, that 'something might be done to harmonise the Rose & Dobbs interests'. But Heath gave a warning that 'it may be that our original difficulties as to W. Dobbs will prove insurmountable'.

The inevitable climax came in a letter from Cuthbert Heath to Bertha Broadwood on 2 July 1901:

We have arranged the rough scheme of the proposed company and so far as I can see both James and Mr Clarke [E.W. Clarke, who had succeeded James Upton as the Broadwood family solicitor] fully agree, tho' of course there are details still to be arranged.

Now I want to make an earnest personal appeal to you. The money department is mine. I have today seen the London manager of the Insurance Co. which is to provide the money . . .I anticipate *no difficulty at all* on that score. Our object was to provide sufficient money to pay off the £11,000 mortgage and the £24,000 to the sisters and about £7,500 to £10,000 cash, and this can be done without any doubt. At the same time we feel—Spottiswoode especially—that we ought to be in a position to lay our hands on an extra £25,000 at any time should the business develop as we all firmly believe it will. To do this we ought to have a margin of borrowing power. Now if you, Amy and Lucy would be content instead of taking the whole of your £24,000 out to leave say half of it in to rank as second mortgage (I am content that my £1,000 should be so, and there seems no doubt that James's £35,000 can also rank similarly) and to carry 4½% instead of 4% as at present, the £25,000 margin can be arranged to be borrowed only in so far as the business expands.

I have written to Amy and Lucy explaining that under this arrangement their remaining capital will be more secure and that their income will be increased. I have also begged them as I beg you now not to let the individual interest stand in the way of that of the whole family. James & his children, Harry & his children & indeed in some ways W. Dobbs himself. As you know Leslie and I have tried hard to reconcile conflicting interests but for *present* purposes you must take it from me that W. Dobbs *cannot* remain in. What the future will bring forth in that respect I cannot tell but Leslie and myself still feel, as we have always felt, that provided the interests of the company are not prejudiced, we should like to make room for him. At present it is impossible.

We have gone quite sufficiently into things to be fairly certain that J. B. & Sons can be revived and that there is no reason at all why it should not make profits similar to those of 15 years ago and you know what that means, but we must have a free hand and a fair start. The latter depends to a considerable extent on you and your sisters. I count on you to help us.

PS I hope you quite understand that if you insist we can pay you off but it will be at the expense of crippling largely the efficiency of the Company.

Although Bertha's first reaction was to fight for Willie Dobbs's retention, it was obvious from Cuthbert Heath's careful postscript that the best that could be done would be to press for generous redundancy pay. After consulting Amy and Lucy, Bertha accepted Cuthbert Heath's scheme; but despite Lucy's pointed comment that 'if WCD is like most men he'll be far too proud to have anything to do with the firm after the dismissal which the partners have given him, so there's not much use in qualifying him for a future directorship I fear!', Bertha insisted that clauses should be written into the Articles of Association of the new company which specifically empowered her to hand over her shares to her nephew William Dobbs.

Willie Dobbs was told of his dismissal by William Leslie at Horseferry

'Enraptured' *(Supplement to Hearth and Home, 28 November 1901)*. A nostalgic evocation of the square piano, nearly forty years after it went out of production.

Road. He wrote to Bertha: 'It is disappointing that this should be the end of the affair which you and I had hoped would end differently. It is no use regretting it however. The main thing is to try to learn lessons from failures, which for all we know may do more real good than harm.. It might have been wiser if I had stepped out earlier, as I might have done if I had followed simply my own wishes, but I thought it seemed best for myself and others to hold on as long as possible.'

It was, Cuthbert Heath agreed, 'a gentleman's letter and I can give it no greater praise than that'. At his aunt's insistence, Willie Dobbs was provided by James and Harry with 150 shares of £10 each, as compensation. Heath thought that a tough bargain: 'After all, Harry has worked as hard. I believe that this last holiday is the only one he has taken for five years . . . '

So it was settled. Willie Dobbs found that 'the absence of uncertainty about the business is an immense relief'. He told his mother later that when, in the first week of August, he went to see George Rose to hand over the keys of the factory he found him anything but triumphant. Rose said: 'Well, I believe *you* have got the best of it after all.' Willie was touched that both Cuthbert Heath and William Leslie took the trouble to talk to him 'very nicely' on his last day.*

Harry's wife Ada held out a small, four-footed olive branch to her sister-in-law Bertha. She wrote from Bone Hill, St Albans, offering her 'a nice little dog—out of the 11 we have—7 of one family and 4 of another!'

A preliminary meeting of the Board of the new company was held on 30 September 1901. Those present were Harry Broadwood, Leonard Bevan, Cuthbert Heath, W. H. Leslie, George Rose, W. H. Spottis-woode, S. H. Walrond (who was to be the new Company Secretary) and Clarke, the solicitor. Leslie was elected Chairman, and the Memorandum and Articles of Association were signed by the new directors—Heath, Leslie, Rose and Spottiswoode—and sent for registration.

George Rose was appointed Joint Sub-Manager with special care of the factory, at a salary of £250 a year and 5 per cent of the profits, with a guarantee that his income for the first three years would be no less than £400, £450 and £500.

Leonard Bevan was appointed Joint Sub-Manager with special care of the sales department at Great Pulteney Street, at a salary of £250 a year and 5 per cent of the profits (but no guarantee similar to that of Rose). He was, however, elected to a seat on the Board 'subject to his acquiring the necessary qualification'.

Then the inevitable pruning began. The office was grossly over-manned with elderly clerks. The first 'compulsory retirement' was that of Algernon Black, the chief clerk, who through the Nineties had been Chairman of the Music Trades Section of the London Chamber of Commerce. Black was given three months' notice, and a pension. He took it badly, and for some time conducted an acrimonious correspondence with the new Company Secretary over the payment of his pension. He sent the correspondence to Bertha Broadwood, who typically started a fund among the family. Four other clerks were also given notice; but in December 1901 'Miss Collingwood was appointed shorthand writer at £1 per week'—the first woman office employee of the company.

But in the event the person who took the change worst was,

*Willie Dobbs had a small private income, and a year later was busy producing a play in London, and then was 'going back to Persia, through Russia this time'. He served in the First World War, with the Middlesex Regiment and then as a Captain in the Royal Fusiliers, when he was twice wounded. He was killed in action on 31 July 1917, aged forty six.

improbably, 27-year-old Leonard Bevan. Ebullient, ambitious, musical, he had hoped that the company would be his. For a time, with the backing of the Pryors, it almost seemed that he had achieved it. Now he was to be a Sub-Manager.

On Sunday, 13 October he went to his parents' house in Kensington, which was empty for the week-end; he first slit his wrists, and then hanged himself. The coroner remarked that he had committed suicide 'in a most determined manner'.[31]

Chapter IX

The Years of Crisis

1901–1931

*E*ngland is like a composite photograph, in which two likenesses are blurred into one. It shows traces of American enterprise and of German order, but the enterprise is faded and the order muddled. They combine to a curious travesty in which activity and perseverance assume the expression of ease and indolence. The once enterprising manufacturer has grown slack, he has let the business take care of itself, while he is shooting grouse or yachting in the Mediterranean. That is his business. The once unequalled workman has adopted the motto, 'Get as much and do as little as possible'; his business is football or betting . . .

Necessity is a great teacher, and we have the energy to respond to her touch when we feel it. We have begun to feel it at home. In the industrial world manufacturers felt it first; years ago the cotton trade felt it and responded. Others have felt it more recently and are responding.

They are rebuilding, reorganising, renewing plant, extending their operations, forming combinations, adopting improvements, employing technical skill and learning from others. At the present time the best of them are, I do not hesitate to assert, more alert than any of their rivals.

Arthur Shadwell [Industrial Correspondent of *The Times*],
Industrial Efficiency, (Longmans, London 1906)

The new company of John Broadwood & Sons Limited was registered on 3 October 1901, with a capital of £100,000 divided into 99,996 Ordinary Shares of £1 each, and four Managers' Shares also of £1. The four managers were Leslie, Heath, Spottiswoode and John E. Talbot; the other directors were shareholders who qualified by holding Ordinary Shares of the nominal value of £4,000—James and Harry Broadwood, and George Rose. The sums invested in the company by Cuthbert Heath and Bertha, Amy and Lucy Broadwood were recognised by the issue of First and Second Debentures.

The injection of new capital enabled work to go ahead rapidly on the building and equipping of the new factory at Stour Road, Old Ford, Hackney. The removal was completed by June 1902, virtually on the day that the Horseferry Road lease expired. The public explanation was that the flourishing business needed to expand from the constricted old premises in Victoria; in that year there was some evidence to support this proposition. Broadwoods supplied a piano to Westminster Abbey for the Coronation of King Edward VII on 7 July (the Royal Warrant was renewed that year). A contract was made to supply pianos for the Peninsular & Oriental steamships, and (following the ending of the Boer War) there was a substantial order for one hundred pianos for the Transvaal, to be supplied within four months.

In that year, too, the company joined with the Automobile Association to experiment with the use of motor vans. The seventeen Broadwood horse-drawn vans in their dark green livery* had long been a familiar sight in London; now Broadwoods were one of the pioneers of the age of the commercial motor.

The new factory at Old Ford was built on a site of one-and-a-half acres, and carefully planned (by George Rose) on a production-line system, with tramways and overhead gantry rails installed throughout. The latest woodworking machinery was introduced, much of it powered by electricity. Visitors also admired the internal telephone exchange and the synchronised clocks. Wood (1,500 tons) was stored in a timber yard across the road beside the Hackney Canal. Reporters invited to the factory in February 1904 noted that the equipment could turn out three thousand pianos a year.

'Messrs Broadwood have provided very thoroughly for the comfort and well-being of the five hundred men and youths employed by them, and they are so trained and organised that everyone becomes a specialist

* There was a slight contretemps when in February 1903 the firm was formally reprimanded for using the Prince of Wales's feathers on the vans; two weeks later they received the Royal Warrant from the Prince of Wales's household.

The Broadwood solid-tyred van, 1903 *(John Broadwood & Sons Ltd)*

in his particular branch,' wrote *The Observer*. Despite the machinery, it was still a labour-intensive industry, and a single instrument could go through eighty pairs of hands in the course of manufacture. The correspondent of the *Pall Mall Gazette* was evidently a musician, and a romantic at that, for he was overwhelmed to discover that the piano, so ethereal in the concert room, was an artifact of man:

> The men who are working in this extraordinary manufactory are extremely intelligent, and understand every detail connected with their employment. It was a pleasure yesterday to discuss detail after detail with various skilled workmen. To realise from their point of view (a point of view which must necessarily be superior to that of the amateur) was to read a new lesson in the liberal education of technical accomplishment, whether that accomplishment was centred in wood, in ivory, or in wool. How many of the great pianoforte players, we wonder, realise that the second shearing of the sheep provides them with better wool for the hammers of their pianofortes than either the first or the third? Here, indeed, one gets to the bed-rock of technique, and here, indeed, one realises how much there is running before artistic interpretation before that which we call fine art is in act accomplished. [1]

The Broadwood factory at Old Ford, 1903 – fixing steel barless frames (*John Broadwood & Sons Ltd*)

The Broadwood factory at Old Ford, 1903 – French polishing the lid of a grand (*John Broadwood & Sons Ltd*)

The Broadwood factory at Old Ford, 1903 – the grand finishing shop (*John Broadwood & Sons Ltd*)

The Broadwood factory at Old Ford, 1903 – Key-cutting *(John Broadwood & Sons Ltd)*

The Broadwood factory at Old Ford, 1903 – Regulating the grand action *(John Broadwood & Sons Ltd)*

The Broadwood factory at Old Ford, 1903 – Regulating the upright action *(John Broadwood & Sons Ltd)*

The workmen were hiding their feelings on this occasion, for the move from Horseferry Road to Old Ford was not popular. One recalled: 'The whole atmosphere had changed from West End to East End—at Westminster they were craftsmen, many came to work in top hats and frock coats; of course, they changed into disreputable garments at their benches—but at the new factory they were just workmen.'[1]

The comment about the 'comfort and well-being' of the workmen caused some cynical laughter: the sole lavatory at Old Ford was a French-style *pissoir* in the middle of the yard, open to the elements and freezing in winter.

In November 1902 the Board of Directors granted leave of absence for the winter to Cuthbert Heath and James Broadwood. James's health, always precarious, was failing; on 23 January 1903 he died at Funchal, Madeira, where he had travelled in search of a drier climate: he was forty eight. Ostensibly life had given him so much; a great name, social position, wealth and intelligence. Then it had dealt him the shattering blows of the death of his young wife and the crumbling of his inheritance. He left his 13-year-old son Evelyn and daughters Joan and Audrey in the guardianship of his sister Bertha. She directed young Evelyn to Wellington College and thence to a career in the Regular Army; and as soon as he was old enough, she required him to read all the family papers which she had methodically filed in labelled envelopes, briefing him on his family's glorious past, its challenging present and a future which she was determined he would restore.

Two of the older leaders of the Victorian firm died soon afterwards, A. J. Hipkins in June 1903 (his widow was provided with a life pension of £200 a year) and Frederick Rose in March 1904. Hipkins's devotion to Broadwoods' past has been described. Fred Rose was a member of the family that had served Broadwoods throughout the century—his father, Daniel Giles Rose, had as a young clerk witnessed old John Broadwood's will; his son, George Daniel Rose, was now a director and works manager. Fred had started with Broadwoods as a boy of fourteen, had reorganised the factory after the fire of 1856, and was generally the company's administrator. In the winter of 1870, at the onset of the London smallpox epidemic, he arranged for every Broadwood workman to be vaccinated; none caught the disease. He was known in Westminster for well-doing. Each Christmas he organised a dinner for 600 men from lodging-houses.

Following James Broadwood's death, William Leslie arranged for one of his City friends to put £12,000 into the company and take a directorship. He was Howard Gilliat, Governor of the London Assurance

Bertha Broadwood, *c.* 1903 *(The Broadwood Trust)*

in 1899 and Chairman (among other interests) of the Trust and
Mortgage Company of Iowa (of which William Leslie was also a
director). Howard Gilliat remained on the Board until his death in 1906
when he was succeeded by his 24-year-old son John Francis Gilliat*.

Another climatic change took place in 1903. After 160 years
Broadwoods left Great Pulteney Street. The freeholds in Bridle Lane and
Silver Street were sold, the leaseholds in Great Pulteney Street and
Golden Square sub-let. As a central London showroom the company
bought the lease of a once-famous house in Conduit Street, Limmer's
Hotel. The Board disposed the company's historic records more wisely
than many other businessmen, resolving: 'With regard to the old

---

* John Francis Gilliat (1883–1948), a Director of the Commercial Union Assurance
Company, 1921–1948 and Chairman 1927–1928 and 1943–1948.

documents &c at Gt Pulteney Street it was decided to invite Miss Lucy Broadwood and Mr Henry Broadwood to sort through the various papers, scheduling all documents: those relating to the business to be left in the care of the Company and those of a private nature to be left in the care of Miss Lucy Broadwood and Mr Henry Boadwood, they undertaking to allow representatives of the Board to have access to them.'

As the building was cleared, various poignant remembrances of the past came to light: an old lead water cistern, bearing Burkat Shudi's monogram and pine-tree crest; and hidden in the eaves of the attic, bundles of crow-quills, placed there by some craftsman more than a century earlier to weather, and then forgotten. Behind the panelling in the Partners' Room were found several old chamber-pots;[3] evidently when the weather was inclement, Burkat Shudi or John Broadwood had not cared to march downstairs to the outside privy in the back yard.

The new showroom in Limmer's Hotel was opened on 2 May 1904 with a dinner attended by agents, the press and musical notabilities. There was a special exhibition of the company's historic instruments. That spring, Leslie took on the general managership as well as the chairmanship. He brought in an auditor, Layton Bennett, and he instructed that 'for the future all instructions for the factory were to be given through him'. Clearly the new Board had not been able to resolve the problem of continuing friction between 'the showroom' and 'the factory'. This culminated when one new model was sent up from the factory, put on show and sold without any member of the Board seeing it. George Rose, at Old Ford, did not take kindly to instructions from Conduit Street.

Meanwhile the directors were making efforts to increase the export sales. They made a deal with the American Aeolian Company to sell Broadwoods in Paris, and on a visit to New York, Spottiswoode met the chairman of the Aeolian Company who 'expressed a hope that at some date in the near future he would be in a position to suggest that his company should take up the Broadwood pianoforte in the USA'—but there was then an American tariff of 25 per cent on the import of foreign pianos.

The question of tariffs was controversial in this decade. The battle for and against 'Free Trade' was particularly bitter in the piano trade, where the import of German upright pianos had become a flood. Broadwoods did not join in the anti-German hysteria, and as early as 1903 the Board agreed that 'no one connected with the Firm shall take any part whatsoever in the Fiscal Discussion in relation to the Pianoforte Trade . . .'

Player upright *(John Broadwood & Sons)*

Three years later, as President of the Musical Instrument Trades Protection Association,* George Rose held to that policy, reminding the members assembled at the annual dinner: 'We have always made it a point to abstain from questions of a political character, as unfortunately there are some of us who do not see "eye to eye".'

Sir Herbert Marshall, Conservative politician and Leicester piano dealer, and President of the Music Trades Association of Great Britain, remarked that 'if the public demand a certain kind of tone, I think they should have it. If they like a German tone, give them a German tone. You can do it.' Many piano-makers, Broadwoods among them, were attempting it.

Simultaneously Broadwoods were developing the player-piano. The player-piano was the means whereby the piano trade attempted to bring the traditional instrument into line with modern technology. The player-

* From 1908, the Piano Manufacturers' Association.

piano was introduced in the United States in the last years of the nineteenth century, and survived until the 1930s when it was finally driven out by the electric gramophone. Broadly its development falls into two periods: the first, when the purpose of the player was to enable the amateur to play the piano 'perfectly' without the trouble of actually learning; and the second, when the piano became a means of 'reproducing' performances by great pianists, of a standard that no amateur could hope to attain. Indeed, some piano rolls were cut of such complexity that the music would have been physically unplayable by human hand.

The early 'players' were cabinets on castors, which were placed up to the keyboard of a conventional piano. Wisely, Broadwoods declined to have anything to do with these devices. It was not until the American manufacturers began to build the 'player' mechanism inside the piano case proper that the firm became involved.

In December 1902 a representative of the Cecilian Company approached Broadwoods, and in the following month the company agreed to sell six piano cases 'in the rough' for the Cecilian Company to adapt. However, Broadwoods were negotiating with other makers, particularly the Aeolian Company and its British offshoot, the Orchestrelle Company. Shortly before, the Aeolian Company had launched the instrument that was to give its name to the whole genre—the Pianola. Broadwoods were making Pianolas in Britain from 1904, but were also buying the British patents from other inventors—the first, in January 1903, from P. Welin.

Though the first player-piano bearing the Broadwood name did not appear in the showroom until January 1907, by that date the factory had made 152 player-pianos. A keen advocate was the sales manager Matthew Sinclair, not least because he had taken out patents for player actions in France, Germany and Belgium. Sinclair's enthusiastic young assistant was an Oxford graduate who had joined Broadwoods a few years earlier, and remained with the firm until the first World War, Harry Tennent*.

The development of the player at Broadwoods has been set down by Dennis Carrier, who having been one of the 'Bedford boys' found himself, still an apprentice, in charge of the despatch department at Old Ford (earning 24s a week):

* Henry M. Tennent (1879–1941). After the war he went into theatrical management, becoming General Manager of Drury Lane and—as founder of H. M. Tennent Ltd—a leading impresario. He was a composer of light music. In the reference books he delighted to list his first job with Broadwoods.

Player grand *(John Broadwood & Sons)*

Orders came in for despatch to all parts of the world and of course to the West End showroom which was the rendezvous of the elite in the musical world. There was no such thing as payment for overtime so, when we had as we often did a rush of orders to get out, I frequently got to the works at 6 am and worked late to clear it.

After about a year of this came the advent of the player piano . . . My firm bought the patent rights of an American built-in job and proceeded to manufacture it at the factory, under imported personnel—very much a closed shop so that although intensely interested I could not get a look in for a long time. However, our directors were not satisfied with the result tone wise, and brought over an expert on this method from Germany, which turned out to be very simple in the end, very like voicing in organ building. Of course, they had to pick on me to assist this old German who could

268

Player grand in 'Queen Anne' case

not speak a word of English—I had to converse with him in German.

Up to this time player mechanisms had only been installed in Upright pianos and we were asked to tackle a very different problem—ie. building into a Grand. Design drawings had been done and a Grand piano built with the necessary modifications, and then the firm started. Full of enthusiasm, we worked for many weeks, hours did not count and often we worked on through the night with liberal supplies by the Management of sandwiches and bottles of beer. Eventually this went into full production alongside the existing players . . . Gradually a regular maintenance contract was built up as a section apart from the regular tuning, this meant an immense amount of travelling and must have been very costly, but the motto in those days was that 'the job had to be right' . . . [4]

The keyboard of Captain Scott's Broadwood player piano being taken on board the *Terra Nova (Syndication International)*

In 1910 Broadwoods provided a player piano for Captain Scott's Antarctic Expedition: 'My old firm had promised them a player piano plus a quantity of music rolls, to while away the tedious hours that would ensue when not on watch. I had to try to anticipate all the things that could go wrong under such trying conditions and take steps possible to avoid breakdowns. In addition I gave a series of instructions to one of the officers, Lieutenant Rennick, on maintenance.'[5]

Rennick* wrote to Carrier from Melbourne on the way out, in October 1910, describing the eventful passage:

I promised to write and let you know how the pianola goes. Well, I never knew that I should have to play around with it, like I have done. After we got well on our voyage, and consequently lightened, the decks began to 'open up', and the rain leaked thro and also salt water from the seas we were shipping, with the result that the

---

* Henry F. de P. Rennick, a regular Royal Navy officer who was in charge of hydrographical surveys and deep-sea soundings on the Scott expedition.

Pianola took the lot. From S. Trinidad on the woodwork took to warping and so consequently the motor was thrown out of line—no sooner was that done than pads (various) melted off and valves started worrying. Tho the machine has been a godsend to us yet I think I have exhausted my vocabulary over it. It has taken up a good many 'watch-belows'*. However it's going strong now and we are fairly working it to death. The next thing will be landing it on the pack which I hope will be a success.[6]

Evidently it was a success, for incredibly the Broadwood player was unshipped from the *Terra Nova* and taken to the tragic expedition's first base-camp on the ice (certainly the first piano in Antarctica). Finally it was brought back to London, repaired, and presented to Captain Evans.

It was not the last piano to make the voyage. Another Broadwood player went with the Shackleton expedition of 1912–1913, and Commander Evans wrote from McMurdo Sound in January 1913: 'I have very much pleasure in informing you of the great benefit we derived from the Player Piano you so kindly supplied us with. Both on the voyage out, in the Antarctic, and on our return it gave the greatest satisfaction and required very little adjustment, notwithstanding the extreme conditions of climate and temperature it had undergone. In the Hut in winter no instrument could have afforded greater pleasure, as we were reminded of home by the tunes we knew so well. In fact it proved an ideal instrument both afloat and ashore'.[7]

The development of player pianos required capital. Unfortunately, though the firm produced a small profit in 1903, it had once again shown a loss in 1904. That Christmas, W. H. Leslie wrote to Harry Broadwood. The new factory, he pointed out, was expensive, increasing the overheads from 18 per cent to 30 per cent. It had been built to produce three thousand pianos a year, but was only producing about two thousand:

Clearly the easiest and simplest form of remedying our present state is to endeavour for all we are worth to extend our field and increase the demand for our pianos. This is to be done in three ways:
1) Make instruments which are as good or better than those of other people;
2) Cultivate the provincial, export and trade dealers;
3) Advertise.
With regard to 1) I think we have done this, or are doing it. 2) This we have done—and I hope you were satisfied that we have not given

* i.e. rest-time not on watch.

away very much to our supporters in the country and trade, i.e. our sole agents—as even of the £900-odd paid to them, only about £500 can be fairly said to have been paid for business which was solely our own.

This expansionist policy lasted through 1905. In May George Rose reported that a new iron-frame upright was ready, that a steel-frame upright would be ready by September, and that the reconstruction of the concert grands was on the way. The Board asked for two smaller pianos—a 3 ft 11 ins upright and a 5 ft grand. George Rose allowed his exuberance to exceed his judgement when he produced yet another new piano, the '8A Honeysuckle'. It had not been sanctioned by the Board, and he was formally reprimanded.

As Leslie noted in the minutes, this had been 'contrary to regulations'. By this time George Rose was a noted figure in the trade, and in no mood to be disciplined by the businessmen of Conduit Street. When in 1906 the Board reversed the policy of expansion and began to search for economies reducing the number of models to six grands and seven uprights, Rose was still more irritated. A further cause of mutual distrust must have been the success of Chappells with their concert grands, since Chappells had been revived as a limited company in 1897, and had recruited a remarkable works manager, Mr Glandt, who had trained at Steinways.[8]

A further unease afflicted the factory. The old paternalism was passing, and the new world of trade unionism was being introduced. In the summer of 1906 George Rose travelled to Germany in search of materials, and then crossed to New York (to look at player-piano developments). On his return he told the *Music Trades Review*, in words that can hardly have improved relations in the factory:

The state of the music trade in the United States appeared to me to be very prosperous, and to promise even greater results in the future . . . The Americans love business for its own sake, not merely for its rewards. The result of this single-hearted devotion to business is the excellent quality of workmen employed at the piano and kindred factories. The difference in appearance between the American and English workman must strike the intelligent observer very forcibly. The former seem to take a much greater pride in their outward appearance and their work. They are encouraged by their employers to think for themselves and to take an active and personal interest in their labours; they are not merely human machines. If any one of them has an idea which might improve the working of a department or benefit in any way the manufacture of an article, he is invited to put his views before his principals, not merely before his immediate foreman. If the idea is favourably received, he can always count upon suitable promotion or reward. Hence, a good workman need never know what unemployment is, and it must be admitted that the relations between master and man are more intimate and friendly in the States than in this country.[9]

Shortly afterward, Rose suggested to the Board that some means should be found of 'bringing us at the factory into closer touch with the opinions and requirements of Conduit Street, and vice versa'. Leslie, with Cuthbert Heath's strong approval, proposed a local Board to meet weekly on Wednesdays at the factory. The chairman of the company was to be ex-officio chairman (though in practice Leslie never attended) with George Rose as his deputy. The first meeting took place in October 1907, with Rose in the chair and Stuart (sales manager) and Sinclair (player-piano specialist) travelling out from the West End.

If George Rose hoped that the factory Board would give him more power, his hope must have faded when in January 1908 the young John Gilliat came down from Conduit Street to say that it was 'essential to reduce expenses at the factory'. A further comment of his was subsequently struck out of the minutes by Rose: 'He had come to the conclusion progress was hindered by friction between the members of the Board and lack of mutual help. He had for a year been studying the business, acquiring knowledge without help, and having now gained the knowledge he had been seeking, he would give his opinion without hesitation.'

In April 1908 Conduit Street ordered a production of 35 to 38 pianos a week during the summer. Rose felt that this would produce too small a stock, and ordered 40 uprights, with grands in addition, and 12 players per week. In effect, he was telling Conduit Street that they did not know their business.

George Rose announced his resignation at the factory Board on 3 June. He put in an appearance at the company Board meeting on 5 November, and 'questioned the possibility of the company being able to contend further with the heavy capital charges necessitated by the new developments'. The Chairman told him that 'economies at the factory were considered by the Managers to be possible'. In any case, it was pointed out, he had resigned as a director two days earlier.

It was a sad breach. George Rose, and his father, uncle and grandfather before him, had worked loyally for Broadwoods. George

Rose was a good piano-maker; enough instruments survive from the early years of this century to testify to that. Perhaps he was a little too much a figure in the trade to take easily to new ways.

For he was a figure; and when in the spring of 1906 he retired as first President of the Music Trades Benevolent Society from its inception in 1902, he was presented with a testimonial averring that 'his untiring zeal and energy have won for him the respect and esteem of all his colleagues'. Subsequently Rose went into partnership with Sir Herbert Marshall, and 'Marshall & Rose' pianos were much admired for thirty years.

Throughout the first decade of this century the name of Broadwood was also kept before the musical public in London and the provinces by the 'Broadwood Concerts'. These carried on the tradition, begun in the rooms at Great Pulteney Street, of inviting notable soloists to give public performances on the company's pianos. Indeed, it might be said that the tradition began when Shudi in 1765 arranged for his new harpsichord to be played by the boy Mozart.

The 'Broadwood Concerts' are remarkable both for the number of distinguished musicians who, when young, found there the chance to make a name and for the fact that contemporary music was introduced.

In London, the series was launched at the St James's Hall on 6 November 1902. The leading soloists were Ernst von Dohnanyi and the 27-year-old violinist Fritz Kreisler. They began with Bach's Sonata for Piano and Violin No. 3 in E, and ended with Brahms—the first Sonata in G major (Op. 78 No. 1). Kreisler, already a bravura performer, included a piece by Tartini, the Fugue in A. The series was underpinned by two established concert singers, the tenor Gervase Elwes and the bass-baritone Harry Plunket Greene.

The first season was notable for the introduction of modern European chamber music. The Bohemian String Quartet (with Josef Suk as second violin) played Dvořák and Smetana, and the Halir Quartet works by Glinka and Rimsky-Korsakov. Nor were contemporary British composers neglected: Kreisler played in Cyril Scott's Quartet in E Minor. Three young British soloists took part in a concert in February 1903— Donald Tovey, Landon Ronald and Haydn Wood.*

The same artists were engaged for the following winter season, with the addition of Henry J. Wood (then conductor of the Queen's Hall Orchestra) as a pianist. Two concerts were added to the series to

---

* (Sir) Donald Tovey (1875–1940), pianist and teacher; (Sir) Landon Ronald (1873–1938), accompanist and conductor; and Haydn Wood (1882–1959), violinist and composer.

introduce notable foreign chamber groups, the Moscow Trio and the Kneisel Quartet, from Boston.

In that season (1903–1904) the concerts were also launched in the provinces. The Manchester music store, Forsyth Bros., were agents for a remarkable series of 'Ladies' Concerts' held twice weekly in the afternoon at the Midland Hotel. A season ticket cost £2 10s and any lady who stayed the full course would have enjoyed some musical treats. These concerts were billed as 'classical' or 'popular'. The same distinguished artists took part as in London—the Bohemian String Quartet, the Moscow Trio, the Brodsky Quartet, Dohnanyi, Henry J. Wood, Plunket Greene and Gervase Elwes. The line between 'classical' and 'popular' was not rigid; Dohnanyi played a 'classical' programme of Schubert, Beethoven and Liszt, but also included Beethoven's Thirty-Two Variations in a 'popular' recital.

Some flavour of the 'popular' afternoons may be gauged from the inclusion of the young actress Constance Collier, reciting to a piano accompaniment (on a Broadwood steel barless grand, naturally); and songs by Mr William Higley, among them 'Where the Swallows Homeward Fly', by Maude V. White.

In 1904–1905 the London series was transferred to the newly-opened Aeolian Hall in Bond Street[10] and was notable for the début of the 22-year-old Australian pianist and composer Percy Grainger (who launched himself with Brahms's Variations on a Theme of Handel). In that season also Sir Walter Parratt, organist of St George's Chapel, Windsor, resurrected the Broadwood 'Pedalier' pedal-grand for a performance of Schumann's Fugue on the notes B A C H.

The Manchester concerts were repeated in 1904–1905, though on a much smaller scale (there were eleven concerts); and there were other series at Birmingham, Leeds and Malvern. In April 1905 Broadwoods took stock of the commercial results, noted a loss of £1,100 on the season (including London and the provinces), but determined to continue, considering that the concerts were 'valuable as an advertisement and as a means of helping the musical profession'.

The 1905–1906 season saw the inclusion of the Kruse Quartet (with Lionel Tertis as viola-player; Tertis also stood in with the Bohemian String Quartet when one of its members was ill). That season too, the choristers of the Temple Church, conducted by Dr Walford Davies, sang a Palestrina Motet. In the provincial series, at Malvern, Gervase Elwes' accompanist was Hamilton Harty*.

* (Sir) Hamilton Harty (1879–1941), accompanist and conductor

There was a break in 1906–1907 (when the Board was imposing economies), but the concerts resumed in the following winter, though only in London, for four more seasons. Frank Merrick and (Sir) George Henschel took part in 1908–1909; the English String Quartet, with Frank Bridge in 1909–1910; the New Quartet led by the 24-year-old Albert Sammons, and the pianist and composer York Bowen in 1910–1911. In that season too, a young vocal quartet included as its bass a pupil of Henschel, nearly twenty three, named Frederick Grisewood*.

The Broadwood Concerts therefore demonstrate a remarkable record in the picking of musical winners, and indeed in musical adventurousness (at one of the last concerts, in 1912, Percy Grainger performed a Dance by Granados, then unknown outside Spain).[11]

When George Rose left, the factory returned to the charge of William Thompson (who had deputised for Willie Dobbs a decade earlier). His assistant, as works superintendent, was Reginald Collen, who had a technical background—he had been apprenticed as a marine engineer. At this time Harry Broadwood's two sons were reaching adult life: Stewart was twenty, and Leopold two years younger. They had not followed their father to Eton, but had been sent to Bradfield College. In November 1908 Harry Broadwood arranged for Stewart to see Mr Thompson, as a preliminary to his taking up work in the factory: but for whatever reason, this approach was not followed up and Stewart began an engineering apprenticeship with Thorneycroft of Southampton. Soon afterwards, Leo started an apprenticeship in electrical engineering with W. H. Allen & Son of Bedford.

It is hardly surprising after the almost continuous trouble and discord of his own years with the family firm that Harry Broadwood was equivocal about his sons joining: he did nothing to force them into the family tradition, but was content to let them expand their individual interests in the new technologies.[12] It was only in the year after Harry Broadwood's death at the sadly early age of fifty four, in 1911, that Stewart became a sub-manager in the factory. Otherwise Bertha (who had been elected a director, at last, in 1910) would have been the only upholder of the family name in the company.

King George V succeeded his father in May 1910, and that December the Royal Warrant was once again bestowed on Broadwoods. Despite dock strikes and coal strikes (the latter caused the factory to be shut on Saturdays) business markedly improved. At last the debts of the previous decade were being repaid; and Evelyn Broadwood, as a young Regular

* 'Freddie' Grisewood (1888–1972), later a broadcaster and for many years chairman of the BBC discussion programme 'Any Questions'.

Army officer attending his first Board in 1912, had the pleasure of hearing that the bank overdraft had been halved in that year, to £10,000. The success of the Broadwood player-pianos had helped this turn-round, and a separate factory to make them was opened at Baldwin's Place in the following year. By that time the Broadwood, with the Pianola and the Hupfeld player-action, was regarded as a brand leader; and in 1914 the company was among the first to introduce an improved piano-roll with 'contiguous perforation' which, by improving the player's control of expression, further increased sales.[13]

The improvement of sales extended to ordinary pianos, particularly in the 'quality' ranges. There was even an increased demand for 'special' pianos with decorated cases. In 1909 it had been decided that the existing stock of 'specials' in various stages of manufacture should be converted to ordinary rosewood grands, since there was no sale for them. Now, in the spring of 1914, eight 'specials' were on order, one of them—a Louis XV grand 'with satinette quartered panels, bordered kingwood, legs solid mahogany'—for Maples, a steady customer.

Throughout the early years of the century the piano trade as a whole had been challenged by increasing imports of German pianos, particularly Bechsteins and Blüthners. Some parts of the trade reacted with a passionate anti-German jingo-ism that intensified as the threat of war with Germany increased. Broadwoods took no part in that campaign; indeed, in 1912 they were negotiating with Langer of Berlin for the supply of piano actions, and in the spring of 1914 with the Deutsche Halbtonwercke for grand rims and wrest planks.

When war was declared on 4 August 1914 the company was buying substantial quantities of materials in Germany—wire, studs, keys and wrest pins. These deliveries ceased, and there was doubt also about the reliability of the supply of actions from Herrburger in Paris. Much of British industry, particularly the 'luxury' industries such as piano-making, came to a virtual standstill in the first few weeks of the war. The Old Ford factory was put on half-time ($22\frac{1}{2}$ hours a week) and wages were halved (although the foremen were given a token 5s extra). The problem of the supply of materials proved not to be an immediate hazard, however; there were 513 actions in stock, there was a good supply of Poehlmann piano wire in London, much of it bespoken by Broadwoods, and Goddards were offering wire that they claimed was as good. For safety's sake a large order for actions was despatched to Herrburger in Paris. The first shortage was of wrest pins, and a search for suppliers was mounted in England and the Unites States (shortly afterwards 500 sets of American wrest pins were ordered on approval). A Toronto maker wrote offering actions. By the end of November 1914 the upright shop was on full time again, though the grands remained on short time.

A problem seemed to be arising over the standards of workmanship, which suggests that international events were having an unsettling effect on the craftsmen. Certainly throughout 1914 there were incidents which implied careless supervision. An agent, Whitehouse, complained that 'most piano actions are dirty, and all pianos still contain half a cupful of sawdust and shavings'. Mr Nicholls, the agent in Barbados, wrote complaining that while he had ordered pianos 'torrified' (made of solid wood and subjected to more than usually intense heat) for the tropics, he had been sent veneered instruments the polish of which had bloomed. One of the 'special' grands, newly completed, was dropped in the factory and split. Finally, shortly after the outbreak of war, when Broadwoods were promoting concerts to entertain the troops, a piano ordered for an army concert in Lichfield was despatched to Liverpool and the local agent had to supply a rival make.

By mid-1915 the main difficulties were in the supply of iron frames, metal parts generally, and actions. This was more a problem of transport rather than materials. No shipping space was available for the import of Herrburger piano actions from Paris; and the budget of September 1915 imposed an import duty of 33⅓ per cent on various goods including musical instruments and parts. Broadwoods began to make their own actions again; they had made twenty five by October[14]. At first, transport was also the main problem in the supply of frames. The railways soon became choked with war materials, and at one time there were four tons of iron frames awaiting despatch at Booth & Brookes, and no way of booking rail delivery. Broadwood vans were sent in relays to collect them.

Apparently minor shortages could be critical. In December 1915 the whole of the British production of methylated spirits was commandeered, which for Broadwoods meant that French polishing became impossible. They turned back to wax polishing, and experimented with paraffin. When meths was released again to the civilian market, it cost 4s per gallon compared with 2s 3d six months earlier.

Prices generally rocketed. Spruce (essential for soundboards) when it could be got cost £33 per standard, compared with a pre-war price of £12 10s; even glue rose by £5 per ton. The wisdom of Broadwoods making their own actions became clear in March 1916 when the Government banned completely the import of such goods. By mid-1917 there was no more brass on the civilian market for studs, no more steel for frames or wires. A New York firm was offering to supply copper-covered and steel

Aircraft propellers being made at Old Ford, 1915 *(John Broadwood & Sons Ltd)*

strings; but there was a total ban on the import of copper. In October 1918 timber rationing was introduced. Throughout 1917 the factory was trying to maintain a target of thirty pianos a week, but did not achieve it. In line with the increases in the costs of materials and wages, selling prices had to be raised; there followed an outcry against 'profiteering in wartime'.

The profitable years immediately before the war had in fact ended; and once again Broadwoods was showing a loss. Yet the factory was busy. What kept it so was the manufacture of ammunition boxes, aircraft propellers and finally aircraft.

On 17 December 1914 the factory noted a 'request from Messrs Vickers & Co to tender for 65 Tool Boxes @ 15s each for British Mines, also 25,000 to 50,000 Ammunition Boxers @ 13s each'. Leslie, the Chairman, had business links with Vickers (through his company Leslie & Godwin) and had no doubt sounded out the arms manufacturers for business. The

The Maurice Farman aircraft, 1915. *(Imperial War Museum)*

materials were supplied by Vickers and there were complaints that the wood was wet; nevertheless 3,500 ammunition boxes had been delivered by April 1915. The factory made boxes for tools and ammunition throughout the war.

In August 1915 there was an approach from Capt. Wheatley of the War Office about the possible manufacture of aircraft propellers, at £33 7s each, complete in case. By the beginning of 1916 war work was taking so much labour that the production of pianos was suffering. The factory Board—Stuart, Collen and Thompson—decided to end munitions production and try to catch up on the growing back-log of piano orders. It was a vain hope. At the end of June the firm was asked to tender for 'nacelles [engine housings and cockpits] for Hendon Aircraft Factory' and a day later the request was followed by a firm order for '30 M F 1914 nacelles, delivery a.s.a.p., they to supply all metal fittings'. Simultaneously there was a warning that 'the Government might require the factory' (Old Ford was indeed to be 'controlled' under the Munitions of War Acts from July 1916).

The inevitable was accepted and the decision made that the mill would be half on Government work, and half on pianos. The 'M F' was the Maurice Farman aircraft, a French design that still bore some family resemblance to the flimsy construction of wood, cloth and wire in which

Aircraft fuselages being loaded at Old Ford, 1916 *(John Broadwood & Sons Ltd)*

Orville Wright had first flown a mere seven years earlier. It was a 'pusher' biplane, with its single engine mounted at the back of the wooden nacelle in which the pilot sat poised on the centre of the lower wing and encompassed by a cat's cradle of wires and struts (see page 280).

¡There was no undercarriage. The aircraft landed on skids made of bent wood which also held up the front elevator (from their appearance they became known as 'Longhorns'). The Broadwood piano factory was equipped with both the machinery and skill to turn out these bent wood skids, and the Aircraft Manufacturing Company (Airco) leant heavily on their production. Orders flooded in; they totalled, that year, 140 nacelles, 480 front skids and 430 tail skids.

Then in November 1916 the orders for Maurice Farman parts were peremptorily cancelled. The reason was that the military aircraft was being redesigned under the stress of war experience. Although the Maurice Farman equipped six Royal Flying Corps squadrons on the Western Front through 1915, and other squadrons of the RFC and the Royal Naval Air Service in Mesopotamia and the Dardanelles,[15] it was being superseded. However, it came to be used as a training aircraft and part of the M F order was re-issued, for 400 tail skids to be delivered as quickly as possible, in February 1917, only three months after the cancellation: more M F orders followed.

The De Havilland 4 aircraft, 1916. *(British Aerospace Hawker Siddeley)*

At the same time, Broadwoods received an Airco order for fuselages for the aircraft that, it was planned, would now become Britain's main fighting machine, the De Havilland 4.

It is a measure of the hand-to-mouth character of aircraft construction at this time that while the rear part of the fuselage was a standard design, the front part had to be tailored to fit an available engine. So the order was for 170 rear fuselages, 60 front fuselages for the Rolls Royce engine, 40 for the RAF (Royal Aircraft Factory) engine, and 50 for the BHP (Beardmore-Halford-Pullinger) engine. The order was given and accepted with only the minimum of financial agreement: 'The price for the 170 rear parts has been settled at £21 each, all the others will be arranged later'. In fact Broadwoods lost financially, and a compensation settlement had to be negotiated later.

The speed of decision in the designing, making and launching of those aircraft was prodigious. The DH4 made its maiden flight in mid-August 1916, with Geoffrey de Havilland at the controls. It passed its official trials in September-October 1916, and first saw active service in France with 55 Squadron RFC in March 1917, one month after Broadwoods, as sub-contractor, had received a large order for it. An aircraft historian says that 'no time was lost in developing the basic design through minor airframe modifications and in fitting engines of progressively higher power.'[16] This was reflected in the Old Ford factory where Collen explained that delays were caused because 'we are continually being asked to make alterations to the structure—there have been three alterations in one part in the course of construction'.

In May 1917 Broadwoods began to build 75 front and rear fuselages for the latest De Havilland, the DH6 (this proved to be an underpowered aircraft and was generally used as a trainer). In June there came an assorted order for DH4 and DH6 fuselages, MF nacelles and assorted skids. It was suggested that they should tender for wings as well, and in June Airco ordered 50 pairs of 'planes' (wings) and ailerons (flaps).

The Airco orders mounted month by month, to a total value of around £26,000 by mid-1917. The works manager, Collen, proposed turning the whole of Old Ford over to aircraft manufacture, and taking another factory at Stratford, East London, for piano-making. As there was little chance of obtaining piano components this was not proceeded with. At the end of November 1917 there was an Airco order for 100 new aircraft, the DH9. This was a modification of the DH4, and more popular with pilots since the cockpit was moved back from its former potentially lethal position between the engine and the fuel tank. The DH9 had made its first flight at Hendon four months earlier. Further DH9 contracts followed from another contractor, the National Aircraft Factory No. 1 (Cubitts). At Old Ford, the factory yard was covered over to allow more storage space: another purpose was to protect the factory from air attack. German Zeppelins had begun bombing London on moonlit nights, and local people in Hackney had been besieging the Broadwood works seeking shelter. The firm pointed out that it was not a secure shelter (rather, it was an obvious target); but the popular belief that the 'great factory would be safe' persisted, and Broadwoods were obliged to shut their doors at six o'clock on moonlit nights.

By March 1918 Broadwoods had aircraft contracts worth £90,000. In the next month, Airco put in a further order for yet another development of the De Havilland, the DH9A, 'complete with undercarriages, cowling, bomb cells &c @ £125 each'. At last piano-making had to be suspended for the duration of the war, 'in view of the Government call for men and so many as may be suitable switched on to aircraft work. Pianos well advanced will be looked over, finished off, and sent up to Conduit Street as they can be taken'. This final qualification was because the company's lorries were fully stretched ferrying completed aircraft to Hendon.

In the preceding year, piano manufacture had been kept going largely by women. A consequence of the war, for Broadwoods as for many industries, was the introduction of women on the shop floor. In October

1915 Collen noted that 'the new recruiting scheme may result in a good many men being called away from the factory' (Lord Derby had introduced his 'attesting' scheme, whereby men of military age were encouraged to 'attest' their willingness to serve if called: full conscription was not introduced until January 1916). By November, women had been brought in, and the national officer of the trade union gave approval of their conditions of work. By February 1916 girls were working in upright finishing, regulating and 'looking over'; a month later, two began to learn french polishing, and others key-making.

They were also involved in the making of ammunition boxes, and a munitions inspector said he was 'surprised at what he found the women able to do here, and expressed his delight with all he had seen'. As a result, the firm was approached by a Senior Lady Inspector of Factories, asking permission for 'a representative of Messrs Pathé to take photos of the girls at work and show, on the cinematograph, processes in which women are now employed in various trades'. By October 1916 the mill was being operated by older men and boys, and piano-making was being carried on by older men and girls; for the rest of the year they kept up an output of 20 uprights and 4 grands a week.

By 1917 this had been reduced to 15 uprights a week. To keep production going, Collen had rationalised production methods. His account marks the end of the traditional detailed (perhaps over-detailed) craftsmanship which had been characteristic of Broadwoods throughout the nineteenth century:

On account of the shortage of labour and difficulty in obtaining certain materials, considerable changes have been made in the methods of piano manufacture. We are doing a number of cases in solid mahogany to save veneering. To cheapen case making the girls are now making the component parts. Backs are squared after frames are fixed and strung. The blocks are glued on by girls and special devices have been designed to enable them to glue on the ends, bottoms and tops—key bottom mouldings will also be done by them and the cheeks glued and screwed on; the fall and back hollow, lock slip and beadings will be erected in one place, and the plinth, toes, top brackets and legs will also be made as one component—all absolutely to gauges.

These four principal components when erected will, with the top and bottom doors, make up the piano. Actions are being made in the factory and we have also fixed up an order with the Clutsam Co. for the supply of these. Keys are now being better supplied by Messrs

Shenstone and we have arranged with the London Action Co. to finish off about 200 sets which we had on hand when our men were called up. Maple rockers are being used instead of steel and the handholds are now being made in wood only, as before.

This entirely does away with the two branches of cheeking and plinthing, and fitting up.

Thus it was under the pressure of events that Broadwoods rationalised the making of upright pianos.

The shortage of skilled men brought about this change. By August 1916, 105 men had joined the army and a further 45 were waiting to go. The Government operated its own press-gang. On 30 March 1917 'the Ministry of Munitions man called and selected six men of military age now on munitions work to be taken away for other work—he may return for more'.

As ever when labour is in high demand and living costs are rising, there was soon industrial trouble of a kind that was wholly new to Broadwoods. The aircraft workers formed a trade union and pressed for higher wages. In July 1917 there was a general pay dispute throughout London aircraft factories, and on Thursday, 5 July the men walked out for ten days. Collen could only stand by watching, since the strike was 'not arising from any dispute here'. The London District Committee of the Aircraft Industry negotiated, and granted a wage increase. The Ministry of Munitions was slow to authorise it. In December 1917 a deputation of aircraft workers went to the works manager and pointed out that their wage rise, negotiated in November, had not been granted. 'The men cannot understand the reason for the delay and are consequently unsettled and dissatisfied.' Collen agreed to pay them an extra 1s 4d per hour 'on their undertaking to increase the production'.

Events moved rapidly in the last weeks of that year. For it transpired that while arranging for action-making to be transferred to Vickers of Dartford, the chairman of Broadwoods, Leslie, had also put together a scheme whereby Vickers would buy out the Managers' shares and in effect take the company over.

The first challenge was to start making pianos again. Four days after the war ended, Collen reported to the factory Board that 400 pianos had been started, the frames cut out from the existing timber stocks. A large timber order for spruce, whitewood, mahogany and maple was sent to Mallinsons, the principal suppliers. Negotiations began with Herrburger about actions; from Paris, he replied that he could supply them at a cost of 188 per cent above pre-war price, plus freight and duty. He was, however,

Leo A.T. Broadwood, *c.* 1917 *(L.A.T. Broadwood)*

planning to make them in London (Herrburger Brooks Ltd was started in 1920).

The second challenge was to sort out the future of John Broadwood & Sons. The Board meeting at Conduit Street on 20 December 1918 was packed with members of the family. Captain Evelyn Broadwood, who had won a Military Cross with the Norfolk Regiment, was elected a director (and his Aunt Bertha re-elected). There were also present Lucy Broadwood, Ada Broadwood (Harry's widow) and her sons Stewart and Leo. Evelyn 'asked for information about the Managers' shares to be given to Messrs Vickers under the proposed agreement'. After this meeting, W. H. P. Leslie ceased to be chairman of the company, and Cuthbert Heath took over the chairmanship. No managers' shares were transferred to Vickers, and the action-making machinery was recovered from their factory.

The third challenge was to cope, in association with the rest of the

Captain Evelyn Broadwood, *c.* 1917 *(The Broadwood Trust)*

piano trade, with the new conditions of industrial relations prevailing. The newly formed Piano Workers Union had faced the Piano Traders Association with the demand that piece work and the 'contract system' (whereby workers were taken on and laid off as seasonal demand dictated) must forthwith be abolished. The Piano Traders Association turned this down on 16 December by 56 votes to 40. The majority were the small makers, the minority the larger firms. On the following day the 40 representatives of the big firms formed a separate alliance (called the London Pianoforte Traders Alliance) 'for the purpose of promoting a prompt settlement with the Trade Union on the terms indicated by the delegates'.

One consequence of the settlement was that the company bought the men's tools, which under the old contract system had been their own property. One man, H. Bowles, was paid £251 5s for hammer equipment, and another, M. J. Paris, £183 15s for cramps. There was still difficulty in obtaining components, not only from the shortage of raw materials but also from the industrial disputes that were as general in the United States and France: Herrburger wrote that it would be fruitless for Broadwoods to travel to Paris for discussions, as he was fully stretched with labour and wages troubles. He despatched 72 actions in July 1919 'which is a great achievement in view of the prevailing conditions'. But he put up the price to a total of 200 per cent over the pre-war level.

Leo Broadwood, who had been persuaded by his brother Stewart to become his *alter ego* in the showroom at Conduit Street, was stung by the public criticism of the increase in the retail price of an upright from £45 to £108 in a decade, and invited a journalist to examine the firm's books.

He pointed out that 'despite the fact that only eighty per cent of Broadwood's men had, as yet, returned to the factory its wage bill had already doubled. Out of a total addition to the costs of a piano of £28 9s 3d, labour accounted for £11 . . . The retailer's profit margin was still 50 per cent, forced upon Broadwood in the past by German competition and now retained in anticipation of its resurgence. The manufacturer's profit was calculated at a mere 15 per cent on the wholesale price'. A leading piano historian has remarked that 'such frankness about costs and prices is rare in the annals of an industry notorious for its secretiveness',[17] but it was typical of Leo's openness and perhaps his impetuosity.

By the end of 1919 it began to seem possible that the prevailing increase in the stock of parts might make it practicable to achieve 3,000 pianos a year by midsummer 1920. There were problems in obtaining good frames—one complete consignment of steel frames from a leading maker proved to be defective—and key-making was re-started in the factory. It was decided to buy in ready-made player-piano actions, and they were obtained from Otto Higel and the Auto Player Co. of New York. Closer links with the principal suppliers were sought, and following this policy W. J. Mallinson*, son of the leading timber merchant, joined the Board.

Unfortunately the potential increase in production was not paralleled by similar increases in sales.

In October 1919 a works deputation went to the factory manager, Collen, and demanded the dismissal of two workmen who had resigned from the union. The deputation was told that the policy of John Broadwood & Sons was 'the open shop'. Eventually both men left the company. One, an exceptional craftsman, started his own repair business and became the leading repairer in London—not least because Leo

---

* (Sir) William James Mallinson (1877–1944), J.P. and Sheriff of Surrey, 1933.

Broadwood saw to it, quietly, that all Broadwood repairs were sent to him.

In December 1919 the union put in a demand for a 44-hour week (a reduction from 50 hours), and wages of 2s 2d per hour for men and 1s 4d for women, with a week's paid holiday in summer. The management offered 2s per hour, with an extra ½d after May, but no paid holiday. There was stalemate; and in the spring of 1920 the Broadwood workmen came out for a strike that lasted for twelve weeks. That year, once again, the company recorded a loss. John Brinsmead & Sons went bankrupt that January. At Broadwoods, after the strike, there was a desperate attempt to find more work of almost any kind—office desks, telephone switchboards, even '3 gross photo frames'. The factory had precisely 17 orders for pianos on hand. A third of the workforce, some 200 people, were laid off: as far as possible the skilled cabinet-makers were retained and women, boys and unskilled men discharged.

So unusual and unpredictable were trading conditions at this time that—briefly—the factory Board took the decision to cease making uprights altogether, and to concentrate on grands. The argument for this lay in a conversation between Clifford Martin, then sales manager, and the Maples buyer. 'Mr Matthews was convinced that the Germans would take a long time to get going with Grands, but that they were undoubtedly seriously cutting into the Cottage [Upright] trade. Therefore our policy should be strict concentration on Grands.'

It was Mallinson who introduced Broadwoods to the manufacture of gramophones. As he told the factory Board in December 1919,

he had called at Marshalls, where he was shown a machine at £70; he also visited the Orchestrelle Co. and ultimately bought one for £53. He then ascertained that Messrs Garrard have been making the motors, and could supply us at the rate of 50s. in quantities as required. He therefore pointed out that as, beyond the case which we could easily produce ourselves, and the motor at the price noted, there was very little cost, it appeared as if the undertaking of this line ought to be a profitable proposition. Designs for the cases would be provided for by getting Mr Crawley to undertake the drawings, Mr Martin [Clifford Martin, the newly-appointed sales manager] to spend the next month organising it.

Five models were produced. The standard model was in a free-standing cabinet, the turntable under a hinged top and the front opening to reveal storage for 180 12 ins. records. The machine played three 12 ins.

The Broadwood gramophone, *c.* 1922 *(John Broadwood & Sons Ltd)*

records without rewinding. Priced originally at 85 guineas, this proved to be above the market and the price was reduced to 78 guineas with fifteen record albums thrown in. The other four models were a 'Grand Table' version in a 'Sheraton design' at 20 guineas, a floor-standing model in 'Chinese Chippendale' at 57 guineas, a 'Sheraton style' floor cabinet at 60 guineas, and one with cabriole legs at 82 guineas.

The clockwork motors (for these were, of course, simple wind-up 'acoustic' models before the days of electrical recording) were bought from the jeweller and clockmaker lower down Regent Street, Garrard.

The advertising literature made much of the 'patent wooden tone arm': 'the Broadwood tone arm is entirely constructed of wood, a material which absorbs extraneous sounds, while metal is inclined to magnify them'.

The *Scotsman* was impressed: 'Those who have listened only to an ordinary gramophone cannot realise the wide gulf that separates it from a Broadwood. The Broadwood gramophone reveals all the delicate nuances of the human voice as exhibited by the great singers with extraordinary fidelity, with the elimination of the unmusical and objectionable sounds which are the invariable accompaniment of the 'popular' article . . . a gramophone which commands the admiration of the musical critic!'[18]

Unfortunately, in America electrical recording and reproduction were even then being developed, and when electrical gramophones were introduced five years later with the massive commercial backing of the increasingly wealthy gramophone companies, the market for acoustic machines almost disappeared and Broadwoods withdrew from the field.

Slowly the piano trade began to improve. By the summer of 1922 the factory was planning to make 275 pianos, uprights as well as grands, and including one full-scale concert grand, during the autumn and winter. But the company had still not returned to profitability and the business was kept going by repeated injections of cash by Cuthbert Heath. As an economy, the large showroom in Conduit Street was abandoned in 1924 and a smaller showroom taken at 158 New Bond Street.

Nevertheless the public face was still brave. When in 1924 the artists and craftsmen of Britain combined to make for Queen Mary 'The Queen's Dolls' House' containing miniature books by leading authors, miniature paintings by notable artists, and miniature furnishings by the best craftsmen, the Dolls' House required a grand piano. It was, of course, made by Broadwoods, and designed by the man who a quarter of a century earlier had designed prize-winning pianos, but was now working on a larger scale (he was building New Delhi)—Sir Edwin Lutyens. The

Miniature by Lutyens for Queen Mary's Dolls House *(John Broadwood & Sons)*

decorated grand, nine inches long, was carved, gilt and painted, with metal frame, soundboard, bridges, strings, action and keys all working, and it could be played with the head of a pin. It was made by the craftsmen at Old Ford.

Industrial unrest, however, continued throughout the country. In May 1926 there occurred the General Strike, and for ten days the factory was at a standstill. On 10 May Stewart Broadwood, who was a keen amateur engineer, was experimenting in his workshop at Bone Hill, St Albans, when the flywheel of an engine broke, struck him and killed him. He was thirty eight, and left a widow and two small children*.

When therefore King George V and Queen Mary paid a Royal Visit to the Broadwood factory at Old Ford on the afternoon of 20 July 1926 it was in the most extraordinary circumstances. It was only ten days after the ending of the General Strike, which explains why contemporary accounts place so much emphasis on the fact that the King and Queen travelled in

---

* Michael Stewart Tschudi, aged ten, and Ann Marion, aged eight. Michael Broadwood was killed as a Naval Officer during the Second World War.

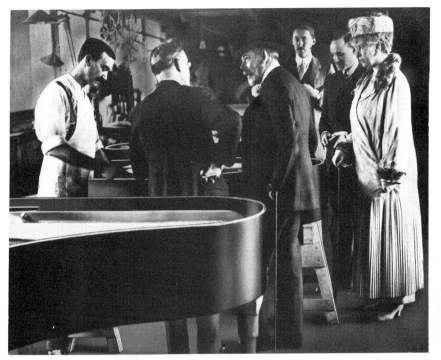

King George V and Queen Mary touring the Broadwood factory, 1926 (*John Broadwood & Sons Ltd*)

an unescorted open car 'though they had to pass through a district which has the reputation of being thickly peopled with "Reds"'. Further, the Broadwood family and also the factory were still stunned by Stewart Broadwood's death, though this was hidden from the visitors.

Understandably the emphasis of the day was on loyalty and tradition. Included among the welcoming party were eight of the longest-serving employees claiming a total service of more than 450 years. One of them was H. Ansell, himself with the firm for thirty seven years, though his father had worked for it for forty five years and his grandfather for more than forty. The 'father of the factory' was George Preston: he had completed sixty one years' service, and still, in his seventy sixth year, used a circular saw in the mill. In age he narrowly beat George Nicholson, senior soundboard maker, who had worked for Broadwoods for fifty nine of his seventy five years.

After the visit, the King ordered a new Broadwood for Buckingham Palace, and Queen Mary a Broadwood-Ampico reproducing player-piano for Sandringham.

The President of the American Piano Company (makers of the Ampico player-piano action), George Foster, had come to London for the visit and was presented to the King and Queen. In the previous year, Stewart Broadwood had visited New York, negotiating the use of the Ampico action in Broadwood player-pianos and discussing yet again the possible export of Broadwoods to the United States.

At this time the standard range of Broadwood pianos consisted of three conventional uprights and one player-upright, a 'quarter-grand' (5 ft 7 ins) and a 'baby grand' (5 ft). The trend towards standardisation had been pointed out to the King, who had shown particular interest in this 'entirely new principle of construction'. This was, in essence, a prefabrication principle whereby the case and action would be manufactured separately and then secured together. It was clearly derived from Collen's experience in simplifying piano-making for the benefit of the women workers a decade earlier, and was registered (as the Collen-Broadwood Patent, No. 267195) in March 1927.

In that year two new subsidiary companies were formed: the Old Ford Engineering and Manufacturing Co Ltd (to attract more work to the under-employed factory), and the British Piano Action Company (to make player-piano actions to a Broadwood design).

No new concert grand had been made by Broadwoods for some years, though there was a large stock of ageing instruments. Evelyn Broadwood liked to maintain the firm's traditional generosity by lending these out to pianists. When in 1928 the British Pianoforte Publicity Committee ran a national piano competition in association with the *Daily Express* the winner was Cyril Smith,* then a student at the Royal College of Music. Subsequently Evelyn arranged for Broadwoods to lend him a piano for his London concerts, and he wrote enthusiastically that 'the Broadwood was simply splendid'.

There were occasions when this spontaneous generosity could produce difficulties, as in the case of the pianist Pouishnoff.† Pouishnoff had first dealt with Broadwoods in 1923, when he asked for a piano for a concert in Bournemouth. This was supplied. Three years later a musical friend of Evelyn's, E. Godfrey Brown, musical director of the BBC radio station in

---

* Cyril Smith (1909–1974), concert pianist, Professor of Pianoforte at the Royal College of Music 1934–1974. A stroke during a Russian tour in 1956 paralysed his left hand, but he made a noble recovery, continuing his playing career with his wife Phyllis Sellick in duets for three hands.

† Leff Pouishnoff (1891–1959), Russian-born concert pianist who made his home in England, but toured widely.

Belfast (and a considerable influence on the development of broadcast music nationally), wrote to suggest that it might be worth talking to Pouishnoff again: 'I know him pretty well and think a good deal of him as a pianist and as a business man—Blüthners pay him £600 a year to play on their pianos he says.'

A scheme was devised for Pouishnoff to tour Spain in autumn 1927. It was a grandiose scheme, in every sense, since it is clear that the pianist was assuming that the wealthy piano-firm would provide the instrument and defray all costs. The negotiations rapidly turned into a nightmare for Evelyn and for Leo Broadwood, who as company secretary was well aware of the financial realities.

Evelyn wrote to a friend:

> I am looking at it from the point of view of whether we can piano him on his tour—for the glory of British pianos in general and of the Broadwood piano in particular and in the sacred cause of his having a really good instrument! . . I don't know much about conditions in that part of the world, but I have told him that I am sure that it would be necessary for his piano to travel with him everywhere, and as a consequence a kind of piano-supervisor would seem to be necessary, wherever he goes, to see to unloading from train, unpacking, putting on to concert platform, and the reverse process.'

The tour did not take place in 1927, fortunately, for it began to look very like the Hallé tour of Australia 40 years earlier—an immense expense, with no possibility of any reasonable return. Nevertheless Pouishnoff was still expressing a willingness to enter into some form of contract with Broadwoods to play their pianos, at a price.

In November 1927 Leo Broadwood put his foot down. 'We are quite unprepared in the matter of concert Grands—we have one old type here . . . Further to this, it would be the first time that we have ever offered money to a professional to play upon our pianos or entered into a binding contract with a professional. Our policy in the past was to supply pianos free. That is as far as we went . . . Others went in for subsidising and contracts.' Evelyn Broadwood was obliged to extricate the firm, making the entirely truthful explanation: 'We are faced here with a somewhat formidable, though optimistic, reorganisation.'

In 1928 Leo Broadwood decided that his future lay elsewhere and resigned his executive post with the company, while remaining a member of the Board, and keenly concerned about the future of the family firm.

Sales in 1927 had shown an increase, and the company returned a small profit (but not enough to pay the Debenture holders' interest). But from 1928 the future once again began to look bleak. The market for player-pianos was becoming more competitive, and another manufacturer—Challen—had achieved a considerable marketing success with a 'baby grand'. In the spring of 1928 Cuthbert Heath commissioned the accountants Layton-Bennett, Chiene & Tait to report on the company, its activities and its future.

On the question of manufacture, nearly half the cost of the average piano was found to consist of the iron frame, the keys and the action. The price of the frame could be kept down by competition between the various makers, but 'with regard to the keys and action, monopolies exist which prevent any reduction. Keys are supplied solely by Shenstone Ltd . . . and the actions by Herrburger Brooks Ltd'.

The accountants were impressed by 'the manner in which Mr Collen has arranged the various processes of manufacture so as to make the best possible use of the somewhat unsuitable conditions at the factory . . . The relationship between the factory manager and the workers appeared to us to be of a high standard, and calculated to obtain the best results from the labour employed.' They concluded that 'the premises are too big and otherwise unsuitable for present production. Either a further outlet for production must be discovered or more suitable premises should be occupied provided the present building can be disposed of without too great a sacrifice . . . The company has a most valuable asset in its patent methods of production.'

Sales were a different matter.

The greater part of the company's turnover is to the trade, sales being made to recognised agents at a discount of 33⅓ per cent. Contact is maintained with the company's agents by means of a single traveller supplemented by occasional visits by Mr Foster [Eric Foster, the sales manager] and Mr Collen . . .

We understand that the prices of the better makes of pianos are fixed, whereas a merchant or agent may bargain over the selling price of a 'commercial' and cheaper piano . . . The probability is, we think, that the better makes of instruments and the 'commercial' pianos serve quite distinct markets . . . One of the most potent factors militating against an increased turnover in pianos is in our opinion the supply of mechanical music. The introduction of wireless to a certain extent, and the great improvement in the gramophone to a much larger extent, has in our opinion definitely curtailed the market for pianos.

A grand *c.* 1885, designed on the Burne-Jones trestle stand, the gesso decoration by Kate Faulkner of the William Morris workshop. The piano is now in the William Morris room at the Victoria and Albert Museum *(Photo: Graham Miller)*

Above The square grand in 'art nouveau' style designed by C R Ashbee for his wife, 1898. The case is of light oak, and the piano has a composite metal frame, bolted together, and painted a pale apple green *(Toynbee Hall, London)* *(Photo: Graham Miller)*

Left The Lutyens design for a grand piano won a gold Medal at the Paris Exhibition of 1900 where it featured in Waring and Gillow's 'Jacobean' room. The original was in oak, but a number of other examples were made, including this (1907) in mahogany, built for Harold Brockbank of Sizedale Hall, Haverthwaite near Carnforth. It is now owned by Robert Welch *(Photo: Graham Miller)*

A modern Broadwood grand at the Wandsworth workshop *(Photo: Clive Barda)*

Concerning the overall management, the survey was acerbic:

We understand that very few Board meetings are held . . . It appears that your [Heath's] continued substantial financial support of the company has possibly caused some of your Directors to be less critical than they would otherwise be . . . A small, active and practical Board of Directors would be of greater assistance to you, and regular meetings of the Board should be held at which essential facts and figures should be considered and a definite policy determined . . .

It has been our experience that a business has a surer prospect of success if entire responsibility is vested in a single capable and practical individual devoting his whole time to the company's affairs . . . a strong managing director is required with sole responsibility to the Board of Directors for the company's success.

There had been no such figure at John Broadwood & Sons for fifty years, since Henry Fowler Broadwood retired from active management. No one had been given the responsibility or the authority, and as a result there had been constant friction between the showroom and the factory. In 1927, Reg Collen was still complaining about the impracticability of the sales department's ordering policy.

The criticism of the Board was probably less than fair, since it was inevitable that as the company was in a state of total financial dependence on Cuthbert Heath, his was the only voice that effectively counted; the rest of the Board did sometimes complain, as Evelyn once wrote forthrightly to Heath, that they seemed to be no more than a rubber stamp.

While the company remained so heavily in debt, of course, it was impracticable to make any substantial investment. There has been criticism,[19] in hindsight, that the leaders of the British piano trade did not, in the years immediately following the First World War, launch themselves into the concert grand market while the German makers were out of the way. Looking at the problems that beset the Broadwood management—shortages of materials, increases in cost, industrial disputes, general discord within the piano trade—and above all, under-capitalisation and indeed heavy debt, it is inconceivable that they could have done so. Bechsteins, with the advantage of the much better coordinated German supply sources, reopened their London agency in 1923.

Cuthbert Heath had indicated to the accountant Layton-Bennett that

Grand with Janko keyboard *(John Broadwood & Sons)*

he would enable Broadwoods to be reconstructed by writing off past loans and debts, thus allowing the company to continue without its increasing burden. He was prepared, therefore, to cut his losses (and very substantial they were, for he had personally taken over loans made to the company in earlier years by his companies, including the Excess Insurance Company and the Phoenix Assurance Company, to a total of about a quarter of a million pounds).

In July 1928 he wrote to the leading City chartered accountant, senior partner of Deloitte, Plender, Griffiths & Co:

Dear Sir William Plender,
I happen to be Chairman of Broadwoods. The piano business has been very bad lately and there is a proposal to amalgamate—at all events for working purposes—four or possibly five of the leading firms.

Now in order to do this it is agreed that some outside person should be called in. Could you help us; I mean quite as a matter of business?

The financial side of things would not apparently present difficulties. What we want is some person competent to advise on what it all comes to—the saving of overhead charges. This person should know all about the reorganisation of factories—which to keep & which to scrap, which officials to get rid of &c &c.

The selling part is more technical & the peculiarities of agents would have to be taken into account, but there is no doubt that very considerable sums could be saved in publicity, travellers & many things of this kind.

I believe myself that a properly arranged combination would lead to prosperity.[20]

Three of the companies involved in these discussions with Broadwoods on a 'working arrangement' were Chappell, Collard & Collard and Cramer. The suggestion was that one factory—Broadwoods proposed Old Ford—should manufacture for the group. In the event, when Plender (or the partner he had designated to act for him, Alan Rae Smith) received confidential sales and financial figures from the various companies, it was clear that all the leading makers were in the same sinking ship. The deal was finally killed when in 1929 Chappells was bought by the American music publisher Louis Dreyfus, largely for its successful popular music-publishing side. The injection of American capital enabled Chappells to buy up Collard & Collard, and also Allisons; this left Broadwoods again isolated.

In September 1930 Louis Sterling,* the energetic founder of the British Automatic Gramophone Company, bought the action-maker Herrburger Brooks; and in an attempt to achieve a monopoly in action production in Britain, bid for the sole other remaining maker, John Malcolm & Son. He was blocked by William Evans of Challen, who in one week assembled enough support from other piano-makers to top Sterling's bid. Sterling achieved his victory a year later, but with specific guarantees to Evans and his friends.[22]

---

* (Sir) Louis Sterling (1879–1958), Chairman of Herrburger Brooks, Director of S. G. Warburg & Co. Born in a poor home in New York, he sold newspapers as a boy, and emigrated to England early in the century. He found a job in the new gramophone industry, first in cylinders and then discs, becoming Chairman of the (British) Columbia Gramophone Company. In 1925 he bought up the American Columbia parent, which owned rights in electrical recording and reproduction. Later he was Chairman of Electrical and Musical Industries Ltd (EMI).[21]

Touring the country during the first three months of 1930 Broadwoods' unfortunate traveller, A. C. Hone, found himself faced not only with stagnant trading conditions leading to few orders [Wall Street collapsed the previous year, precipitating a world recession], but also with rumours that the firm was closing down. He wrote back to the sales manager, Eric Foster: 'I met Ray in Leicester, and as usual he was full of rumours. He volunteered the information that Broadwoods were selling up. Cook of Marshalls also mentioned that he heard a rumour that the factory was closed down and that we were up for sale. It's a pity that some people cannot attend to their own business of selling pianos.' Later, from Sheffield: 'Mr Fair is still very sore about the Harrods advt. and he would not accept any explanation to justify our action in the matter. He has also heard rumours re Broadwoods being offered for sale, and apart from my feigning absolute ignorance of this fact, he made it fairly obvious to me that he would be very careful about placing orders with us, until he knew definitely what was happening.' Harrods had not only broken the Broadwood price-fixing agreement, but had placed a national advertisement to announce the price-cutting, thereby harming Broadwoods with the provincial dealers.

By late 1930 Cuthbert Heath was coming to the end of his benefactions, writing that 'there is no doubt that the Debenture holders are entitled to foreclose and I think they ought to do'. The general position of the piano trade encouraged this view: 'Mallinson writes that he saw Sterling who is very pessimistic as to the piano trade and tells me . . .that Herrburger's sales are halted.'

Sterling, better than most, knew why. For the principal agent in the decline in sales of the piano was the electric gramophone. Sterling had been a leader in recording classical music, and as Ehrlich says, 'English gramophones and records were acknowledged to be among the world's leaders. Prices were falling as quality improved, reflecting enormous strides in technology (notably the transition from acoustic to electric reproduction), skilled management, mass production and increased productivity. By 1928, shares in gramophone companies were "the liveliest of stock exchange propositions"—the Columbia Gramophone Company declared a divident of forty-eight per cent.'[23]

Early in 1931 there were negotiations with Murdochs. This company, with its large chain of retail music shops, also manufactured pianos through its subsidiary John Spencer & Co. James Murdoch went round the Old Ford factory and found some 500 old Broadwood grands in store, relics of the large trade in hirings during the Victorian and Edwardian era. Many, he understood, had been played only once and then stored. Murdochs refused to take over the stock and negotiations foundered.

There were discussions with Marshalls, who proposed to take Broadwood production into their own factory. But their financial position, too, proved to be 'very weak'.

In March 1931 Alan Rae Smith was appointed Receiver and Manager of John Broadwood & Sons 'to enable those reorganisations to be effected which the altered conditions in the Piano Industry of today necessitates. It is thereby hoped to ensure the continuance of this famous business which has existed for the last 200 years.' The West End showroom (for the previous two years at 227 Regent Street) was closed and Broadwoods moved in briefly with Marshall & Rose at 233.

Discussions continued with other manufacturers; and a proposal came from William Evans of Challen. He offered to take over the manufacture of Broadwood pianos: 'our desire would be to put the Broadwood piano where we feel it rightly belongs, as the premier British instrument'.

Evans was in a position of strength. In the previous two years the sales of Challen pianos had topped £100,000, and he could claim that 'in the beginning of this year [1931] we were selling about two-thirds or even three-quarters of the total number' of grands sold in Britain. 'In January, February and March we sold just over four hundred Grand Pianos', and he suggested that Broadwoods confirm this with Herrburger Brooks.

William Evans could be proud of his achievement in countering the trend. By a combination of efficient mass-production and effective marketing he had made the 'baby grand' a status symbol. The son of a police inspector in Wales, he had learnt the piano-making trade at Chappells in Chalk Farm. In 1926 he had joined Challen, designed a small grand, and by producing it in quantity cut the price from £125 to £65. He increased sales by intensive advertising, and put the Challen baby grand into the BBC studios.

Broadwoods was therefore reconstructed. Michael Holland resigned from the Board in October 'in view of the . . . desirability of reducing the size of the Board to a few experts'; R. H. Collen, less willingly, resigned in November 1931. At Old Ford, all except two dozen or so craftsmen were laid off, and the factory let as 'industrial units'. The two dozen who remained transferred to the Challen works at Hendon, to make Broadwood pianos. With William Evans as manufacturing director, and Capt. Evelyn Broadwood as Chairman, John Broadwood & Sons was still in business.

Chapter X

Survival and Resurgence

1931–1982

*I*n the last analysis the piano's status depends upon what is happening to music, and here it is difficult to reach a balanced judgement. There are abundant signs of vitality, particularly in England, where musical standards have risen immeasurably since the 1920s, and the piano has benefited from this. It has never been better played or, to be more precise, has never been so well played by so many professionals . . . Fewer amateurs learn the piano but they are better taught, thanks to more qualified teachers . . . Moreover, their repertoire is more likely to reflect a broader musical culture, thanks to the influence of records and the waning but still beneficent influence of broadcasting. Many schools are equipped with adequate instruments, and some attempt to inculcate an appreciation of music which rises above commercial pop.

Cyril Ehrlich, *The Piano, a History*

The firm's attempt to change to meet a new market had been frustrated not by endemic weaknesses but by the collapse of that market, following the Wall Street crash and the international recession that was its consequence. In the summer of 1929 two new pianos had been launched: a 'Dainty 3 ft 9 ins Overstrung Pianette . . . a beautiful tiny upright piano for a tiny space' retailing at 57 guineas; and the Model 'O' Elfin grand, 4 ft 6 ins long, retailing at 123 guineas. The concept of smallness was emphasised: 'Owing to the restricted space in many new homes under the new housing schemes throughout the country, the House of Broadwood have had repeated demands for a tiny piano for a tiny space.' Ironically, the piano was returning to the size from which John Broadwood had developed it; the gap between the concert grand and the domestic instrument was widening. Broadwoods were hard pressed to maintain quality in a world that was crying out for cheapness, and a world, too, that found other diversions in the shape of the gramophone, the 'wireless' and the £100 motor car. In 1930 the baby grand was re-launched as the 'Minim' miniature grand, its price cut to 95 guineas.

The manufacturing agreement with Challens licensed them to be sole manufacturer of the Broadwood piano for a period not exceeding fifteen years, at the end of which time Challens would have the option to purchase the goodwill of the business for £10,000. The pianos to be manufactured were to be not inferior to the Challen piano, and the agreement was that the best grade of instrument produced by Challen would carry the Broadwood name, lesser grades to be identified as Challen 'in order so far as is possible to eliminate direct competition between the two makes of instrument'.

John Broadwood & Sons were to retain the right to a retail establishment for the sale or hire-purchase of instruments to private purchasers (as distinct from dealers or exporters) and also the sole right 'to carry on under the Broadwood name the business of tuning and of letting out of Broadwood Pianos on hire'. A new retail showroom was subsequently opened at 9 Hanover Street.

The arrangement was approved unanimously by the shareholders and then by the Debenture holders at meetings held at Hanover Street in May 1932. It was a drastic pruning. The capital of the company was reduced from £100,000 to £27,998 11s, divided into 24,209 Ordinary Shares of £1 each, 75,787 Ordinary Shares of one shilling each, and four Managers' Shares of one shilling each. This was to be achieved by writing down the existing £1 shares to one shilling.

As Chairman, Capt. Evelyn Broadwood held the largest single

shareholding, of 19,477; he also held proxies for a further 41,824 shares including those of Cuthbert Heath, the Excess Insurance Company and, among the family, Mrs Ada Broadwood. He therefore held a voting strength of nearly 70,000 of the issued shares (75,787) and was in an impregnable position, apart from the moral advantage that much the greatest loss was his own, among the shareholders.

The Debenture holders similarly approved the arrangement without dissent, not least because nearly £70,000 of the Debentures were in the name of Cuthbert Heath personally, or of companies under his control. Some time before, the auditors of the Excess Insurance Company had questioned the reliability of these investments and it had been explained to them that it was a personal and family interest of Mr Heath's, which he was prepared to underwrite personally. The Inland Revenue similarly pressed C. E. Heath & Co., no doubt suspecting that a wealthy man would hardly make such large payments out of generosity. Yet it was so.

In May 1932, with a final magnanimous gesture, he relinquished his claims as a second Debenture holder in favour of creditors, which gesture was largely instrumental in persuading the meeting to accept the arrangement. He was not at Hanover Street, but recuperating from an illness in the South of France. One notable figure was present—Bertha Broadwood, aged eighty six; she attended, and she voted in favour, her last act of duty to the family company, for she died in the following year.

Some two dozen of the craftsmen from Old Ford transferred to the 'new Broadwood factory' at The Hyde, Hendon (despite the grandiose letterheads, which gave an illusion of independence, this was a section of the Challen factory). To the Broadwood workmen, this was a dismal fall; traditionalists to a man, they had been proud to be working for the greatest piano firm in Britain with its incomparable history and standards, and were dismayed to transfer to the apparent control of a comparatively new company whose standards, so they believed, were below their own. But it was something, in the depression, to have a job at all; and while the numbers employed at Old Ford had been dropping through the 1920s, the closure for piano-making of the great Broadwood factory threw several hundred men, women and boys out of work. There was little other work available in Hackney and families suffered severe distress.

Nevertheless, the first half-year results of the new company showed an encouraging trend—a profit of £3,400. Miniaturisation seemed to be the way forward, as William Evans had anticipated; one musical authority wrote at that time that the small grand was becoming so popular that it might drive out the upright.[1]

That it did not succeed was in part due to a popular novelty: the Minipiano, a six-octave bichord upright introduced by Percy Brasted in 1934. Other makers followed, and in January 1936 William Evans launched a Broadwood 'miniature upright grand' (though the back of the brochure described it as the 'Evans miniature upright Grand').

Broadwoods continued to fulfil their duties as Royal Warrant-holders, tuning in alternate months at Buckingham Palace (seven pianos) and Sandringham (four pianos). Throughout 1935 it was a duty performed for King George V; in 1936 it was for King Edward VIII (afterwards the Duke of Windsor) except for the final tuning of the year at the Palace, four days before Christmas, which was for the new King, George VI. On 10 May 1937 Queen Elizabeth* hired a 'decorated case Grand Pianoforte' for Buckingham Palace. The Coronation took place two days later, and this hiring was for the celebrations that followed. In December 1937, to the pleasure of Capt. Broadwood, a pleasure shared by Willie Evans, the Royal Warrant for the new monarch was after due time awarded.

The Broadwood tuners were a notable body of individualists. There were some 40 'outdoor tuners' at this time, 36 of them tuners proper and 4 regulators. They covered the whole of England (though never ventured into Scotland) and there were several tuning contracts in Ireland. Few of the great country houses were not on one or another of the Broadwood itineraries.

Each tuner had his own round. He would be given his work in bulk at the beginning of a month, and it was up to him how he organised it. The tuner was thus to a great extent master of his own time. The Broadwood tuner was a welcome guest in houses great and small, schools, colleges and institutions, and if the piano did not in fact need tuning, he would be welcome for a cup of tea and a chat. One great individualist among them, proud of his 'best connection' since he had the special 'beat' of the Royal palaces, was Charlie Jeykell. Another was Joe Dyke, who devised his own form of tuning wedges which he manufactured as a cottage industry and sold profitably to his fellow-tuners.

Once a year the outdoor tuners (as an élite, they did not include the factory tuners who were a lesser breed to them) met together. Usually in March the OTSF (Outdoor Tuners' Sick Fund) spent part of its corporate savings on a convivial dinner at the Victoria Hotel, where the members would wine, dine and exchange the tales of the past year that are the conversational currency of men whose working lives are largely spent independently: travellers' tales.

* Now (1982) H.M. Queen Elizabeth the Queen Mother, whom the company still serves as Pianoforte Tuners.

There was a traditional 'Broadwood' method of tuning. Grands were tuned with the right hand, uprights with the left—the latter because this gives an upward pressure which, countered by the tension of the string, offers less risk of distorting the bedding of the wrest pin. This principle, it is said, was handed down among Broadwood tuners from at least the early years of the nineteenth century.

Despite the distressing problems of business, Capt. Broadwood was becoming a familiar figure in the piano trade and a propagandist for the piano, and the Broadwood, in the world of music. It is a measure of his influence at this time that he was asked by his friend Edward Dent,* perhaps the leading academic musical authority of his time, to referee a Doctorate of Philosophy thesis by a young graduate of Newnham, Rosamond Harding, whose dissertation was on the history of the piano to 1851.

Evelyn Broadwood wrote in 1931: 'this massive work seems to me to be admirable. It is very readable and at the same time contains a mass of valuable exhaustive information. Its particular value is that it covers a period in the evolution of the pianoforte which has so far never been properly recorded. I should like to recommend to the Degree Committee that this work should be recognised by the award of a suitable degree.'

His judgement has been amply vindicated. When Dr Harding's great book was published two years later, it immediately established itself as the standard work, as it remains to this day.†

Once again, in the autumn of 1938, there were threats of war. Business was poor, and William Evans decided to terminate his agreement with Broadwoods. Capt. Broadwood, supported by his fellow directors, decided to continue to manufacture. The Broadwood workmen led by Albert Lodge were extracted, with a quantity of pianos in course of construction, from the Hendon factory and a new factory was rented on a trading estate at Brunel Road, Acton. John Broadwood & Sons were once again independently piano-makers.

It was the worst of times. Capt. Broadwood, with typical verve and disregard of the advice of architects and his company secretary, insisted on a main wall of the new factory being raised up an additional storey so that the name of Broadwood could be prominently displayed upon it, together with the Royal Arms of a Warrant-holder. The new factory opened in January 1939.

* Professor E. J. Dent (1876–1957), Professor of Music at Cambridge 1926–1941.

† R.E.M. Harding (1898–1982), *The Piano-forte, Its History Traced to the Great Exhibition of 1851* (2nd edition, Gresham Press, 1979).

Three months later, on the eve of his eightieth birthday, Cuthbert Heath died. There can be do doubt that but for his intervention almost forty years earlier, the company would have gone into liquidation; and many times, in the years that followed, it faced disaster only to be pulled back by his injection of money and encouragement.

Nevertheless there is an irony in the fact that the man who kept Broadwoods going into the twentieth century seems to have had no appreciation of music whatsoever; because of the deafness that afflicted him throughout his life, he was quite unable to assess the virtues of a piano, or indeed hear it.

Manufacture in the new factory was of course soon overtaken by the exigencies of the Second World War. Many of the craftsmen were called up for military service; and within a year, having paid a dividend of $2\frac{1}{2}$ per cent during the 1930s, the company was once more unprofitable. Yet it kept going, despite shortages of basic materials.

In August 1941, with the agreement of the Board, Capt. Broadwood took over the management of the company, as well as its chairmanship. It was a difficult year. The Government under its wartime powers had brought in a 'Concentration of Industry' Act, and under its provisions Broadwoods joined with other manufacturers in a consortium—George Rogers, Marshall & Rose, and Whelpdale, Maxwell & Codd. The instruments of all four makers were manufactured for the remainder of the war at the Welmar factory at Clapham. Broadwoods alone had enough orders for two years' normal production, but the conditions did not allow them to be fulfilled.

The Brunel Road factory was sub-let, and the tuning department became the mainstay of the business, other than the rents from the Old Ford factory; although that too was in hazard, since in 1941 two large bombs dropped outside the factory, and one inside. The negotiations over war damage compensation went on for many years. Meanwhile the tuning department, under the Concentration of Industry Act, took over the concessions of Bechstein and Erard.

In 1944 a further Royal commission was added: 'The company had been honoured with the tuning of all the pianos in Windsor Castle including the instruments used by HRH Princess Elizabeth and HRH Princess Margaret Rose.'

The war with Germany ended in 1945, but the company was not able to re-occupy the Brunel Road factory and recommence manufacturing on its own account until the following year. Albert Lodge, who had managed the factory in the months before the war, had with other Broadwood workmen gone to De Havillands (where their skills were applied to building the Mosquito, the leading wood-framed aircraft of the Second World War); he decided to stay in aircraft manufacture. The company negotiated an early release from the forces for Bernard Carrier (who had joined the company in 1927, and whose father had worked for Broadwoods as one of the 'Bedford boys' at the turn of the century) and he was instructed to start up the factory again.

It was a formidable assignment. The factory had been used during the war by an optical-lens manufacturer and when it was handed back, the building was knee-deep in cullet and rubble, the floors punched with hundreds of holes where machinery had been bolted down, and dotted with mounds of jeweller's rouge which had set hard as concrete. Preparing the building was itself a mammoth task. Carrier himself built many of the conduits and installed much of the wiring, apart from adapting for piano-making such machinery as was available.

Piano parts had to be bought in as and when they could be found; there was no mill, and jigs had to be built. But soon from the nucleus of 'work in progress' transferred back from Welmar they were producing two pianos a week, with Gus Mickisch (who had come from Murdochs, where he started at the age of twelve) as marker-off and bellyman, one fitter-up and one action-maker, and two polishers (Pat Jessup and Sid Harrup), soon to be joined by Wally Zeale (who had done a post-war course at the Northern Polytechnic) as action finisher. They were making two models of upright, No. 8 and No. 10, with an 85-note scale.

Bernard Carrier was the liaison between the factory and the showroom, where he created a positive working relationship with the General Manager, 'Tommy' Watkin. It was a frustrating time for both of them, since the company had export orders worth £40,000 and it was not possible to complete them. It was a necessarily makeshift form of manufacture. When the Cunard liner *Queen Mary* was re-equipped for civilian use after its wartime service as a troopship, Broadwoods built an upright for it; but it had only 87 notes instead of the full scale, because of the space limitations in getting it on board.

The full scale of 88 notes was reintroduced to Broadwoods in 1951, the models being labelled 8F and 10F (for 'full scale'). In all this difficult period Bernard Carrier strove to maintain the firm's traditional high standards. His drawings were meticulous in their accuracy and detail. Frequently he would take a problem home, and return early the following morning carrying full working drawings. When reports came of a string breaking in an export piano, he built a machine to assess the break-point of strings. He devised an oscilloscope to study the action of hammers. Faced with new wood, he would bow it to test is resonance.

Factory outing in the 1950s (from left) Bernard Carrier, Leo Broadwood, Jack Draper.

Typically, when in the 1950s the showroom asked for a piano that closed up like a bookcase, with a folding keyboard, he designed and built one; and true to the Broadwood tradition, he personally inlaid the monogram 'JB & S' in veneer on the doors.

But in the years immediately after the war the climate was not favourable to piano-making. Such materials as were available were directed by the Government to 'non-luxury' trades. There was a shortage of skilled men, since training in piano-making had ceased during the war. Finally, Government diverted all industrial produce in the luxury trades to the export market. Therefore until 1951, all pianos sold on the home market were re-conditioned (even King George VI had to be content with two re-conditioned Broadwood pianos). For the first five years after the war, home piano sales carried 100 per cent purchase tax; this was only reduced (to 33⅓ per cent) in 1950, and abolished in the following year.

The trade was able to learn some lessons from wartime manufacture, notably in the introduction of heat-resistant glues which had been developed for aircraft building. Soon effective plastics were being used for keys and actions. These developments simplified, rationalised and standardised production across the trade, though it retained a larger element of hand-work and craft skill than other types of manufacture.

Once the piano was able to be sold again in the home market it soon faced a most substantial challenge from that form of entertainment that was to dominate so much of domestic life—television. The BBC had re-started its television service (with one channel) in 1946; but it was in 1953, with the televising of the Coronation of H.M. Queen Elizabeth II,

HM the Queen at the Broadwood stand at the British Industries' Fair, 1955 with Sir Ernest Goodale (Chairman, BIF) and T.B. Watkin (general manager of Broadwoods)

that the nation began to transfer its allegiance to television as the main focus of domestic amusement. The TV set finally took over the social position once held by the piano as the prime symbol of any conventionally well-equipped home in Britain in 1956, with the introduction of independent television. From that date, the possession of a piano, and more particularly the purchase of one, became a deliberate act of a family whose parents wanted the children to appreciate the satisfaction of playing music, as distinct from listening to it or watching great executants 'on the box'. However, the vogue for folk music re-established the guitar as a favourite and portable instrument among the young; and the pop world capitalised on the rapid development of advanced electronics to create wholly new sounds that could be emulated, with cheap tape equipment, in any back bedroom, so that the piano seemed to a mass public an historic oddity, if not an anachronism. Only the tenacious survival of 200 years of a great classical piano repertoire, and the emergence in each new generation of brilliant new executants to perform it and inspire amateurs to attempt it sustained the piano in many homes and every concert-hall.

Upright provided for the Royal Tour in SS *Gothic*, 1952

Queen Elizabeth II succeeded her father in February 1952, and after due time the Royal Warrant for Pianoforte Making was once more given to Capt. Broadwood who, fittingly, served his year as Master of the Worshipful Company of Musicians. Soon afterwards the company supplied pianos for the liner *Gothic* in which the Queen and the Duke of Edinburgh made their first overseas tour. When it was fitted out in 1954, Her Majesty's Yacht *Britannia* was provided with Broadwood pianos.

Despite the extreme difficulties of trade in this post-war period, the company was sustained by a body of workmen who could claim almost unequalled service, particularly in the tuning department. For example, J. G. Lendon, who died in 1954 aged ninety four, continued to work as transport manager until his ninetieth year, having started with Broadwoods as a young shipping clerk, and achieving seventy four years' service. Maturity was valued; but it was the fact that Capt. Broadwood was in his sixty ninth year that impelled the Board, at an Extraordinary General Meeting in April 1957, to pass a resolution that 'no person shall be disqualified from being appointed a Director by reason of his age, and no Director shall be under obligation to retire by reason of his age.'

In 1960 the seventh generation of the family was elected to the Board, in the person of Leo Broadwood's son Stewart Evelyn Hardress

313

Study of a tuner:
W. Seymour joined Broadwoods in 1889
and served the company for 66 years.
(*John Broadwood & Sons Ltd*)

Broadwood; it was, as Capt. Broadwood remarked on that occasion, a particular pleasure to him to see a further generation joining the company.

These were years of great difficulty for the piano trade in general. Certain overseas markets, notably Australia and New Zealand where the company had in the past enjoyed considerable sales, were closed by tariffs. But the company continued to manufacture, to find, recruit and train young craftsmen, and to search for the basic materials, which were often hard to find. In those years T. B. 'Tommy' Watkin was the mainstay of day-to-day management; having joined Broadwoods in 1932, he was a well-liked and trusted figure in the trade, a popular member of the trade associations and of the golfing society. R. F. R. Barrow was company secretary, later succeeded by A. M. McElaney; and until 1965, when he retired after forty six years' service, E. C. Sloggett was tuning and repair manager.

If the problems of manufacturing new instruments were a constant challenge to the company's inventiveness, there were many thousands of old ones still performing yeoman service all over the world. One cabinet piano came to light in a jazz bar in the Southern States of the USA, having probably started life in some naval quarter in the West Indies, and then been transported to Georgia to be the favoured instrument of early syncopation. In 1960 there was a Broadwood in the rehearsal studios of Columbia Pictures, and Dirk Bogarde suffered agonies at it as he tried to learn to mime the keyboard technique of Liszt.*

In the mid-1960s there was an increase in sales. By good fortune the factory was able to answer this challenge, first because in 1964 a quantity of piano-making machinery was bought in from a North London manufacturer who was closing down, and secondly because in 1968 a larger factory next door in Brunel Road (Nos. 1–5) became available and was duly leased.

Bernard Carrier was able to supervise the removal and to supervise the manufacture of pianos with machinery rather more adequate than the makeshift methods of the previous years. He retired in 1973, his devotion to the Broadwood tradition unswerving after forty six years. Others continued into the 1980s, notably H. T. Viner, who began as a youngster in the showroom in 1924 and in 1980 was head of the still prosperous tuning department; and father of them all, Sid Weight, still tuning in the factory at the age of eighty four, his ear as fine and his hand as firm as ever.

* *Song Without End*, a Columbia picture begun by Charles Vidor and completed after Vidor's death by George Cukor. The piano soloist (Bogarde mimed with truthful agony) was Jorge Bolet, and Morris Stoloff conducted the Los Angeles Philharmonic Orchestra. Bogarde subsequently described the film as 'a fiasco' (*A Postillion Struck by Lightning*, Chatto & Windus, London 1977).

Wally Zeale, action finishing foreman *(John Broadwood & Sons Ltd)*

Ron Mickisch, marking-off foreman *(John Broadwood & Sons Ltd)*

Captain Evelyn Broadwood, *c.* 1970 *(Turner Gee Studios)*

Capt. Broadwood in his eighties was a doyen of the British piano trade, and with many other interests in the world of the arts (Senior Governor of the Old Vic and Sadler's Wells) and of various charities (Governor of the Royal Normal College for the Blind, and Vice-President of the Royal Hospital and Home for Incurables, Putney). He had been High Sheriff of Surrey in 1957, and represented Britain on the International Congress for the Standardisation of Concert Pitch.

He was immensely proud of the Broadwood inheritance.[2] He delighted to entertain musical groups at Lyne and to expound on the historic past of his family. It may be that he preferred to overlook the

317

Piano in HMY *Britannia (Royal Navy)*

business problems of the twentieth century in enjoyment of the undoubted triumphs of past years. This did not make life comfortable or easy for those who served him in business, and it is to their credit that the business continued through difficult times. Captain Evelyn Henry Tschudi Broadwood died in June 1975, in his eighty sixth year. He had willed his body for medical research; and a memorial service was therefore held, as he had wished, at the Unitarian Church in Brighton.

Capt. Broadwood was succeeded as Chairman by Adam Johnstone, a professional management consultant and former Professor of Marketing at the International Business School at Fontainebleau. Mr Johnstone set in train a programme of modernisation.

One result was an increase of exports to Germany and Japan, two homes of quality piano-making. Inroads were achieved in other European countries, particularly Holland and Switzerland (the last especially satisfying in view of the origins of the founder of the company), and also Singapore and Thailand. In the face of the challenging commercial conditions of the time, these results were encouraging.

318

Princess Margaret with Adam Johnstone *(John Broadwood & Sons Ltd)*

In 1977, to mark the Silver Jubilee of H.M. Queen Elizabeth, a special grand (a new model, named the '250'), was manufactured, with the frame appropriately silvered. The Queen graciously accepted this piano, which now stands in the drawing room of Balmoral Castle. In spring 1979 the company once more returned to the West End of London, with the re-opening of a showroom at 56–57 Conduit Street. The opening ceremony was performed on 12 April by H.R.H. Princess Margaret.

Celebrations of the 250th anniversary of the founding of the company by Burkat Shudi in 1728 began, suitably enough, with a dinner for the workmen. On 29 April 1978 some 150 of the Broadwood craftsmen and staff, their families and friends, sat down for a cheerful evening in the restaurant of the London Zoo in Regent's Park.

A musical celebration was a concert at the Queen Elizabeth Hall, on London's South Bank, on 4 May 1978 when Malcolm Binns played five Broadwood pianos made at various dates from 1787 to 1978. Haydn was played on a five-octave grand of 1787, perhaps the oldest Broadwood

Beethoven's Broadwood on a stamp

grand still in playing order; Beethoven was played on a grand of 1819, similar to the one given to the composer by Thomas Broadwood; Mendelssohn was played on the square piano made by the company for Prince Albert's domestic use; and Chopin on one of the grands made by Broadwoods for the composer's recitals in London in 1848. Finally, Malcolm Binns played pieces by Herbert Howells and Claude Debussy on one of the modern Broadwood grands.[3]

A particularly happy gesture was the presentation to Broadwoods of an engraved silver salver by C. E. Heath & Co., to mark the long association between the two companies. In this year, 1978, a medallion was struck, bearing the head of John Broadwood; all purchasers of pianos from the company in the anniversary year received one and their names were recorded in a commemorative book. A gramophone record, 'The Broadwood Heritage', was produced by Decca, on which Malcolm Binns played a variety of historic and modern Broadwoods. A special Broadwood prize was also awarded to the BBC's 'Young Musician of the Year'.

The culmination of this year was a banquet at the Savoy Hotel, London, on 15 November, when some 500 friends of the company, including the directors of most leading pianoforte companies, and dealers and agents from throughout Britain and many parts of the world, joined to celebrate the first 250 years. The holding of this dinner had been a particular wish of Capt. Broadwood.

Guest of honour at this occasion was the pianist and former Prime Minister, Edward Heath. In a felicitous speech he expressed his pleasure at the presence of members of the Taphouse family from whose store at

Adam Johnstone (Chairman) with Edward Heath and Monica Johnstone
(Photo: Tomas Jaski)

Oxford, as Organ Scholar of Balliol, he had hired his piano. He recalled
that the first item moved into No. 10 Downing Street when he became
Premier had been his piano; and he asserted his admiration for the
continuing tradition of Broadwood. The toast of the company was
proposed by Gerald Brasted, Director and Secretary of the Piano
Manufacturers Association; Adam Johnstone, as Chairman of John
Broadwood & Sons Limited, responded, with a particular reference to
the presence beside him of his wife, the great-great-great-granddaughter
of John Broadwood.

After a dinner, as generous a meal in food and wines as any supplied by
Shudi for Handel, a Broadwood grand became the focus of
entertainment, played in turn by Malcolm Binns, Aleksandra
Klaczynska, Georgie Fame and Ian Stewart.

The unique and particular place which Broadwoods have held for so
long in Britain's musical life was symbolised in an exchange of messages
read out to the assembly by the Chairman, that may well stand as
an appropriate conclusion to this history, and an anticipation of
future enterprise.

A Message to the Queen

Having served Your Majesty and Your Majesty's Family for over 240 years, and on this 250th Anniversary of our Company at a celebration Dinner at the Savoy Hotel, I send Your Majesty loyal greetings from all who are employed by our Company and those who will be present at the Dinner. We are proud to have served Your Majesty and the Royal Family throughout eleven generations, and hope that we shall continue to do so for many more.

Adam Johnstone

The Reply

On the occasion of your Dinner celebrating the 250th Anniversary of your Company, I thank you and all those employed by John Broadwood & Sons for your kind message of loyal greetings. I hope that your remarkable record of service to the Royal Family as Pianoforte Manufacturers over 240 years will long be continued, and I send you and your Company my best wishes for a successful evening and greatest possible future prosperity.

Elizabeth R.

Modern upright – 'Buckingham'

Postscript

So, after 250 years, the piano manufactory of John Broadwood & Sons continues to uphold the standards so brilliantly set by its founders. As the company passed this milestone, a trade recession no less challenging than any that had faced it in the past brought new problems and difficulties. To face them, the directors moved production from the Acton factory, and arranged that the bulk of manufacture of uprights should be continued by a Broadwood team of craftsmen within the Gloucestershire factory of the Bentley Piano Company. The Bentley company had been founded 70 years earlier in an old Cotswold mill at Woodchester by Douglas Grover, whose family had worked in the London piano factories (including Broadwoods) for the previous hundred years. David Grover, the present managing director of the Bentley Piano Company, is a past President of the Institute of Musical Instrument Technology and of the Piano Manufacturers Association.

Despite the challenges of the recession which for several years afflicted the whole of the piano trade, the company was able to streamline its efficiency and consolidate its activities. This was exemplified by the introduction of computerisation in the management of several thousand tuning contracts.

The appointment in December 1981 of Anthony Card as managing director brought back to the company one of its former apprentices, who had trained both on manufacturing and administration with the company 30 years earlier. After working for a period as a Broadwood tuner in the North of England, he became works manger for the Kemble piano company; one of the largest British manufacturers, Kembles were for a period associated with Broadwoods in making uprights.

Throughout the difficult years, Broadwoods continued to be represented at the major trade fairs such as Frankfurt, where they were proud to observe the continuing international interest in and support for the company and its instruments.

History is, at best, no mere nostalgic recital of past glories, but a strong springboard for the future. Probably no piano manufacturing company can boast a history as long and as rewarding as this of John Broadwood & Sons. But this is only Part One—the great beginning from which, those who are concerned with the company are determined, further successes will spring.

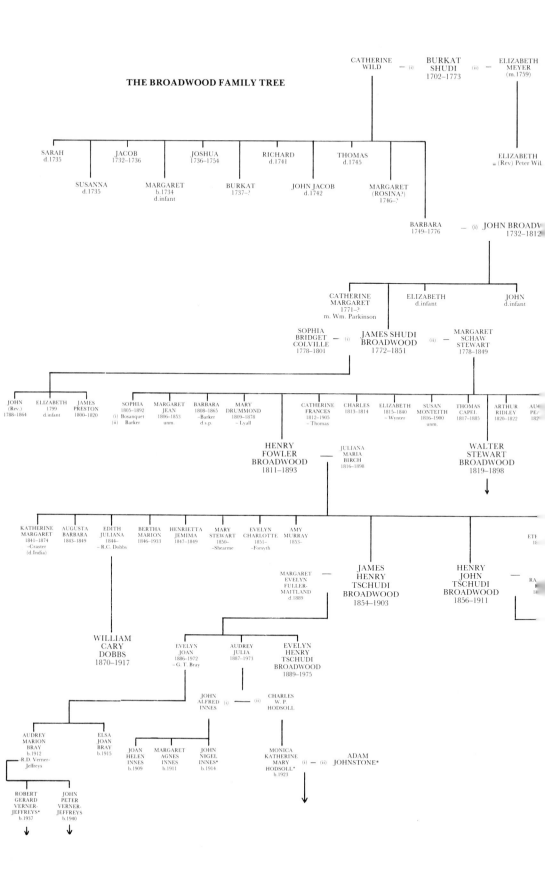

THE BROADWOOD FAMILY TREE

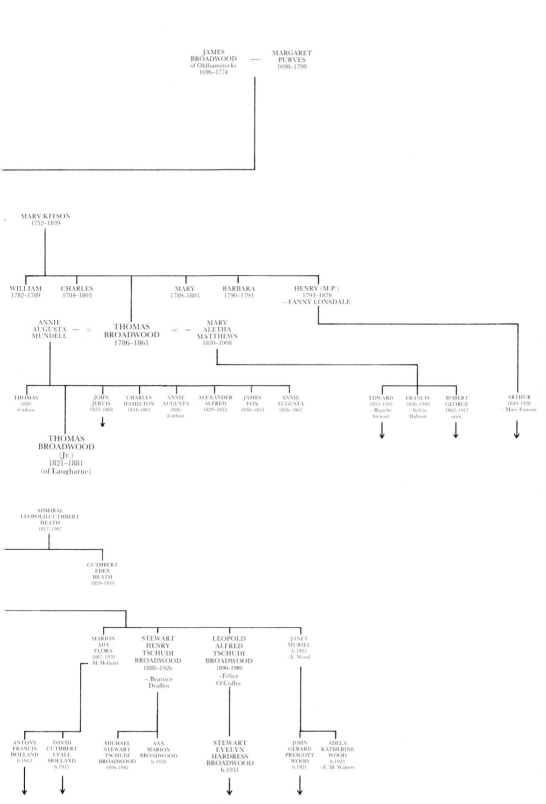

JAMES
BROADWOOD
of Oldhamstocks
1696–1774

MARGARET
PURVES
1698–1799

MARY KITSON
1752–1839

WILLIAM
1782–1789

CHARLES
1784–1803

MARY
1789–1803

BARBARA
1790–1793

HENRY (M.P.)
1793–1878
– FANNY LONSDALE

ANNIE
AUGUSTA — (i)
MUNDELL

THOMAS
BROADWOOD
1786–1861

(ii) —

MARY
ALETHA
MATTHEWS
1830–1908

THOMAS
1820
d.infant

JOHN
JERVIS
1823–1868

CHARLES
HAMILTON
1824–1861

ANNIE
AUGUSTA
1826
d.infant

ALEXANDER
ALFRED
1829–1833

JAMES
FOX
1830–1833

ANNIE
AUGUSTA
1836–1867

EDWARD
1853–1916
– Blanche
Stewart

FRANCIS
1856–1940
– Sylvia
Dalison

ROBERT
GEORGE
1862–1917
unm.

ARTHUR
1849–1928
– Mary Frances

THOMAS
BROADWOOD
(Jr.)
1821–1881
(of Laugharne)

ADMIRAL
LEOPOLD CUTHBERT
HEATH
1817–1907

CUTHBERT
EDEN
HEATH
1859–1939

MARION
ADA
FLORA
1887–1970
M. Holland

STEWART
HENRY
TSCHUDI
BROADWOOD
1888–1926

– Beatrice
Draffen

LEOPOLD
ALFRED
TSCHUDI
BROADWOOD
1890–1980
–Felice
O'Coffee

JANET
MURIEL
b.1895
–E. Wood

ANTONY
FRANCIS
HOLLAND
b.1913

DAVID
CUTHBERT
LYALL
HOLLAND
b.1915

MICHAEL
STEWART
TSCHUDI
BROADWOOD
1916–1941

ANN
MARION
BROADWOOD
b.1918

STEWART
EVELYN
HARDRESS
BROADWOOD
b.1931

JOHN
GERARD
PRESCOTT
WOOD
b.1921

ADELA
KATHERINE
WOOD
b.1923
–E. M. Walters

Technical Appendix

The most authoritative source for any study of the technical development of the piano is Dr Rosamond Harding's *The Pianoforte: Its History Traced to the Great Exhibition of 1851* (2nd edition, Gresham Press, 1979). A. J. Hipkins's *A Description and History of the Pianoforte* (Novello, London, 1896) is of great value in its particular emphasis on Broadwoods. The other source from which I have drawn substantially is an anonymous MS notebook (referred to as The Notebook), which is No. 23 in the collection of documents held by John Broadwood & Sons Limited. This is undated, but was evidently compiled in the early years of the present century by reference to ledgers, not all of which I have been able to identify. The information given has proved correct where verifiable.

Broadwood Patents

1769 (Eng. 947) B. Shudi (Venetian) swell.
1783 (Eng. 1379) J. Broadwood Action Dampers Hammers, arrangement of Forte Pedal, Sordino Pedal, Two or more Sound-Boards, Sound Brd with Sound-Post or Bridge, Wrest pins, arrangement of
1825 (Eng. 5261) J.S. Broadwood, Action, Check
1827 (Eng. 5485) J.S. Broadwood, Hitch pins, Frame, Metal Hitch pins, arrangement of Hitch pin in metal.
1842 (Eng. 9245) H.F. Broadwood, Schoolroom Pianoforte.
1888 (Eng. 1231) H.J.T. Broadwood, Barless Grand.
1894 (Eng. 20504) G.D. Rose, Grand Action.
1927 (Eng. 267195) Collen/Broadwood, Simplified manufacture.

The Square Pianoforte

The earliest recorded Broadwood square was sent out of the workshop to 'Miss Pelham at Brighthelmstone' on 9 August 1770. This was the simple Zumpe pattern with the English single action and the 'over-damper', of five octaves FF to f³. The case was veneered in mahogany with fruitwood stringing, and measured 5 ft 2½ ins by 1 ft 9¼ ins.

In 1783 John Broadwood took out an English patent (No. 1379) for eight developments in pianoforte manufacture. These concerned the action, the dampers, the arrangement of hammers, two or more soundboards, the soundboard with soundpost, the arrangement of wrest pins, the forte pedal and the sordino pedal. The last controlled a piece of wood hinged to the case, lying along the soundboard bridge.

The first recorded sale of a piano with the brass under-damper is on 29 September 1783, when Miss Gibbs of Cork bought one for £21.

The first mention of a pedal is in relation to a square which Mr Robert Buckley of Manchester ordered on 24 March 1786 for Mr Keynes of Deans Gate: 'It is to have a pedal the wire of which is to come through the cheek and not to have leather.' For the wire 'to come through the cheek' implies that the device was to be worked by a stop-knob beside the keyboard rather than a foot-pedal.

Other customers demanded other old-fashioned controls. Thus as late as 26 May 1796 a Mr Bartolozzi ordered 'a pianoforte ornd. without addl. keys with 2 pedals to act by the knee, one of them to raise the lid, the other the dampers.' A pedal 'to lift the lid' was similarly ordered by Lord Despencer in 1797.

In 1784 John Broadwood introduced other patented innovations, for in that year he made No. 200 (now in the possession of C. F. Colt) with a double soundboard and soundpost in the style of a violin. Not many of these seem to have been made, and few survive. It is particularly interesting, therefore, that in the patent specification, this innovation is described as 'the most essential part of the said improvements on the said instrument'. The expansion of production is demonstrated by the fact that although pianos of this period were not numbered on the nameboard (consecutive numbering for squares, as for grands, was introduced in 1796), the Notebook on dating gives No. 409 as having been made in 1785; this implies that in one year, the factory made as many square pianos as had been made in the previous fourteen years.

The other datings given in the notebook are:

488	591	901	1266	2000
1785	1786	1788	1790	1793

The English double action was introduced into squares in the 1780s and offered as an optional alternative until the early years of the nineteenth century, when it superseded the single action.

Broadwoods were offering 'additional keys' on the square from late in 1793, bringing the keyboard up to 5½ octaves (up to c⁴ or 'CC in alt'). John Broadwood wrote to a correspondent in Charleston on 13 November 1793: 'We have just begun to make some of the small Pianofortes up to that compass.' (Harding credits this development to William Southwell of Dublin in 1794, but Broadwoods began earlier.)

Cases were becoming more decorative from 1794; thus in October of that year Pascal Taskin bought four squares, 'one plain and three inlaid'. By 1790 Broadwood was supplying actions to be fitted into cases by furniture manufacturers: thus on 2 March 'Mr Chippendale for a P.F. to be put in a sideboard, £18 18s.'

By 1814 most square pianos were 5½ octaves, and the case had become more substantial (and larger: 5 ft 6 ins by 2 ft 1½ ins). The instrument had six legs, was sometimes decorated with brass mouldings and borders, had built-in drawers for music, and a forte pedal suspended from the case.

The first metal hitch-pin plate was applied to a square piano by Samuel Hervé while working for Broadwoods in 1821, and this became general practice the following year. From the mid 1820s most squares were six octaves (FF to f⁴) and measured 5 ft 7½ ins by 2 ft 2 ins.

Production of the square ceased in 1866 at No. 64161.

The Grand Pianoforte

James Shudi Broadwood writes in his notes of 1838 that 'the Grand Piano may be called an English instrument, it having been invented by Americus Backers, a Dutchman, who resided in Jermyn-street about 1776. He was a maker of Harpsichords, and on his first application of hammers, to gain the jingling music of the Harpsichord, then so much admired, he did not clothe them, but struck the strings with soft wood or cork; he afterwards clothed them slightly with leather.'

Annotating this account in the version he printed for private circulation in 1862, Henry Fowler Broadwood asserted that the date given is 'a decided clerical error; the date is 1767'. This seems highly likely as the date at which Broadwood and Stodart, both then workmen of Shudi, were helping Backers to develop what became the 'English Grand Action'.

The earliest English patent in which the word 'Grand' appears in association with the piano is that by Robert Stodart dated 1777 (No. 1172).

The Notebook gives the date of the first Broadwood grand sent out as 1782, and quotes an entry from the Journal that on 20 April in that year 'Mrs North hired a large Pianoforte'. The first reference to pedals is on 12 January 1785 when 'Mr Tyler of Bath' paid £48 6s. for 'a large p.f. with *two pedals*, desk inside etc.' These pedals would have been attached to the front legs of the piano; that on the left bisected to control the bass and treble *sourdin*, that on the right the *forte* pedal.

The instruments were of five octaves, FF to f³. The increase to 5½ octaves, to c⁴ or (as Broadwood referred to it, CC in alt) happened about 1790, apparently to please Dussek. He ordered his piano on 20 November 1789, and John Broadwood wrote to a correspondent in Charleston on 13 November 1793: 'We now make most of the Grand Pianofortes in compass to CC in Alt. We have made some so for these three years past, the first to please Dussek which being much liked Cramer Jr. had one of us so that now they are become quite common . . .' The extension of a further half-octave (in the bass) to give a six-octave compass probably took place in 1794. The factory notebook indicates that on 7 May 1794 'A Grand piano in compass from C in the bass below the common to C in alt' was sent to Mrs Cuss Major at Cannons: this was No 607 and cost £73 10s. The description is ambiguous since it is given as 'C in alt' and not the 'CC in alt' which would have clearly indicated six octaves; but as the notebook compiler comments, probably CC in alt is meant, since the 'Prince of Peace' piano made to order less than two years later is certainly six octaves (though grands were made of 5½ octaves as late as 1805).

The harpsichord tradition evidently lingered on in some quarters, for there were demands for the Venetian Swell to be added to Broadwood grand pianos well into the 1790s (which says much for the reputation of Shudi's invention). When it was specially ordered, Broadwoods added it to the grand at an additional charge of 10 guineas. This finally ended in 1799, with a letter to a Mr Tyler: 'We hope you will not be offended with our declining to put a swell in future to any GPF being convinced they deaden the tone & appearance and being exceedingly troublesome to manufacture which however we should not mind did it answer to satisfaction'.

The Notebook records:

The earliest numbers of Grand Pianofortes recorded in the 1796 day books are

40	220	335	367	405	656	521
1788	no date	1792	1792	1792	1794	1793

By 1796 the numbers had reached 1000 and the series continued until 1890 when it ceased at 22579 after which all Grands were included in the one set of numbers commencing 24/6/90 at 42001.

The Long Bichord Grands were numbered in this series and the new D.R. [Drawing Room] Grands of 1875. About the years 1809–12 Grands were mentioned with numbers below 400, one as old as 42 [see Upright Grands, below]. They were numbered by Mr J. Black in the same series as the Upright Grands which he commenced to make about 1805 when purchased by the firm. See Upright Grands 1279 No 3992 Satin wood Gd. with Wedgwood plaques 3992 date 1807 by J. B. & *Son.* No. 4037 by J. B. & *Sons* and has Venetian swell and three pedal feet from a cross bar centre, one open swell.

Semi-Grands began at No. 1 in 1831, continued to 1108 in 1839, when the series ceased.

New Patent Semi-Grand & Improved Semi-Grand began at No. 1 in 1831 and continued to 1546 in 1848 when the series ceased.

Boudoir and Cottage Grands began at No. 1 in 1834. The series continued to 11670 in 1890 and was continued in the new series 42001.

Short Bichord Grands were numbered with the series also.

Royal Boudoir Grands 7 ft 6 ins long, 6⅞ C to A in 1863, and

Short Drawing Room Grands in 1865. In 1866 the Royal Boudoir Grands were made 7 octave. In 1871 the small C to A Semi-Grand was discontinued and the Royal Boudoir Grands thenceforward were called Semi-Grands and a new series of

Boudoir Grands being commenced, as 7 octave.

Cottage Grands 6⅞ octave began at No. 3 in 1863. The first two being numbered in the preceding series. The numbers reached 2185 in 1890 and were continued in the new series commencing and continued with 42001.

The 7 Octave Cottage Grand began in 1878 and were continued in this series.

Boudoir Grands 7 Octave began at No. 5 in 1871. The first four were numbered in the series next preceding but one. The numbers reached 3167 and were continued with 42001.

Baby Grands C. S. Barless were made in 1912.

Full Concert Grand, 'Jumbo', 9 ft long, made 1891.

Cross or Overstrung Grands first made in Sept 1895.

Square Cross Strung Grands (fiddle tail-piece) 1901.

Spinet Grands 6 octave, 4 ft 6 ins, 1903.

Baby Grands (barred) 7 octave to f, October 1905.

The development of the metal frame for the grand piano during the nineteenth century was conducted in the context of a 'battle of the bars'. Who introduced strengthening bars of metal, and in what disposition, became matters of high contention. The need for such strengthening was acknowledged early. Hipkins records (and the statement is corroborated by correspondence quoted in the text) that 'James Shudi Broadwood tried iron bars to resist the treble strain in 1808, and again in 1818, but was not successful in fixing them'.

Probably as a result of the success of Samuel Hervé in fixing a metal string-plate to the square piano in 1821 (see above), experiments were made to add metal strengthening to the grand. In a correspondence in *The Times* following the Great Exhibition of 1851, Broadwoods wrote that 'We have in our house a piano, constructed in 1823, with steel tension bars above the strings.'

Erards introduced steel bracing bars in 1824, and took out an English patent in 1825. Broadwoods' patent (No. 5485) was not taken out until 1827, but it is clear that the firm had made pianos with this strengthening four years earlier.

Hipkins reports that it was Henry Fowler Broadwood's ambition to get rid of the iron bars altogether, since they broke into the scale and needed to be fitted with extreme precision if they were not to affect the tone.

In 1847–9 he succeeded in making a grand piano with an entire upper framing of iron, and in this instrument two bars sufficed, neither breaking into the scale, one parallel with the lowest bass string along the straight side of the instrument, the other presenting the entirely new feature of a diagonal bar, fixed at the bass corner of the wrest-plank and again on the string-plate, and having its thrust at an angle to the pull of the strings. But in the grand pianos he afterwards made with his diagonal bar, he also used a straight bar towards the treble, of the ordinary type, to avoid any possible sacrifice to durability. This was the Broadwood Iron Grand model of 1851—the first to be made in England in a complete iron framing, but not solid; it was in wrought and cast-iron, wedged up with gun-metal at the points of juncture, and not in a single casting as is the American plan.

Of the four Broadwood grands shown at the Great Exhibition, two had three bars parallel with the strings; one had a single parallel bar and a diagonal; and the fourth had a single parallel bar and two radiating diagonals.

In 1888 Henry John Tschudi Broadwood patented the 'barless' piano. The metal plate was of mild or cast steel turned up round the sides to form a continuous flange, without requiring bars. The steel frame proved to be increasingly expensive, and the 'American' cast iron frame was subsequently adopted.

The Upright Grand

The upright grand was an attempt to save room-space by placing the body of the piano upright; in effect, therefore, it is a grand piano folded through 90 degrees at the back of the keyboard, with the wrest pins immediately above it. John Landreth patented such a design in 1787; and a typical example is that patented by Robert Stodart in 1795 'in the form of a bookcase'. This demonstrates the general characteristic of the genre—its extreme height, tending to instability, particularly when music was placed on the shelves provided at the top right of the case. H. F. Broadwood wrote (1862): 'These were . . . Pianos hoisted up vertically on a box with four legs, the mechanism causing the hammers to strike through the space left, as in Horizontal Pianos, between the sound-board and pin block [wrest plank]'. It has been suggested (see text) that John Broadwood was not enthusiastic about this development. The Notebook records: 'Upright Grands [were] first made regularly in 1805 by Mr James Black of Percy Street and purchased from him in March 1805 to March 1813, together with some Grands, both Instruments being numbered in one series.

Grands are mentioned with numbers below 100. An Upright Grand No. 188 is numbered in 1810, the series continued in the Upright Grands from 1813 to 1831 when it ceased at 940.' From this it seems that Broadwoods made few upright grands in their own factory; those bearing the Broadwood name, at least to 1813 (i.e. to John Broadwood's death) were manufactured on an 'own name' basis by James Black, a former Broadwood workman.

The Cabinet

In the cabinet piano the lay-out of the upright grand was inverted so as to bring the heavier part of the instrument down to the floor and reduce the overall height to not much more than six feet.

J. S. Broadwood noted (1838) that: 'the Vertical or Cabinet Piano was first produced by William Southwell, from a sketch given him by James Broadwood in 1804; so little was it then appreciated, that the first manufactory in the line refused to purchase the patent he took out. It has since become a great favourite, both from its peculiar quality of tone, and its comparatively superior ornamental appearance; and bids fair to take generally the place of the present Small or Square Piano.'

H. F. Broadwood (1862) added a gloss that: 'The Upright Cabinet Piano of Southwell, differed from the Upright Grands, in having the pin block transferred to the upper end of the instrument; the interval between plank and soundboard being suppressed; the soundboard was glued firmly to the pin-block, and the mechanism placed in front instead of behind the strings. From this sketch of 1804, and Southwell's invention, date all modern upright Pianos of English and French makers.'

As Harding indicates, this lay-out had been tried as early as 1735, but was most successfully introduced by Southwell from 1807, with a refinement of the 'English Sticker Action'. The ornamental feature of this design came from its open front, infilled with a panel of pleated silk or brocade.

The Notebook records: 'Cabinets began in 1812. The first [was] sent away 16 Jan 1812, having no recorded number, nor are numbers recorded of 13 sent away subsequently. The first number recorded is 106, afterwards lower numbers are mentioned, but no lower than 89. The series continued until 1856 when it ceased at 8963.

The Upright

The upright (as distinct from the upright grand or the cabinet, see above) was originally and for many years known as the cottage piano. Harding describes its development from the square, since the original versions were based on the square action placed on its side. The originators seem to have been William Southwell, Robert Wornum and Frederick William Collard, all of whom devised 'cottage' pianos. Harding gives the main credit to Wornum, with his particular improvements in 1826 and 1828.

Broadwoods began making them comparatively late, and continued with the traditional straight stringing and sticker action, with its leather hinge, until late in the nineteenth century.

The Notebook records:

Cottages began at No. 1. In the old number books, of the first 150 only 13 are marked off and the earliest date there given is 1823. These were however first sent away in 1819. The first sent away are:

1	2	6	4	9
11.8.19	23.8.19	25.9.19	18.10.19	23.10.19

7	8	16
6.1.20	24.1.20	4.2.20

The series continued to 68876 in 1890 when the new series commenced at 80001.

From the years 1853 to 1857 a second number appears against some Cottage pianos to mark certain instruments purchased from Mr John Reid [who subsequently, though briefly, became a partner]. The series began at No. 1 and ends at No. 1562. The numbers do not interfere with the principal series but were put in addition.

Chilled Steel Upright (welded &c) made
Sept 1893.
Overstrung Cast Steel Upright Nov 1897.
Steel Barless 21 Oct 1905.

Among the many variants of the standard designs is one illustrated by Harding (Plate XIV) with a dip in the top, presumably so that the performer's voice would project over it. This was made c. 1825.

The Strings

Hipkins gives the general history:
The wire used in [the eighteenth] century,

whether iron or brass, was of feeble tenacity and up to the middle of the [nineteenth] century it was easy to break the treble strings and force a piano out of tune . . . Early in [the nineteenth] century Nuremberg wire was in use, but about 1820 it had to give way to Berlin wire. In 1834 a great stride was made by Webster of Birmingham, who brought out a steel wire to replace the iron wire, the tensile properties of which it much exceeded. It is true that steel wire had been tried in Germany, but presumably with little success, as iron wire, previous to Webster's improvement, prevailed everywhere. In 1850 Müller, of Vienna, took the lead. In 1854 Webster and Horsfall, of Birmingham, introduced an invention, attributed to Horsfall, of a tempered cast steel music wire of great value; but the preference has again reverted to Germany, the wire of Pöhlmann, of Nuremberg, being the most in favour at the present time (1896) with the leading pianoforte makers.

Harding points out that the bass strings were usually overspun from the early years of the nineteenth century, though at first this was done loosely, and with a core of brass wire overspun with copper. Danchell (1838) says that 'we are indebted for a valuable improvement, namely, the covering the bass strings with wire, to the suggestion of a literary gentleman connected with the British Museum'. The attribution is cryptic, though as Dr Gray of the British Museum 'by his experiments, established the due proportions in the gravity and vibration of the bass and steel strings . . .' (Broadwood 1862) it seems possible that the overspinning of bass strings was one of the improvements he suggested to John Broadwood in the 1780s.

The question of the disposition of the strings, and in particular overstringing, is dealt with in the text.

The Action

The earliest type of piano action manufactured in England was the 'single action' based on the original by Cristofori, and known in England as 'Mason's action' (see Harding for detailed descriptions and diagrams of this and other actions). The key raises two levers, one of which propels the pivoted hammer towards the string, while the second raises the over-damper. This was known as the 'English Single Action' and was used for Broadwood's square pianos from 1770 to 1783. As part of his 1783 patents, John Broadwood introduced the brass under-damper, which has a closer relationship to the hammer.

The English Grand Action, which was the culmination of the experiments of Backers, Broadwood and Stodart, first appears in a patent of Robert Stodart of 1777. The refinement of this action was the introduction of an escapement or hopper to restrain the falling hammer, a check to prevent the hammer from bouncing back and sounding the string a second time. This action also includes a rail, similar to the harpsichord 'jack rail' to restrain the damper from flying upwards.

The English Double Action introduced the escapement into the square piano in about 1815.

The next major development was the repetition action or double escapement action, invented by Sebastian Erard and patented by Pierre Erard in 1821. The effect of the Erard repetition action was to add a second escapement mechanism which held the hammer firmly after its first note, but enabled the pianist to repeat the note far more quickly than with the older form of action, thus providing far more sensitive control over repeated notes. This action, modified and simplified by Henri Herz of Paris, was adopted by most makers of grand pianos, including Broadwoods.

Broadwoods introduced their own modification of this action in 1838 by adding a spring-check; and an under-damper mechanism was introduced in 1867, continuing until 1891.

The standard mechanism for the upright piano throughout most of the nineteenth century was the cumbersome 'sticker' action. The key was linked to the hammer mechanism by a long rod or 'sticker'. A check action was invented for the upright by Robert Wornum in the 1820s, involving a tape to pull back the hammer: thus, the 'tape-check' action.

Acknowledgments

Two illustrations are reproduced by gracious permission of Her Majesty the Queen: that of the harpsichord made by Shudi in 1740 for Frederick, Prince of Wales, and now in Kew Palace; and Shudi's bill to the Royal Household in 1750, from the Royal Library, Windsor Castle.

My greatest debt is to the Broadwood Trust for inviting me to research and write this book, and in the process offering me unrestricted access to this remarkable archive of original business and family documentation. In particular I thank Adam and Monica Johnstone for their interest, encouragement and hospitality.

At John Broadwood & Sons Limited I am grateful to the staff who have taken time and trouble to help.

All members of the Broadwood family whom I have approached have been generous of their time and interest. I remember warmly an encounter over luncheon with the late Captain E. H. T. Broadwood, long before this book was thought of. The late Leo Broadwood helped me greatly. I also thank Stewart Broadwood, Mrs Janet Wood, Miss Ann Broadwood, Miss Elizabeth Broadwood, and Colonel John Hay Broadwood for their assistance.

The research and writing of this book coincided with the transfer of a vast archive of uncatalogued original material from Lyne to the Surrey Record Office. I am especially indebted therefore to the Surrey County Archivist, Dr David Robinson, and his staff: Mrs E. A. Stazicker, Mrs A. A. Doughty, Mrs A. K. McCormack, Miss E. Silverthorne, Mrs D. G. Sutton, A. J. George, R. V. Shrigley, M. G. Vine, and Mrs L. Trodd.

The London Library has been, as so often, a reliable, rich and friendly source of reference. Among other libraries and institutions that have provided ready assistance are the Albany Institute of History and Art, New York; the British Library; the British Museum (A. Hopley, Archivist); the Colonial Williamsburg Foundation (Mrs Margaret S. Gill, Registrar); The Provost and Fellows of Eton College (Patrick Strong, College Archivist); Historic Deerfield Inc., Massachusetts (Peter Spang, Curator); the Historich Museum, Rotterdam (A. M. Meyerman, Director); the Household Cavalry Museum (Lt Col A. D. Meakin, Curator); Kensington and Chelsea Borough Libraries (B. Curle); Mount Vernon Ladies' Association of the Union (Harrison M. Symes, Director); National Galleries of Scotland; National Museum of Hungary, Budapest (Dr F. Fülep, Director); National Portrait Gallery; Patent Office; Public Record Office; Royal Society (N. H. Robinson, Librarian); Scottish Record Office (J. D. Galbraith, Assistant Keeper); Smithsonian Institution, Washington (Mrs Helen Rice Hollis); United States Embassy, London (Stephen L. Roberts, Librarian); Victoria and Albert Museum (Maurice Tomlin and Michael I. Wilson); and Yale Collection of Musical Instruments (Nicholas Renouf, Assistant Curator).

For permission to quote I thank the following, with apologies for any omissions:

Professor D. C. Coleman for Gentleman and Players, article in the *Economic History Review*; Henry Marcy Collard Esq. for *A Short History of a Great House – Collard & Collard*, by Edward Lamburn; Professor Cyril Ehrlich for *The Piano, a History* (J. M. Dent & Sons Ltd); Jonathan Gathorne-Hardy for *The Public School Phenomenon* (Hodder and Stoughton Ltd); Mrs Gilbert Russell and Faber and Faber Ltd for *The Harpsichord and Clavichord* by Raymond Russell; Professor Christopher Smout for *A History of the Scottish People* (William Collins Sons & Co Ltd); A. & C. Black (Publishers) Ltd for *Mozart: A Documentary Biography* by Otto Deutsch; the Cambridge University Press for *A Concise Economic History of Britain* by W. H. B. Court; William Collins Sons & Co Ltd for *The Years of Endurance* by Sir Arthur Bryant; The Indiana University Press for Technology and Liberal Education by George Haines IV in *1859 – Entering an Age of Crisis*; Macdonald and Janes Publishing Group Ltd for *The Organ* by W. A. Sumner; Macmillan Administration (Basingstoke) Ltd for *The Letters of Mozart* by Emily Anderson; The Oxford University Press for *Makers of the Harpsichord and Clavichord 1440–1840* by Donald Boalch, *Dr Burney's Musical Tours of Europe* and *The Great Dr Burney* by Percy A. Scholes, and the *Oxford Companion to Music* edited by Percy A. Scholes and John Owen

Ward; A. P. Watt Ltd for *The Song of the Banjo* by Rudyard Kipling; and The Society of Authors on behalf of the Bernard Shaw Estate for *Shaw's Music* by George Bernard Shaw, edited by Dan H. Laurence.

For other information and assistance in various ways, I record my gratitude to John Barnes (Edinburgh), Mrs Mary Baxter, J. B. Bennett (East Mersea), Dirk Bogarde, Antony Brown (historian of C. E. Heath & Co), Douglas Brown (Groton School, Massachusetts), Christoph H. Brunner (Mitlodi Switzerland), Dr George C. Cameron (Edinburgh), Mrs Capsey, Mr & Mrs Bernard Carrier, David Castell, Mrs Florence C. Chambers, Donald Chesworth (Warden, Toynbee Hall), R. M. Childs, Commander G. J. T. Creedy RN (H. M. Yacht *Britannia*), Ralph Dopmeyer, Laurence Elvin, Sheila Fermoy, R. S. Finlayson, John Gifford (Edinburgh), Lt Col Sir Martin Gilliat, Michael Harris (Commercial Union Assurance Co), Sir William Heseltine, Sir Robin Mackworth Young, Colin Mair, Raymond Mander and Joe Mitchenson, Commander R.S. Markes RN (H.M. Yacht *Britannia*) the late Stanley Murdoch, the Rt Hon the Earl of Oxford and Asquith, Mrs Mary Potts, Peter Powell, Mr & Mrs Brian Richardson (Reeves Hall), L. Simmonds (bookseller), Mrs M. P. Snetzler, L. C. Squibb (Steinway & Sons), Brian Thompson (Secretary, C. E. Heath & Co), Richard Usborne (Fenton House), Christopher Wall (National Trust), Robert Welch, K. B. Watkin, and Mrs Penelope Wilkinson.

Dr Charles Mould kindly read the chapters on the harpsichord, allowed me to read and make notes from his unpublished thesis on Jacob Kirkman, and made a great many helpful suggestions, as did Professor Cyril Ehrlich who commented usefully on the early draft of the book. C. F. Colt kindly read the chapters on the early development of the piano. I particularly thank Ann Carter who has been a firm but sympathetic editor.

Finally, my thanks are due to Frank de Mengel, who has generously tolerated the author's obsession with the subject of this book.

Photo Credits

Notes

Chapter I 'The Shudi Workshop'

(1) Bertha Broadwood MS
(2) *History of Northumberland*, Vol. IV, New-castle and London, 1897
(3) Smout, T. C., *A History of the Scottish People 1580–1830*, Collins, London 1969
(4) *Ibid.*
(5) Dale, William, *Tschudi the Harpsichord Maker*, Constable, London 1913
(6) Defoe, Daniel, *A Tour Through England & Wales, 1724–6*, Everyman edition, London 1948
(7) *Some Notes Made by J. S. Broadwood, with Observations and Elucidations by H. F. Broadwood*, London 1862
(8) Boalch, Donald, *Makers of the Harpsichord and Clavichord 1440–1840* (2nd. ed., Clarendon Press, Oxford 1974)
(9) Delaney, Mrs, *Diary*
(10) Flower, Newman, *George Frideric Handel*, Cassell, London 1959
(11) Hawkins, Sir John, *A General History of the Science and Practice of Music*, Vol. V, London 1776
(12) *Survey of London*, Vol XXXIII, St Anne, Soho, London 1966. The *Survey* quotes Dale as the authority that Shudi lived at No 1. But Dale says only that it was in "one of these houses" on the south side
(13) *Some Notes Made by J. S. Broadwood, op. cit.*
(14) *Ibid.*
(15) Dale, *Tschudi the Harpsichord Maker*
(16) *Survey of London*, Vol. XXXI, St James, Westminster, north side, London 1963
(17) *Ibid.*
(18) *Ibid.*
(19) *The Daily Advertiser*, Tuesday, 5 October 1742

Chapter II 'John Broadwood Joins the Business'

(1) Rees, Rev. A. (ed.), *The New Cyclopaedia*, article on harpsichord, 1819
(2) James, Philip, *Early Keyboard Instruments* (Peter Davies, London 1930). The probability is that John Broadwood took the job in Shudi's workshop that Zumpe had vacated to start his own business. James points out that 'an inspection of the rate-books of Princes Street, Hanover Square, shows the regular entry of Zumpe's name from 1761 to 1780, when he moved to Princess Street, Cavendish Square. This admits Fetis's statement that he learned to play on one of Zumpe's pianos, dated 1762.'
(3) *Some Notes Made by J. S. Broadwood*
(4) Dale, *Tschudi the Harpsichord Maker*
(5) Deutsch O. E., *Mozart, a Documentary Biography* (A. & C. Black, London 1965)
(6) *Ibid.*
(7) Shudi patent, Broadwood papers (SRO)
(8) Anderson, E. (ed.), *The Letters of Mozart and his Family* (Macmillan, London 1938)
(9) Scholes, P. A. (ed.), *Dr Burney's Musical Tours in Europe* (Oxford University Press 1959)
(10) Dale, *Tschudi the Harpsichord Maker*
(11) *Some Notes Made by J. S. Broadwood*
(12) *Ibid.*
(13) Rate books of St James's, Piccadilly
(14) Lt. Col. A. D. Meakin, Curator of the Household Cavalry Museum, letter to the author

Chapter III 'Shudi and Broadwood'

(1) Bodleian MS Eng misc c 529
(2) Miller, Edward, *History and Antiquities of Doncaster and its Vicinity* (Doncaster *c*. 1804), quoted in Sumner, W. L., *The Organ* (4th ed., Macdonald, London 1973)
(3) Bodleian MS Eng misc b 107
(4) Boalch, D. H., *Makers of the Harpsichord and Clavichord, 1440–1840* (2nd ed., Oxford University Press 1974)
(5) Burney, quoted in Boalch
(6) Hipkins, A. J., 'Personal Notebooks'. In the nineteenth century there were more Broadwood books at Great Pulteney Street than now survive. A. J. Hipkins, as showroom manager, studied them *c*. 1881 and filled two small pocket notebooks with references derived from these books. The references to books that survive are accurate, and in view of Hipkins's reputation as an accurate historian it is reasonable to take his notes made from the books now lost as correct, particularly as some references are confirmed by Dale who had

the opportunity to check them from the originals when preparing his book (1913). The Hipkins notebooks were evidently given to the Broadwood family by his widow after his death, and contain pencil emendations in the hand of Lucy Broadwood. The notebooks are now with the Broadwood papers (SRO)

(7) Lamburn, Edward, *A Short History of a Great House – Collard & Collard*, privately printed, London 1938

(8) Russell, Raymond, *The Harpsichord and Clavichord* (2nd ed. Faber & Faber, London 1973)

(9) *Ibid.*

(10) *Ibid.*

(11) This instrument is said to have been stored in a loft of an old college building at Annapolis from 1828 to 1878. In 1878 it was shown by William Knabe & Co. of Baltimore at the Centennial Exposition in Philadelphia. It was restored in 1909 by Arnold Dolmetsch when he was employed by Chickering & Co. of Boston. It was bought from Nils Ericsson of Chickering by Mrs Fanny Reed Hammond (a friend of Miss Belle Skinner) who in 1939 gave it to the Groton School of Groton, Massachusetts, where it remains. In 1970 Douglas Brown, Chairman of the Arts Department at Groton, discovered the instrument under a stairwell of the headmaster's house in unplayable condition. Mr Brown, with the assistance of the harpsichord-maker Jeremy Adams, has restored it to playing order (information by M. Sue Ladr on the sleeve of Titanic Records TI/49)

(12) Hipkins 'Notebooks'

(13) John Broadwood & Sons Letter Book 1801–1810

(14) Bodleian MS Eng misc 529

(15) Register of Baptisms solemnised in the Scottish United Secession Church, Wells Street, Oxford Street, in the County of Middlesex (this register, in the Library of the United Reform Church, 86 Tavistock Place, London, W.C.1, is a nineteenth century register into which earlier entries dating from 1771 to 1856 have been transcribed in the same hand)

I am indebted to Dr George C. Cameron for the following account of the origins of the Wells Street Chapel:

The practice of patronage in the appointment of ministers in the Church of Scotland, abolished by the Revolution Settlement of the Church in 1689 and one of the important issues on which the 1707 Treaty of Union safeguarded the continued rights of that Church, was nevertheless reintroduced by the British Parliament and imposed on the Church, *nolens volens*, five years after that Treaty. In protest against the intrusion by patrons of unworthy men upon unwilling congregations, and also against the spirit of 'moderatism' which was then growing within the ministry, four ministers seceded, soon to be joined by many more, and formed the first Associate Presbytery in 1733 (Archibald Hall was taught by one of these, James Fisher, who became the seceders' Professor of Divinity). Unfortunately dissent arose within the Associate or Secession Church, first of all over the question of whether or not it was right to take the Burgess Oath of 1747, and further splits on similar issues of conscience followed so that at one time there were six branches of the original Secession. The last surviving remnant reunited with the Church of Scotland as recently as 1955. Despite its unhappy history of internal divisions the Secession played an important part in the Scottish story, and many of its congregations sprang up in parts of England where Scots were numerous. Of these, Wells Street was certainly one of the most important.

Alexander Waugh's family remained significant. His daughters married the painter Holman Hunt and the sculptor Thomas Woolner. Other descendants include the managing director of Dickens' publishers, Chapman & Hall, and also Evelyn, Alec and Auberon Waugh

(16) Kensington and Chelsea Borough Libraries Collection

(17) *Philosophical Transactions of R.Soc. London*, Vol. 78 (1788), pp. 238–254

(18) James, *Early Keyboard Instruments*

(19) *Some Notes Made by J. S. Broadwood*

(20) Hipkins 'Notebooks'

(21) Scholes, P. A., *The Great Dr Burney* (Oxford University Press, London 1948)

(22) Scholes, P. A. (ed.), *Oxford Companion to Music* (7th ed., Oxford University Press London 1947)

(23) Hipkins 'Notebooks'

(24) Uncertainty about the accepted spelling of 'pianoforte' at this time is reflected in the contemporary novels of Jane Austen. In *Mansfield Park* and *Pride and Prejudice* she uses 'pianoforte' and 'piano-forte', in *Northanger Abbey* 'pianoforte', and in her brief *Plan of a Novel* 'Piano Forte'. In *Emma* it is 'pianoforté' or

'piano-forté'. *Sense and Sensibility* has the greatest number of variants: 'pianoforte, pianoforté, piano-forte, piano-forté, piano forté, grand pianoforté'. The term 'instrument' is used by fashionable characters, by a housekeeper when referring to a new piano sent for her mistress, and once by Jane Austen herself as narrator

(25) Alexander Reinagle was also a Scot by residence. His father was state trumpeter in Edinburgh. He emigrated to the United States in 1784 where he founded opera-houses in New York and Philadelphia—and dealt in musical instruments, at least in the latter city (see Johnson, David, *Music and Society in Lowland Scotland in the Eighteenth Century* (Oxford University Press, London 1972)

(26) Porter, Kenneth Wiggins, *John Jacob Astor, Business Man*, Harvard Studies in Business History, 1931 (reissue by Russell & Russell, New York, 1966)

(27) James, *Early Keyboard Instruments*, quoting Dent, E. J., in *The Dominant*, June 1928, p. 15

(28) The 'Day' book (a record of daily activities at Great Pulteney Street) was started on 25 April 1792; an 'Order' book on 1 March 1793; a 'Letter' book on 13 November 1793; a 'Tuning' book on 8 November 1795; and a 'Porters' book on 25 April 1796. These dates are given in a notebook in the possession of John Broadwood & Sons, evidently dating from the late nineteenth century. Not all the ledgers listed here survive, and unfortunately many of the ledgers have been irretrievably damaged by damp

Chapter IV 'John Broadwood and his Sons'

(1) The order for the Godoy piano appears in the books as (on 8 February 1796) from 'The Prince of the Peace, Le Comte de Mopox el de Jarnico, at Grenier's Hotel, Jermyn Street'. The entry in the Day Book for 22 June reads:

Mopox,

A G.P.F addl. keys from C to C in sattinwood case superbly ornamented. A cover of green striped leather and stockings for the legs. A Green baize Cover and two quires of silver paper in two very strong deal cases, the frame in one and case in ye other marked C.D.S.C. No 1 and 2. Delivered at the Bull, Porters Galley Key for the Esperanza, Belotte, Bilbao.

The Count Mopox Grenier's Hotel. Dr.-

A Grand Pianoforte 6 octaves C to C, in sattinwood case ornamented with different woods with water gilt mouldings and Wedgwood's and Tassie's medallions, etc. The Prince of Peace's arms chased and gilt in burnished gold rich carved frame, etc.	£223	13	0
The Prince's portrait in front by Taylor	10	10	0
A Cover of green striped Leather and stockings for the legs	9	9	0
A Green baize Cover	1	7	0
A Deal case very stout for the Instr.	5	10	0
A Deal case very stout for the frame	5	7	0
Strings, forks, etc.	1	1	0
Cartage to the Key	0	7	6
	£257	4	6

The piano was in London, in private ownership, *c*. 1912 when it was examined by William Dale, who found it in 'splendid preservation . . . The satinwood has mellowed with age, the keys are unworn, and the medallions perfect . . . The Prince's portrait in front by Taylor, alas, is no longer there . . . Above the keyboard, surrounded by beautiful decorated work, is an oval, where it was usual to engross the maker's name and date. In this case the unusual course has been taken of inscribing the name on the rail covering the dampers. The oval is now filled with a device, somewhat clumsily put on, which occupies the place where once was Taylor's miniature of the Prince of the Peace'. The piano is now (1982) owned by Mrs Florence C. Chambers, and on loan to the Museum of Fine Arts, Boston, Massachusetts

(2) Jourdain, M. & Rose, F., *English Furniture—The Georgian Period 1750–1830* (Batsford, London 1953)

(3) Cecil, David, *A Portrait of Jane Austen* (Constable, London 1978)

(4) Carpenter, T. Edward, *The Story of Jane Austen's Chawton Home*, Jane Austen Memorial Trust, undated

(5) These transactions are listed in what appears to be a private account book of John Broadwood's—Bodleian MS Eng misc e 663

(6) Cox, H. Bertram & C. L. E. Cox, *Leaves from the Journal of Sir George Smart* (Longmans Green & Co., London 1907)

(7) Information from Mr and Mrs Brian Richardson of Reeves Hall, and Mr J. B. Bennett of East Mersea

(8) Private diary of Thomas Broadwood

(9) Muzio Clementi had started his own business (with the Collard brothers making for him) in 1802; Thomas Tomkinson started his business in 1800

(10) *Some Notes Made by J. S. Broadwood'*

(11) Hipkins 'Notebooks'

(12) *Ibid.*

The page on 'upright grands' reads:

up' grand No 4   16 April 1800
   No 5   5 Feb   1801
   No 1   19 Mar   1801
   No 6   11 Nov   1801

Some experiment was tried in 1802 as 5 were made without number. In 1803 the grand numbers were taken up for upright grands. In 1805 they were bought from James Black. From 19 Mar 1805 to 4 March 1813 he supplied upwards of 400 instruments. About 150 were horizontal, the remainder upright grands at 45 & 50 guineas.

The first six UGs were Nos 1 to 6.

   19 with no numbers
   26 numbered with true grands
   89 or so described as 'N.Bk'

and No 151 and upwards to the end disturbed during 1805 to 1810 by James Black's horizontal grands being numbered with them, and by his 100 consecutive grands made 1810–12. The upright grand ended at 940 in 1831.

No Cabinet PF *so called* left Pulteney Street until 16 Jan 1812. No number is given to it or to the next 13 which left. Then comes 106 and after that lower numbers, 89 being the lowest

(13) Public Record Office, Lord Chamberlain's Office papers, LC 3.68 (54), LC 3.68 (152), LC 3.68 (170), LC 3.72 (17), and correspondence with Sir Robin Mackworth Young

(14) Cooper, A., 'Old Chalk Farm Tavern', article in *Camden History Review* No. 6 (1978)

(15) Scholes, P. A., *The Great Dr Burney*

Chapter V 'The Brothers in Partnership'

(1) The Great Review took place on 31 March 1814

(2) He bought Juniper Hall from a Mrs Worrell on 18 March 1815 for £8,236 10s. Juniper Hall has another musical association. In 1792 it became the home of progressive French aristocrats who had fled the Revolution, among them Mme. de Stael, Alexandre d'Arblay and Talleyrand. While visiting her sister at Mickleham, Charles

Burney's novelist daughter Fanny met and fell in love with d'Arblay whom she married at Mickleham Church

(3) Letter from Thomas Broadwood to the music publisher V. Novello. The original, with a contemporary translation of the report from the Vienna *Gazette of Arts*, was sent to E. H. T. Broadwood in June 1952 by W. J. Huttl of Barnet

(4) The original of this letter (in French) remained in the Broadwood files until some date before 1847. Then W. Watts (Secretary of the Philharmonic Society 1815–1847) who collected autographs asked James Shudi Broadwood if he might go through the company's letter-boxes to look for 'franks', i.e. the signatures of Members of Parliament and Peers which were put on letters to authorise free despatch before the days of the Penny Post. Watts found the Beethoven letter and (with or without Broadwood's knowledge) abstracted it for his personal collection. After his death, his collection was bought at auction by a Mr Holloway, who allowed the Beethoven letter to be photographed for Grove's biography of Beethoven, and also gave a copy to Broadwoods. It was reproduced in facsimile in the Beethoven issue of the *Musical Times* (15 December 1892) but its present whereabouts are unknown. (Information from a MS note by A. J. Hipkins in the company guardbook, 5 March 1877 (SRO); Hipkins notes that he was told the story by the clerk, Joseph Ries)

(5) Young, Percy M., *Beethoven: A Victorian Tribute* (Dennis Dobson, London 1976)

(6) *Thayer's Life of Beethoven* (revised and edited by Elliott Forbes, Princeton University Press 1964)

(7) *Ibid.*

(8) Moscheles, C. (ed.), *Life of Moscheles with Selections from his Diaries and Correspondence* (Hurst & Blackett, London 1873)

(9) Nohl, Ludwig, *Beethoven Depicted by his Contemporaries* (W. Reeves, London 1880)

(10) *Musical Times*, 15 December 1892

(11) Gábry, György, *Old Musical Instruments* (Corvina Press, Budapest 1969)

(12) Monrad-Johansen, D., *Edvard Grieg* (trans. Madge Robertson) (Tudor Publishing Co., New York 1945)

(13) Thomas Broadwood paid £38,700 for the Holmbush estate. The house cost him £17,004 16s 11½d

(14) Martin, T., *The Circle of the Mechanical Arts*, quoted in Jourdain, M., *Regency Furniture 1795–1820* (Country Life, London 1934)

(15) *Furniture*, Board of Trade Working Party

338

Report, H.M.S.O. 1946

(16) Jourdain, M. & F. Rose, *English Furniture*

(17) Hipkins, A. J., *A Description and History of the Pianoforte* (Novello, London 1896)

(18) Hollis, Helen Rice, *The Piano* (David & Charles, Newton Abbot 1975)

(19) *Music Trades Review*, 15 July 1893—probably Hipkins

(20) *Ibid.*

Chapter VI 'The Years of Triumph and Challenge'

(1) Niecks, F., *Frederick Chopin as a Man and Musician* (Novello, London 1888)

(2) Ehrlich, C., *The Piano, a History* (Dent, London 1976)

(3) Davison, H. (ed.), *From Mendelssohn to Wagner, the Memoirs of J. W. Davison, music critic of* The Times, (London 1912)

(4) Sterndale Bennett, J. R., *The Life of William Sterndale Bennett* (Cambridge University Press 1907)

(5) *Ibid.*

(6) Bassett, Marnie, *The Hentys: an Australian Colonial Tapestry* (Oxford University Press, 1954). The Hentys' piano survives in the Warnambool Museum, next to one formerly belonging to Governor La Trobe

(7) A list of pianoforte-makers in London and its environs from 1760 to 1851 is given in Harding, *The Pianoforte* (Appdx G). An analysis of that list shows the following:

Firms founded pre-1800 48

1800–1809	21
1810–1819	16
1820–1829	29
1830–1839	89
1840–1851	222

Miss Harding compiled her list from London Directories and other sources. It may not be exhaustive, but is an interesting indication of the increase in small firms making pianos in London in the 1840s. The years of foundation of some of Broadwoods' principal competitors are given below (year of termination in brackets, where known):

Pre–1800	Erard
	Kirkman (1896—merger with Collard & Collard)
	Stodart, M. & W. (1862)
1800–1809	Tomkinson, Thomas (1854)
	Wilkinson & Co (1835)
	Wornum, Robert (1900)
1820–1829	-

1830–1839	Allison & Allison (as Ralph Allison, 1910)
	Cadby, Charles (1885)
	Challen, William (1864)
	Collard & Collard (1929—bought by Chappell)
	Strohmenger, J. (1929—bought by Chappell)
1840–1851	Brinsmead, John
	Hopkinson, John & James

(8) Curtis, G, *A Chronicle of Small Beer, the early Victorian Diaries of a Hertfordshire Brewer* (Phillimore, London & Chichester 1970)

(9) The clause reads:

That it shall be lawful for every or any of the said Partners at any time during the said copartnership to require that any son of his or any two or more of his sons respectively shall be admitted a partner or partners in this copartnership without any premium and thereupon to assign to such son or sons respectively any part or parts or the whole of his share in the capital of the said copartnership And immediately thereupon the son or sons who shall be required to be so admitted a partner or partners shall be substituted in the place of his or their father respectively so far as relates to the part or parts or whole so assigned

(10) Peel, Mrs C. S., 'Homes and Habits', in *Early Victorian England*, Vol. i (Oxford University Press 1934)

(11) L. A. T. Broadwood, conversation with the author, 1978

(12) *Music Trades Review*, 15 July 1893

(13) *Ibid.* The list reads:

Henry Broadwood took counsel, and submitted the results of his experiments to musicians of note, such as Sir Sterndale Bennett, Boehm (inventor of the improved key-system in the flute), Molique, Pauer, Sir Charles Hallé, Ferdinand Hiller, Stephen Heller, Ernst, Sainton, J. B. Cramer, Sir George Macfarren, and others. Edward Schultz, in particular, followed Henry Broadwood's investigations with much interest.

This was probably written by A. J. Hipkins, but there must be some doubt about the names, since (for example) Hallé did not arrive in London until 1848

(14) Pole, W., *Musical Instruments in the Great Exhibition of 1851* (1852)

(15) Ehrlich, *The Piano*

(16) (Dodd, G.) '*A Day at a Piano-factory*', *Supplement to The Penny Magazine*, April 1842 Reprinted in Dodd, G., *Days at the Factories, or*

the Manufacturing Industry of Great Britain Described (C. Knight, London 1843), and in Dodd, G., British Manufactures, Series IV Ch. VI: 'Piano-manufacture' (C. Knight, London 1845).

(17) Diary in the possession of John Broadwood & Sons Ltd

(18) Westminster Times, 22 March 1895

(19) Ibid.

(20) Piano, Organ and Music Trades Journal, March 1895

(21) Stratton, S. S., Mendelssohn (Master Musicians Series: Dent, London 1934)

(22) International Exhibition 1862, List of Pianofortes exhibited by John Broadwood & Sons (W. S. Johnson, London 1862)

(23) Hallé, C. E. & M. (eds.), Life and Letters of Sir Charles Hallé (London 1896)

(24) Niecks, F., Frederic Chopin

(25) Ibid.

(26) Murdoch, W., Chopin (John Murray, London, 1934)

(27) Manchester Guardian, 30 August 1848

(28) Hueffer, F., 'Chopin', essay in Musical Studies (London 1880)

(29) Ehrlich, The Piano

(30) Official Descriptive and Illustrated Catalogue of the Great Exhibition of the Works of Industry of All Nations, London 1851. Class 10, Philosophical, Musical, Horological and Surgical Instruments, pp. 451–454

(31) Protest to H.R.H. The Prince Albert KG &c., President, and to the Royal Commissioners of the Great Exhibition, London, 1851

(32) Illustrated London News, 16 August 1856, 'Destruction of Messrs Broadwood's Piano Manufactory by Fire'

(33) Ibid., 23 August 1856, 'The Late Fire at Messrs Broadwood's'

(34) Ibid., 6 September 1856, 'Fund for Broadwood's Workmen'

Chapter VII 'The Competitors Emerge'

(1) Ehrlich, The Piano

(2) Ibid.

(3) Music Trades Review, 15 July 1893

(4) Ibid.

(5) International Exhibition 1862. List of Pianofortes . . . exhibited by John Broadwood & Sons, London 1862

(6) Some Notes Made by J. S. Broadwood

(7) Music Trades Review, 15 July 1893

(8) Ibid.

(9) Ibid.

(10) Ehrlich, The Piano

(11) T. H. Burnham & G. O. Hoskins, Iron and Steel in Britain 1870–1930 (Allen & Unwin, London 1943)

(12) Ibid.

(13) Theodore E. Steinway, People and Pianos: a Century of Service to Music, (Steinway, New York 1953)

(14) Manchester Guardian, August 1871

(15) Musical World, September 1871

Chapter VIII 'The Partnership Breaks Up'

(1) Music Trades Review, 15 July 1893

(2) Pall Mall Gazette, 20 February 1890

(3) Henschel, (Sir) George, Musings and Memories of a Musician (Macmillan, London 1918)

(4) Wilson, Michael I., 'The Case of the Victorian Piano', article in Victoria and Albert Museum Year Book, 1972

(5) Journal of the Society of Arts, Vol. LV 1906–7, pp. 365–6

(6) Fitzgerald, Penelope, Edward Burne-Jones, a Biography (Michael Joseph, London 1975)

(7) Journal of the Society of Arts, op. cit.

(8) Earl of Oxford and Asquith, conversation with the author, 1979

(9) Burne-Jones, G., Memorials of Edward Burne-Jones, Vol. II (Macmillan, London 1904)

(10) Wilson, 'The Case of the Victorian Piano'

(11) Music Trades Review, 15 March 1893

(12) Journal of the Society of Arts, Vol. LV 1906–7, p. 371

(13) Ehrlich, The Piano

(14) Henschel, Memories of a Musician

(15) Hipkins, A. J., 'Guithas, the Fold of the Hill and other Extracts from a Brief Notebook 1867–1870' (privately printed, London 1903)

(16) Hipkins, A Description and History of the Pianoforte

(17) Ibid.

(18) Ehrlich, The Piano

(19) Ibid.

(20) Ibid.

(21) Reports from Her Majesty's Diplomatic and Consular Officers Abroad on Subjects of Commercial and General Interest, Part IV, House of Commons Paper C 4530, 1885, p. 61

(22) Ibid., pp. 75–6

(23) Ehrlich, The Piano

(24) Ibid.

(25) Hallé, C. E. & M. (eds.), *Life and Letters of Sir Charles Hallé* (Smith Elder, London 1896)
(26) *Musical Opinion*, December 1890
(27) *The Scotsman*, 15 September 1893
(28) *Pall Mall Gazette*, 12 November 1895
(29) Carrier, Dennis, MS autobiographical notes in the possession of his son Bernard Carrier
(30) L. A. T. Broadwood, conversation with the author, 1979
(31) *Kensington Express*, 18 October 1901

Chapter IX 'The Years of Crisis'

(1) *Pall Mall Gazette*, 4 February 1904
(2) Dennis Carrier MS
(3) L. A. T. Broadwood, conversation with the author, 1979
(4) Dennis Carrier MS, *op cit*
(5) *Ibid.*
(6) Letter from Lieut. Rennick to D. Carrier, in the possession of Bernard Carrier
(7) Letter in the possession of John Broadwood & Sons
(8) Ehrlich, *The Piano*
(9) *Music Trades Review*, 15 August 1906
(10) The St James's Hall closed in 1905. Broadwoods bought some furnishings, which musicians remembered with nostalgia, and installed them in the concert-room at Conduit Street. In particular George Henschel recalled 'the dear old uncomfortable, long, narrow, worn-out, green-upholstered benches, with the numbers of the seats tied over the straight back with red tape'
(11) Artists appearing at the Broadwood concerts 1902–12 included (with ages where known):

1902–3
Ernst von Dohnanyi (25)
Fritz Kreisler (27)
Fanny Davies

1903–4
Harry Plunket Greene (38)
Bohemian String Quartet
  with Josef Suk
Donald Francis Tovey (28)
Landon Ronald (30)
Henry J. Wood (34)
Haydn Wood (21)
Frank Bridge (24)
Halir Quartet
Gervase Elwes (37)
Moscow Trio

Kneisel Quartet
Brodsky Quartet

1904–5
Sir Walter Parratt (63)
Percy Grainger (22)

1905–6
Kruse Quartet
  with Lionel Tertis (29)
Dr Walford Davies (36)
Hamilton Harty (26)

1908–9
St Petersburg Quartet
Frank Merrick (22)

1910–11
Jelly von Aranyi
York Bowen (26)
Maggie Teyte
Frederick Grisewood (22)
New Quartet
  with Albert Sammons (22)
(12) L. A. T. Broadwood, conversation with the author, 1979
(13) Ord-Hume, Arthur W. J., *Player Piano* (Allen & Unwin, London 1970)
(14) Ehrlich, in *The Piano*, doubts the assertion that British piano-makers began to make their own actions again; but Broadwoods did
(15) Munson, Kenneth, *Fighters, Attack and Training Aircraft 1914–1919* (Blandford Press, Poole 1976)
(16) Lewis, Peter, *The British Bomber since 1914*, (Putnam, London 1974)
(17) Ehrlich, *The Piano*
(18) *The Scotsman*, 21 September 1920
(19) Ehrlich, *The Piano*
(20) C. E. Heath & Co. archives
(21) Gelatt, Roland, *The Fabulous Phonograph 1877–1977* (2nd rev. ed. Cassell, London 1977)
(22) Stanley Murdoch, conversation with the author, 1974
(23) Ehrlich, *The Piano*

Chapter X 'Survival and Resurgence'

(1) Percy M. Scholes, Article on 'Pianoforte (6)', in the *Oxford Companion to Music* (Oxford University Press, 1st edition, London 1938)
(2) Captain Broadwood delighted in retailing family anecdotes. In particular he was fond of the story of Chopin's first visit to Bryanston Square. He used to say that this was told by his

'Uncle Tom' about his grandfather, Henry Fowler Broadwood. In fact, it was his great-grandfather, James Shudi, who played this trick.

The historian has to be wary of Evelyn Broadwood's reminiscences, which often seem to have concertinaed a generation—a not uncommon experience in family legend. Thus he used to tell a story that his 'Aunt Susan' had woken one night at Lyne to hear a voice saying, as she thought, 'Pay, pay, pay Burney—pay, pay, pay Burney'. It was a wood-pigeon. But she told her father, James Shudi, and the books were examined, and sure enough the firm did owe money to Dr Burney, which was then paid. A good story, except that Susan Broadwood was born in 1816, and Burney died two years earlier. Presumably someone—perhaps her mother Margaret—told Susan the story, she told Bertha, and Bertha told Evelyn. He was very cavalier about facts. For years Burke's *Landed Gentry* gave John Broadwood's birthplace as 'near Dundee'. It is near Dunbar, on the opposite coast of Scotland; but no one could persuade Evelyn Broadwood to have it corrected. He had great charm. One of the minor pleasures of his life was to devise his own salad dressing; and the present author recalls an occasion in the dining room of the Athenaeum when, with much play with tablespoon, oil and vinegar the then 82-year-old Captain demonstrated this skill. But he could also be idiosyncratic; when the whim took him, he would refuse to answer letters, or even open them. To the despair of his colleagues and family, his desks at Hanover Street and Lyne would pile up with ignored correspondence, sometimes for weeks

(3) The programme of the concert at the Queen Elizabeth Hall on 4 May 1978 was:

Sonata No 52 in E flat major — Haydn
Sonata in A flat, Op 110 — Beethoven
Songs Without Words — Mendelssohn
(Op 19 No 1; Op 62 No 6)
Twelve Etudes, Op 10 — Chopin
Rhapsody — Howells
L'Isle Joyeuse — Debussy

The 1787 and 1819 pianos were loaned by the Colt Clavier Collection; the other pianos are in the possession of John Broadwood & Sons Ltd

Bibliography

I The Broadwood Archives

The Broadwood archives, including both company and family papers, are now housed in three depositories: the Bodleian Library, Oxford; the Surrey Record Office; and the Broadwood factory.

(i) Bodleian Library

The three oldest surviving documents concerning John Broadwood & Sons have been placed in the Bodleian Library. These are:

MS Eng misc b 107—John Broadwood's Journal 1771–1785;
MS Eng misc c 529—Barbara Broadwood's Account Book; and
MS Eng misc e 663—John Broadwood's personal financial dealings e.g. in shipping, loans etc.

(ii) Surrey Record Office

When the Broadwood Trust became responsible for the Lyne Estate following the death of Captain Evelyn Broadwood, the Victorian house and outbuildings contained some hundreds of ledgers, minute books and financial records of the company, dating back to the late 1790s. There were also many thousands of family and business papers, almost inextricably mixed together. Under the supervision of the Surrey County Archivist they have been stored in the Surrey County Record Office, the papers in some 280 boxes and the ledgers on shelves. At present (1982) the papers have not been sorted or catalogued and until this immense task is completed, access to the papers must be restricted. The ledgers (the earliest is dated 1794) are primarily financial, though they contain sets of Partners' Books from 1848 to 1901, and company minute books thereafter. Some are illegible through damp, and since most of the index volumes have been damaged, the analysis of these ledgers in detail will be a slow and laborious process.

(iii) Broadwood factory

The most important records at the factory consist of some 30 volumes of Porters' Books from 1800 to c. 1864, listing all movements of numbered pianos from the factory. The factory also holds a letter-book, partly in the hands of John Broadwood and his son James Shudi Broadwood, from 1801 to 1810. Other Broadwood relics, including the Shudi snuffbox, the Broadwood table snuffbox, gold medals from the nineteenth century, and an array of Victorian sporting silver trophies, are stored in safe deposit. Since the factory is a place of work, and not an historical archive, access to these materials is necessarily limited by the day-to-day pressures of business. Within this understandable constraint, the company does make every practicable effort to help enquirers. A small charge is made for searches, e.g. for the dating of particular pianos.

II General

BRYANT, Arthur *The Years of Endurance 1793–1802* (Collins, London, 1944); *Years of Victory 1802–1812* (Collins, London, 1944); *The Age of Elegance 1812–1822* (Collins, London, 1954)

BURNHAM, T. H. and G. O. Hoskins *Iron and Steel in Britain 1870–1930* (Allen & Unwin, London, 1943)

CAMERON, George C. *The Scots Kirk in London* (Mowbray, London, 1979)

CHANCELLOR, E. Beresford *The Romance of Soho* (Country Life, London, 1931)

COLERIDGE, A. *Chippendale Furniture* (Faber, London, 1968)

ELKIN, R. *The Old Concert Rooms of London* (Edward Arnold, London, 1953)

GELATT, Roland *The Fabulous Phonograph 1877–1977* (2nd revised ed., Cassell, London, 1977)

GREAT EXHIBITION, 1851 Catalogue and Jury Reports (London, 1851)

HALL, Peter G. *The Industries of London since 1861* (Hutchinson, London, 1962)

HAWKINS, Sir John *A General History of the Science and Practice of Music*, (Vol. V, London, 1776)

HENSCHEL, Sir George *Musings and Memories of a Musician* (Macmillan, London, 1918)

HOBSBAWM, E. J. *Industry and Empire* (Pelican Economic History of Britain, Vol. 3, London, 1969)

JOHNSON, David *Music and Society in Lowland Scotland in the Eighteenth Century* (Oxford University Press, London, 1972)

JOURDAIN, M. *Regency Furniture 1795–1820* (Country Life, London, 1934)

JOURDAIN, M. and F. Rose *English Furniture – the Georgian Period 1750–1830* (Batsford, London, 1953)

KELLY, A. Alison *Decorative Wedgwood in Architecture and Furniture* (Country Life, London, 1965)

Lectures on the Results of the Great Exhibition of 1851 (David Bogue, London, 1852)

LEVINE, A. L. *Industrial Retardation in Britain 1880–1914* (Weidenfeld & Nicolson, London, 1967)

LEWIS, Peter *The British Bomber since 1914* (Putnam, London, 1974)

MITCHELL, B. R. and P. DEANE *Abstract of British Historical Statistics* (Cambridge University Press, 1962)

MUNSON, Kenneth *Fighters, Attack and Training Aircraft 1914–1919* (Blandford Press, Poole 1976)

MUSGRAVE, Clifford *Regency Furniture 1800–1830* (Faber, London, 1970)

RIMBAULT, E. F. (ed. Clinch) *Soho and its Associations* (Dulau & Co., London, 1895)

RUDÉ, George *Hanoverian London 1714–1808* (Secker & Warburg, London, 1971)

SCHOLES, Percy A. (ed.) *Oxford Companion to Music* (7th ed. 1947, and 10th ed. revised J. O. Ward, Oxford University Press, 1977)

SHADWELL, Arthur *Industrial Efficiency: a Comparative Study of Life in England, Germany and America* (2 vols., Longmans, London, 1906)

SHAW, George Bernard *The Bodley Head Bernard Shaw: Shaw's Music* ed. Dan H. Laurence (3 vols., Max Reinhardt: The Bodley Head, London, 1981)

SHEPPARD, Francis *London 1808–1870: the Infernal Wen* (Secker & Warburg, London, 1971)

SHEPPARD, F. H. W. (ed.) *Survey of London*, Vol. XXXI, The Parish of St James Westminster, Part 2, North of Piccadilly—Great Pulteney Street (Athlone Press, University of London, 1963) *Survey of London*, Vol. XXXIII, the Parish of St Anne Soho—Meard Street (Athlone Press, University of London, 1966)

SMOUT, T. Christopher *A History of the Scottish People 1560–1830* (Collins, London, 1969)

SUPPLE, Barry (ed.) *Essays in British Business History* (Clarendon Press, Oxford, 1977)

TOMLIN, Maurice *English Furniture* (Faber, London, 1972)

TURBERVILLE, A. S. (ed.) *Johnson's England* (2 vols., Oxford University Press, 1967)

WILSON, Charles *Economy and Society in Late Victorian Britain*, in Econ Hist Review (2nd series, Vol. XVIII)

YOUNG, G. M. (ed.) *Early Victorian England 1830–1865* (2 vols., Oxford University Press, 1934)

III Keyboard Instruments

BARTHOLD, Kenneth van and D. BUCKTON *The Story of the Piano* (BBC Publications, London, 1975)

BOALCH D. H. *Makers of the Harpsichord and Clavichord 1440–1840* (2nd ed., Clarendon Press, Oxford, 1974)

CAMPBELL, Margaret *Dolmetsch, the Man and his Work* (Hamish Hamilton, London, 1975)

CLOSSON, Ernest (ed. R. Golding) *History of the Piano* (Paul Elek, London, 1974)

COLT, C. F. *Catalogue of the Colt Clavier Collection* (Bethersden, Kent, undated)

DALE, William 'The Artistic Treatment of the Exterior of the Pianoforte', in *Journal of the Royal Society of Arts* (Vol. LV 1906–7)

DANCHELL, F. L. Hahn *Latest Improvements in the Pianoforte—Broadwood & Sons' New Action* (C. Ollivier, London, 1838)

DODD, G. 'A Day at a Piano-factory' (supplement to the *Penny Magazine*, London, April 1842), *Days at the Factories, or the Manufacturing Industry of Great Britain Described* (C. Knight, London, 1843) *British Manufactures*, Series IV, Ch. VI 'Piano-manufacture' (C. Knight, London, 1845)

DOLGE, Alfred *Pianos and their Makers* (California, 1911, reprinted by Dover Books/ Constable, London, 1972)

DOLMETSCH, Mabel *Personal Recollections of Arnold Dolmetsch* (Routledge & Kegan Paul, London, 1958)

EHRLICH, Cyril *The Piano, a History* (Dent, London, 1976)

GÁBRY, György *Old Musical Instruments* (Corvina Press, Budapest, 1969)

GALPIN, Francis W. *Old English Instruments of Music, their History and Character* (Methuen, London, 1910)

GEIRINGER, K. *Musical Instruments, their History from the Stone Age to the Present Day* (trans. B. Miall) (Allen & Unwin, London, 1943)

GILL, Dominic (ed.) *The Book of the Piano* (Phaidon, Oxford, 1981)

GROVER, David *The Piano* (Robert Hale, London, 1975)

GROVE'S DICTIONARY OF MUSIC AND MUSICIANS (5th ed., Ed. E. Blom, Macmillan, London, 1954)

HARDING, Rosamond E. M. *The Piano-Forte, its History Traced to the Great Exhibition of 1851*

(Cambridge University Press, 1st ed. 1933; 2nd ed., Gresham Press, London, 1979)

HARRISON, Sidney *Grand Piano* (Faber, London, 1976)

HIPKINS, A. J. *A Description and History of the Pianoforte* (Novello, London, 1896)

HIPKINS, Edith J. (ed) *How Chopin Played—from Contemporary Impressions Collected from the Diaries and Notebooks of the late A. J. Hipkins F.S.A. (Dent, London, 1937)*

HOLLAND, Frank M. *Introduction to the Collection at the National Musical Museum* (British Piano Museum Trust, Brentford, undated)

HOLLIS, Helen Rice *The Piano, a Pictorial Account of its Ancestry and Development* (David & Charles, Newton Abbot, 1975)

HUBBARD, Frank *Three Centuries of Harpsichord Making* (Harvard University Press, Cambridge, Massachusetts, 1965)

JAMES, Philip *Early Keyboard Instruments* (Peter Davies, London, 1930)

LAMBURN, Edward *A Short History of a Great House—Collard & Collard* (privately printed, London, 1938)

LOESSER, Arthur *Men, Women and Pianos, a Social History* (Gollancz, London, 1955)

MAIR, Carlene (ed.) *The Chappell Story 1811–1961* (Chappell, London, 1961)

MELVILLE, Derek 'Beethoven's Pianos', in D. Arnold and N. Fortune, *The Beethoven Companion* (Faber & Faber, London, 1971)

MICHEL, N. E. *Old Pianos* (Rivera, California, 1954)

MONTAGU, J. *The World of Baroque and Classical Musical Instruments* (David & Charles, Newton Abbot, 1979)

NALDER, L. M. *The Modern Piano* (Unwin Bros, Woking, reprint in 1977 of 1927 original)

NEWMAN, S. and P. WILLIAMS *The Russell Collection of Early Keyboard Instruments* (Edinburgh University Press, 1968)

ORD-HUME, A. W. J. *Player-Piano: the History of the Mechanical Piano and How to Repair It* (Allen & Unwin, London, 1970)

POLE, W. *Musical Instruments in the Great Exhibition of 1851* (London, 1852)

PURCELL, K. 'The Design of Grand Pianos', in L. WEAVER (ed.) *The House and its Equipment* (Country Life, London, 1911)

REES, Rev. A. (ed.) 'The Harpsichord' from *The New Cyclopaedia* (London, 1819)

RIMBAULT, E. F. *The Pianoforte* (R. Cocks & Co., London, 1860)

RIPIN, Edwin M. (ed.) *Keyboard Instruments: Studies in Keyboard Organology 1500–1800* (Dover Publications Inc., New York, 1977)

RUSSELL, Raymond *A Catalogue of Early Keyboard Instruments: the Benton Fletcher Collection at Fenton House* (National Trust, London, 1976) *Early Keyboard Instruments in the Victoria & Albert Museum* (H.M. Stationery Office, London, 1959) *The Harpsichord and Clavichord* (2nd ed., Faber, London, 1973) *Victoria & Albert Museum Catalogue of Musical Instruments*: Vol. 1, *Keyboard Instruments* (H.M. Stationery Office, London, 1968)

SMITH, Eric *Pianos in Practice* (Scolar Press, London, 1978)

STEINWAY, Theodore E. *People and Pianos: a Century of Service to Music* (Steinway, New York, 1961)

SUMNER, W. L. *The Organ* (4th ed., Macdonald, London, 1973) *The Pianoforte* (Macdonald, London, 1966)

TAYLOR, S. K. (ed.) *The Musician's Piano Atlas* (Omicron, Macclesfield, 1981)

WILSON, Michael I. 'Burne-Jones and Piano Reform', in *Apollo Magazine*, November 1975 'The Case of the Victorian Piano' in *Victoria & Albert Museum Year Book*, 1972

IV Biography

ANDERSON, E. (ed.) *The Letters of Mozart and his Family* (Macmillan, London, 1938)

BASSETT, Marnie *The Hentys, an Australian Colonial Tapestry* (Oxford University Press, 1954)

BAUER, W. A. and O. E. DEUTSCH (eds.) *Mozart, Briefe und Aufzeichnungen* (Barenreiter, Kassel, 1962)

BURNE-JONES, G. (Lady) *Memorials of Edward Burne-Jones* (2 vols. Macmillan, London, 1904)

CECIL, David *A Portrait of Jane Austen* (Constable, London, 1978)

COOPER, Martin *Beethoven, the Last Decade 1817–1827* (Oxford University Press, London, 1970)

CORRI, Domenico Cox, H. Bertram and C. L. E. Cox *Leaves from the Journal of Sir George Smart* (Longmans Green & Co, London, 1907)

CURTIS, Gerald *A Chronicle of Small Beer: the Early Victorian Diaries of a Hertfordshire Brewer* [the Pryor family] (Phillimore, London and Chichester, 1970)

DALE, William *Tschudi the Harpsichord Maker* (Constable, London, 1913)

DAVISON, H. *From Mendelssohn to Wagner, the Memoirs of J. W. Davison, music critic of* The Times (London, 1912)

DAWSON, Capt. L. *Lonsdale: the Authorised Life of Hugh Lowther, 5th Earl* (Odhams, London, 1946)

DEUTSCH, O. E. *Mozart, a Documentary Biography* (A. & C. Black, London, 1965)

DURAND, Sir Mortimer *Life of the Rt Hon. Sir Alfred Comyn Lyall P.C., K.C.B., G.C.I.E., D.C.L., L.L.D.* (William Blackwood, Edinburgh and London, 1913)

FITZGERALD, Penelope *Edward Burne-Jones, a Biography* (Michael Joseph, London, 1975)

FLOWER Newman *George Frideric Handel, his Personality and his Times* (revised ed., Cassell, London, 1959)

FORBES, Elliott (ed.) *Thayer's Life of Beethoven* (Vol. 2, Princeton University Press, New Jersey, 1964)

HALLÉ, C. E. and M. HALLÉ *Life and Letters of Sir Charles Hallé* (Smith Elder & Co., London, 1896)

LONGFORD, Elizabeth *Wellington, the Years of the Sword* (Weidenfeld & Nicolson, London, 1969)

MACFARREN, Walter *Memories, an Autobiography* (W. Scott, London, 1905)

MONRAD-JOHANSEN, D. *Edvard Grieg* (Trans. M. Robertson) (Tudor Publishing Co., New York, 1945)

MOSCHELES, C. (ed.) *Life of Moscheles with Selections from his Diaries and Correspondence* (Hurst & Blackett, London, 1873)

MURDOCH, W. *Chopin* (J. Murray, London, 1934)

NIECKS, F. *Frederic Chopin as a Man and Musician* (Novello, London, 1888)

NOHL, Ludwig (ed.) *Beethoven Depicted by his Contemporaries* (trans. E. Hill) (W. Reeves, London, 1880)

OMAN, Carola *Nelson* (Hodder & Stoughton, London, 1947)

PORTER, Kenneth Wiggins *John Jacob Astor, Business Man* (Harvard Studies in Business History, reissued by Russell & Russell, New York, 1966)

RENNERT, Jonathan *William Crotch 1775–1847* (T. Dalton, Lavenham, 1975)

SCHOLES, Percy A. (ed.) *Dr Burney's Musical Tours in Europe* (Oxford University Press, 1959) *The Great Dr Burney* (Oxford University Press, 1948)

STERNDALE BENNETT, J. R. *The Life of William Sterndale Bennett* (Cambridge University Press, 1907)

STRATTON, Stephen S. *Mendelssohn* (Master Musicians series, Dent London, 1934)

SYDOW, Bronislaw Edward (ed.) *Selected Correspondence of Fryderyk Chopin* (Heinemann, London, 1962)

YOUNG, Percy M. *Beethoven, a Victorian Tribute* (D. Dobson, London, 1976)

Recordings

The Shudi harpsichord
Bath's Musical Heritage. 18th century keyboard music (Chilcot, Holcombe, Storace, Linley, J. C. Smith and J. C. Bach) played by Gerald Gifford
This instrument, owned by Mrs Mary Potts of Cambridge, is probably a Shudi & Broadwood of *c.* 1775 (two manuals); the dating in Boalch (1749) is improbable
> BATH UNIVERSITY RECORDINGS, BUR 1001 (recorded 1976)

Harpsichord Music of Handel and Scarlatti played by Mark Kroll
The instrument is a two-manual Shudi & Broadwood of 1789 at the Groton School, Groton, Massachusetts
> TITANIC RECORDS (Cambridge, Massachusetts) TI/49 (recorded 1979)

The Broadwood Heritage—Prelude and Minuet by Handel played by Malcolm Binns
> EDITIONS DE L'OISEAU-LYRE/ DECCA, DSLO 540 (recorded 1978)
The instrument is a two-manual Shudi & Broadwood of 1790

The early pianoforte
No recording of an early Broadwood square seems to exist, but the sound may be judged by:
Early Pianos, Vol. II of the Collection of Historic Instruments at the Victoria & Albert Museum: pieces by J. C. Bach, Arne and C. P. E. Bach played by Esther Fischer on a 1767 Square Pianoforte by Zumpe
> ORYX 1811 (recorded 1968).

The Broadwood Pianoforte
The Broadwood Heritage, played by Malcolm Binns (Clementi on a Broadwood grand pianoforte of 1787, Haydn on a Broadwood grand pianoforte of 1794, Beethoven on a Broadwood grand pianoforte of 1819, Chopin on the Broadwood grand pianoforte of 1847 used by Chopin on his 1848 London visit, Mendelssohn on a Broadwood square pianoforte of 1854 made for Prince Albert)
> EDITIONS DE L'OISEAU-LYRE/ DECCA, DSLO 540 (see above)

The Colt Clavier Collection, Vol. VI; Haydn's La Dernière Sonate played by Celia Bizony on her Broadwood grand pianoforte of 1805

(elsewhere on this record is a Broadwood grand pianoforte of 1806)
ORYX 1706

The Colt Clavier Collection, Vol. IV; Beethoven, Sonata (1804) in F minor Op. 57, The Appassionata, played by Malcolm Frager on a Broadwood grand pianoforte of 1806
ORYX 1804

Beethoven, various piano works played by Barbara Holmquest on a Broadwood grand pianoforte of 1819
ORYX EXP 18

Chopin, piano music played by Kenneth van Barthold on Chopin's Broadwood grand
ARGO ZK 59

Music for Organ and Harpsichord, and Fortepiano and Guitar, in the German National Museum, Nuremberg
Diabelli and Kuffner played by Mario Sicca (guitar) and Rita Maria Fleres, the latter on a Broadwood grand pianoforte of 1815.
ORYX EXP 58

Ludwig van Beethoven, The Piano Sonatas 1809–1822, played by Malcolm Binns on contemporary instruments from the Colt Clavier Collection, including Broadwood grand pianofortes of 1794, 1815 and 1819
Twelve records, in four boxes, 1981
EDITIONS DE L'OISEAU-LYRE/ DECCA,
vol. 1 Sonatas 1–7 D182D 3
vol. 4 Sonatas 24–32 D185D 3

Ludwig van Beethoven, Sonata Quasi una Fantasia Nr.14 Op.27 No.2 (Moonlight), and Andante from Sonata No.15 Op.28, played by Paul Badura-Skoda on a Broadwood of 1815.
DEUTSCHE HARMONIA MUNDI 1C 065–99769 (recorded 1967).

Beethoven, Piano Concerto No.1, played by Mary Verney on a Broadwood grand of 1798, with the Hanover Band.
NIMBUS RECORDS 2150 (recorded 1982)

Index